4-
α

Risk and Technological Innovation:

American Manufacturing Methods during the Nineteenth Century

Risk and
Technological Innovation:

American Manufacturing Methods
during the Nineteenth Century

By W. PAUL STRASSMANN

Michigan State University

Cornell University Press

ITHACA, NEW YORK

© 1956 by W. Paul Strassmann

© 1959 by Cornell University

CORNELL UNIVERSITY PRESS

First published in book form 1959

PRINTED IN THE UNITED STATES OF AMERICA BY

THE VAIL-BALLOU PRESS, INC., BINGHAMTON, N.Y.

To E. S.

Acknowledgments

FOR friendly counsel over a period of years and for detailed comments on an early draft of the manuscript I am indebted to Professor Dudley Dillard of the University of Maryland. I am grateful for an intriguing variety of suggestions and criticism provided by various members of the Research Center in Entrepreneurial History of Harvard University and by Professors Forest G. Hill of the University of Buffalo; Joseph Dorfman and Karl Polanyi of Columbia University; E. A. J. Johnson of Johns Hopkins University; W. Rupert Maclaurin, John B. Rae, and W. W. Rostow of the Massachusetts Institute of Technology; C. E. Ayres of the University of Texas; and John E. Sawyer of Yale University.

Special thanks are due to the Social Science Research Council for a generous fellowship, to the Library of Congress for providing facilities, and to Michigan State University for research grants and time released from teaching duties. I appreciate the permission to quote extracts from Joseph A. Schumpeter's *Capitalism, Socialism, and Democracy* published by Harper and Brothers; *The Autobiography of Andrew Carnegie* published by the Houghton Mifflin Company; *The Autobiography of John Fritz* published by John Wiley and Sons; and *The Sources of Invention* by John Jewkes, David Sawers, and Richard Stillerman published by the St. Martin's Press.

My warmest thanks go to my wife for her willingness to participate in the idolatry of deadlines and for pruning the first raw growth of manuscript.

W. P. S.

East Lansing, Michigan
November 1958

Contents

Risk and Technological Innovation:

*American Manufacturing Methods
during the Nineteenth Century*

For months past, crowds have been hastening across every latitude, on their way to the newly-discovered realms of gold. An epidemic rages to gather and hoard that, which except as a symbol, has little more value than its weight of inert sandstone or granite. A people's treasure is in useful labor; there is no wealth, and can be none but what it creates. . . . There is no wealth but labor—no enjoyments but what are derived from it.

But, to those who are ambitious of ennobling themselves and really enriching their country, placers inexpressibly more precious than any to be found on the Sacramento, are invitingly open. Let them dig in THE MINES OF THE MOTORS, and they will bring to light, active, fruitful, and everlasting sources of true opulence.

THOMAS EWBANK, Commissioner of Patents,
Annual Report, 1849

Introduction

AT the heart of an industrial revolution are new machines, new processes, and new materials that transfigure the economic landscape. In 1800 small craft shops stood in rows along American streets, each with a handful of employees using simple tools. By 1900 these shops, if they remained at all, stood in the shadow of smoking industrial plants crowded with thousands of workers and filled with massive, intricate, and semi-automatic machines. The skilled weaver of 1800 had made one pick a second with his hand loom. By 1900 a factory worker could supervise twenty Northrop automatic looms that together made sixty picks a second. Skilled locksmiths and watchmakers had been replaced by automatic milling machines, universal grinders, and multiple-spindle lathes that shaped gears, screws, cams, and levers with haste and precision. Indeed, these machine tools were mechanisms which, if properly fed, could reproduce themselves. Their proper diet was iron and steel, the output of another transformed industry. In 1800 iron had been made deep in the Appalachian forests in small charcoal furnaces and in forges with water-powered wooden trip hammers. By 1900 blast furnaces were one hundred feet high and integrated with the giant steel mills that rose above the Monongahela, Lake Erie, and Lake Michigan. Pulling a lever or turning a wheel was virtually the only manual labor needed from the time tons of coke, iron ore, and limestone reached a plant until the finished beams, plates, and rails were lifted on freight cars. The power that energized production came no longer from muscles or carpentered water wheels but from steam engines, steam turbines, and hydroelectric power stations. It was applied by some electric motors weighing tons and by others weighing ounces. At Niagara Falls the largest hydroelectric power station had a generating capacity of 50,000 horsepower and was being expanded to 110,000 horsepower. Between 1800 and 1900 the classic Industrial Revolution had swept across the United States.

Behind this revolution were changes in business organization and a spectacular advance in science and technology. This book is concerned with the interaction of these two social forces: business enterprise and technological change. It seeks to demonstrate when and for what reasons the introduction of new manufacturing methods led to business losses and risks.

The study does not cover the entire process of technological change from a scientist's first vague hunch to the scrapping of a last obsolete machine. It is concerned only with the phase of innovation—that is, only with the time when a first decision was made to alter the routine of production, when funds were staked on an untried novelty, when new technical knowledge was first applied on a commercial scale. The study is based on the records of technological innovation in methods of producing iron and steel, in textile machinery, in machine tools, and in electric power equipment. It is a detailed empirical examination of business and technology during a period that has attracted the broad speculations of many economists but particularly of Joseph A. Schumpeter and Thorstein Veblen.

Schumpeter believed that leading American businessmen were a creative factor or "propelling force" in developing new manufacturing methods and that they gambled boldly in promoting their visions. He included a wide variety of innovations outside the area of manufacturing in his descriptions; but he felt that the typical innovator of the nineteenth century was "the man who put into practice a novel method of production." In his formal analysis he always treated innovations as new and less costly ways of making old goods. All major attempts at innovation were as risky as "shooting at a target that is not only indistinct but moving—and moving jerkily at that." If innovations were to be undertaken at all, therefore, they had to be protected by a variety of legal and financial maneuvers, including even "the securing of advantages that run counter to the public's sense of fair play." [1]

Veblen conceded that leading businessmen might have risked much in their financial maneuvers and "pecuniary stratagems"; he insisted, however, that they risked little or nothing in promoting the serviceability of an industry. Inventions occurred

[1] Joseph A. Schumpeter, *Capitalism, Socialism, and Democracy* (2d ed.; New York: Harper and Brothers, 1947), pp. 81–110. The entrepreneur did not necessarily gamble with his own funds but, more typically, with funds borrowed from others or created by banks. In Schumpeter's formal theory the basic danger to innovation comes from inertia and vested interests in a community that dislikes change. Otherwise, innovations would not appear in clusters, and there would be no business cycles (*Business Cycles* [New York and London: McGraw-Hill, 1939], I, 11 ff., 130–157). On the other hand, as observed historically, danger comes from the "perennial gale of creative destruction," that is, unpredictable obsolescence in a community that is highly dynamic (*Capitalism, Socialism, and Democracy*, pp. 81–87). See also "The Creative Response in Economic History," *Journal of Economic History*, VII (Nov. 1947), 154, and Burton Keirstead, *The Theory of Economic Change* (Toronto: Macmillan, 1948), p. 96.

in a steady stream as knowledge and experience made the economy an integrated, expanding machine process; but business
strategy generally delayed, and at times "sabotaged," the introduction of already practicable techniques. Particularly after
1860, according to Veblen, the entrepreneur's role with respect
to technology was at best permissive, not creative, although
there were "comparatively slight and infrequent" exceptions.
These exceptions were in the nature of philanthropic aberra-
tions because they interfered with financial maneuverability
and therefore limited business success.[2]

According to the evidence to be presented here, it should be
apparent that both Schumpeter and Veblen were partly right
and partly wrong. The leading promoters of new manufacturing methods were neither gamblers nor passive exploiters of
the creations of others. They were a creative factor in economic development; but, by and large, they proceeded with
a degree of caution that, with certain exceptions, reduced the
chance of error to negligible proportions.

In arriving at this conclusion for several basic manufacturing methods, all innovations on which information was avail-

[2] Thorstein Veblen, *The Theory of Business Enterprise* (New York:
Charles Scribner's Sons, 1904), pp. 30–45, 228, and *Absentee Ownership
and Business Enterprise in Recent Times: The Case of America* (New
York: B. W. Huebsch, 1923), pp. 80–81, 103, 256. Schumpeter disagreed
with Veblen, charging that it would be absurd for businessmen to "sabo-
tage" technological progress in order to maintain capital values. He
pointed out that capital values are themselves determined by the expected
stream of future returns and that the interests of consumers and businessmen coincided in having this stream made as large as possible (*Capitalism,
Socialism, and Democracy*, pp. 96–98). But in making this charge,
Schumpeter failed to make Veblen's distinction between serviceability
and pecuniary value. If demand is insufficiently elastic, the interests of
consumers and producers might very well diverge. An innovation leading
to economies of scale might increase serviceability or "use value," but
the market could be spoiled, and profits could decrease. See Alfred
Marshall's analysis of sharply increasing returns, *Principles of Economics*
(8th ed.; London: Macmillan, 1920), pp. 469–472, 805–812.

able were studied. There was a great range in the precision and reliability of information, and the material was therefore not quantified. Numbers are useful when they attain a level of subtlety and precision beyond that of words. Forcing innovations of unequal importance, based on records of unequal reliability, into simple categories would confront the reader with a superfluous obstacle in appraising the author's definitions. For example, a distinction would have to be made between "important" and "unimportant innovations" and between "precise" and "vague but useful" sources of information. How should one define "important," "precise," and "useful"? In constructing tables, for example, how much weight should one give to, say, *"precise* information about *unimportant* innovations" compared with *"vague but useful* information about *important* innovations"? A formula must be found. Such a formula would then merely reflect the author's impression based on his familiarity with his material. When it comes to this, the reader can evaluate a comprehensive chronological account more easily than a series of tables based on arbitrary definitions to be interpreted by a subjective formula.[3]

The first chapter of this book will explore the meaning of "risk" and "innovation" and will try to make these terms useful for historical analysis. Later chapters will sift the evidence for particular industries. This evidence consists of material from patent applications, census reports, court records, business archives, personal memoirs, the transactions of various engineering societies, and such journals as *Iron Age, American Machinist,* and *Electrical World.* Much weight will be given to the findings of historians who have devoted years of study to individual men, firms, and industries.

[3] This position is similar to that of Professor John Jewkes and his associates: "The study of invention must necessarily be qualitative, selective and impressionistic, more historical than scientific" (John Jewkes, David Sawers, and Richard Stillerman, *The Sources of Invention* [London: Macmillan and Co., 1958], p. 25).

Professor W. W. Rostow has observed that

in the three quarters of a century or so since we created our graduate
schools, and the professional study of history and the social sciences,
based on German models mixed with native American empiricism,
we have managed to create many barren acres of factually accurate
volumes, bearing on interesting issues, in which the authors left the
problem of synthesis to someone else. Ironically this persistent philo-
sophical disease—apparently a disease of modesty and intellectual
scruple—has left American academic life, by default, particularly
vulnerable to the brilliant, casual, and not wholly responsible in-
sights of a Veblen, a Beard, or a Schumpeter who did not fear to
generalize.[4]

And as Schumpeter himself once advised:

I would commend to economic historians—and for that matter, to
economic theorists, if they will interest themselves in the problem—
that they examine the already available secondary literature for
data upon entrepreneurial characteristics and phenomena. A mis-
cellany of such writings—from general economic histories to biographies of businessmen, and from local histories to studies of
technological change—all hold information, which sifted and arranged with definite hypotheses in mind will carry us a goodly
distance toward our goal. New facts will doubtless be needed in
the end, but already we have a multitude that have as yet not been
digested.[5]

[4] W. W. Rostow, "The Interrelation of Theory and Economic History,"
Journal of Economic History, XVII, *The Tasks of Economic History*
(1957), 520.

[5] Joseph A. Schumpeter, "Economic Theory and Entrepreneurial History," *Change and the Entrepreneur*, R. Richard Wohl, ed. (Cambridge:
Harvard University Press, 1949), p. 83.

I

Basic Concepts

Technological Innovation

TECHNOLOGICAL innovations in manufacturing methods are changes in the way machines and materials are used in production, changes that necessarily involve alterations in the design or use of durable equipment or in the choice of materials. Such changes may lead to radical product changes—synthetic rubber, extra-hard alloys, alternating current—or they may reduce the production costs of a known commodity.

The present study is less concerned with the general process of technological change than with a series of more or less particular acts of innovation. The word "series" is used because, except in a very loose sense, innovation itself is not a general economic process. "Process" implies continuity over time, but innovations in different firms, industries, and geographical areas are continuous with one another only as part of the general process of technological change, which also includes scientific experimenting and theorizing, precommercial invention, adaptive imitation,. and copying.[1]

The distinction between "invention" and "innovation" that one chooses to adopt is of particular importance. There has been a tendency to think of invention as a technological matter, involving the application of scientific principles to the contrivance of a new device or process, and to think of innovation as a business matter, involving the organization of markets, capital, labor, and supplies for the production or use of a new device or process.[2] The inadequacy of this distinction was readily noticed by students of technological development. Marketing and other business problems are often wholly inseparable from technological problems so that the solution of one involves solution of the others. At times, such as at the beginning of coke smelting or cast steel making in America, this interdependence of solutions stymied progress; but more often, as in the development of interchangeable manufacturing, partial solutions of commercial problems were accompanied by partial solutions of technical problems. As Professor Usher has pointed out, major inventions were often developed by those who had previously attained tentative commercial acceptance for a tentative and minor invention.[3]

---

[1] For a discussion of the subjective and objective aspects of innovation, imitation, and copying, see Fritz Redlich, "Innovation in Business: A Systematic Presentation," *American Journal of Economics and Sociology*, X (April 1951), 285–291.

[2] Joseph A. Schumpeter wrote, "The making of the invention and the carrying out of the corresponding innovation are, economically and sociologically, two entirely different things . . . . innovation is . . . . in capitalist society, purely a matter of business behavior" (*The Theory of Economic Development*, Redvers Opie, trans. [Cambridge: Harvard University Press, 1934], pp. 85–86).

[3] Abbott Payson Usher, "Technical Change and Capital Formation," in *Capital Formation and Economic Growth* (A Conference of the Universities—National Bureau Committee for Economic Research; Princeton: Princeton University Press, 1955), pp. 533–538.

Although Usher would reject the terms "innovation" and "invention" as useful categories of analysis, others have tried to redefine these concepts as part of the function of "engineer-entrepreneurs." Dr. Harold C. Passer, for example, has described the "engineer-entrepreneur" as a person who can visualize the place in the economy which a new product might occupy, who can decide what technical features this product should have to assure commercial success, and who can invent a product which possesses these technical features.[4] In other words, the engineer-entrepreneur solves commercial and technical problems in terms of one another.[5]

The word "invention" may therefore be used as the contrivance of a new device with certain technical features, and the word "innovation" as all activities of a business enterprise

[4] Harold C. Passer, *The Electrical Manufacturers, 1875–1900* (Cambridge: Harvard University Press, 1953), pp. 1, 66–67, 180–181, 356–360. Professor John B. Rae has added the qualification that the engineer-entrepreneur must have some systematic training in the practical application of science. See his "The Engineer-Entrepreneur in the American Automobile Industry," *Explorations in Entrepreneurial History*, VIII (Oct. 1955), 1.

[5] The term "engineer-entrepreneur" was originally coined by Professor Fritz Redlich in his study of business leaders in the American iron and steel industry as applying to ironmasters with both technical understanding and business acumen. See Volume I of his *History of American Business Leaders* (Ann Arbor, Mich.: Edwards Brothers, Inc., 1940), especially p. 101. Redlich in turn gives credit to Schumpeter and to Veblen's concept of the captain of industry as "a person of insight—perhaps chiefly industrial insight—and of initiative and energy, who was able to see something of the industrial reach and drive of that new mechanical technology that was finding its way into the industries, and who went about to contrive ways and means of turning these technological resources to new uses and a larger efficiency, always with a view to his own gain from turning out a more serviceable product with greater expedition" (Thorstein Veblen, *Absentee Ownership and Business Enterprise in Recent Times: The Case of America* [New York: B. W. Huebsch, 1923], p. 102, quoted by Redlich in *History of American Business Leaders*, p. 14). It should be noted, of course, that Veblen considered the captain of industry a significant figure only until about 1860.

in developing a product or production method to the point at which it gives reliable service and allows sales at a price greater than cost.[6] With respect to novel manufacturing methods introduced by a producer for himself, successful innovation would mean that the cost of installation has been justified by the earnings as compared with alternative investment opportunities. Clearly, these definitions of "innovation" and "invention" are not mutually exclusive. Technological innovation includes all the actions taken as a consequence of a decision, perhaps tentative at first, to bring a device or process into commercial use. Among these actions may be scientific theorizing, experiments, and the building of working models to develop and perfect an invention.[7] On the other hand, all inventions need not be directed toward immediate commercial production. They may be inspired by academic curiosity, military urgency, or simply a desire to control patents for encouraging, exploiting, or preventing innovations by others. Thus, the two concepts overlap. Invention includes technical changes made before, during, and after attempts to introduce a new process or product commercially; and innovation may or may not involve technical development as part of other activities.

The present study is concerned with the risks assumed by

[6] See Passer, *op. cit.*, p. 356.

[7] Professor John Jewkes and his associates have made an interesting distinction between "invention" and "development": "The essence of invention is the first confidence that something should work, and the first rough tests that it will, in fact, work. . . . Development is the stage at which known technical methods are applied to a new problem which, in wider or narrower terms, has been defined by the original invention. . . . Development is the stage at which the task to be performed is more precisely defined, the aim more exactly set, the search more specific, the chances of final success more susceptible to measurement than is true at the stage of invention. Invention is the stage at which the scent is picked up, development the stage at which the hunt is in full cry. . . . There seems to be a fundamental distinction between the two" (John Jewkes, David Sawers, and Richard Stillerman, *The Sources of Invention* [London: Macmillan and Co., 1958], pp. 17–21).

the entrepreneurs who introduced new methods of production in nineteenth-century America; and from this point of view, the broad, commercially oriented definition of innovation seems adequate. It includes only experiments and inventions financed by entrepreneurs for proposed innovations.[8] It is not concerned with the chance of loss, sustained as part of the process of technical change, by inventors in garrets, employees, or the community at large.

Risk

Like "innovation," the word "risk" has its ambiguities. In its actuarial sense it means chance of loss as a knowable parameter of a frequency distribution. In another sense, however, it indicates possible disappointment, which, of course, could not occur when risks are known and fully insured. Risk will be used in the second sense as a significant but to some extent unpredictable chance of loss. This is the type of risk that is generally called "uncertainty." [9]

[8] The activities of government armories and the like constitute borderline cases. Although the Springfield Armory, for example, was not organized by an entrepreneur for making a profit and although its products were not for sale to the highest bidder, it was nevertheless competitive with private arms makers and its contributions to manufacturing techniques were practical and significant. These contributions were innovations that might have failed and that might have caused losses to the government. See Felicia J. Deyrup, *Arms Makers of the Connecticut Valley* (Smith College Studies in History, vol. XXXIII; Northampton, Mass., 1948).

[9] For analyses of the role of risk in economic decision making, see Frank Knight, *Risk, Uncertainty, and Profit* (Boston and New York: Houghton Mifflin Co., 1921); Burton Keirstead, *An Essay in the Theory of Profits and Income Distribution* (Oxford: Basil Blackwell, 1953); A. G. Hart, *Anticipations, Uncertainty, and Dynamic Planning* (Chicago: University of Chicago Press, 1940); G. L. S. Shackle, *Expectations in Economics* (Cambridge: Cambridge University Press, 1952), and *Uncertainty in Economics* (Cambridge: Cambridge University Press, 1955); Evsey D. Domar and Richard A. Musgrave, "Proportional Income Taxation and Risk-Taking," *Quarterly Journal of Economics,* LVIII (May

For acts of innovation the chance of loss is formally unpredictable because the innovator lacks reliable knowledge of the results of procedures like his in identical situations. If he had such knowledge, he would either be imitating a success or duplicating a failure. One is not innovation, and the other is not plausible. The act of innovation may therefore be called unique, not necessarily because it is unprecedented or because recurrence is inconceivable, but because the innovator, by definition, must be attempting something he considers new and because, if unsuccessful, he will not repeat his action in exactly the same manner in an identical situation.[10]

But uniqueness or lack of knowledge make application of the laws of probability impossible. In one formal and strictly definitional sense, therefore, innovation must be regarded as totally unpredictable and uncertain. This formal uncertainty indicates nothing about the actual chance of loss, if any. Nor does it suggest that guesses about the outcome must be totally irrational. The entrepreneur and his expert advisers may have a great deal of other information which they can, with some confidence, project into the future. The financial success of a producers' goods innovation depends on its serviceability and timeliness with respect to a number of factors. About each of these factors a great deal of information may have been compiled; and although the laws of probability may not apply to the innovation per se, they may nevertheless cover some of the component factors. If the entrepreneur and his advisers can

---

1944), 388–422; J. Fred Weston, "The Profit Concept and Theory: A Restatement," *Journal of Political Economy,* LXII (April 1954), 152–170; Martin Shubik, "Information, Risk, Ignorance, and Indeterminancy," *Quarterly Journal of Economics,* LXVIII (Nov. 1954), 629–640; Nicholas Georgescu-Roegen, "Choice, Expectations, and Measurability," *Quarterly Journal of Economics,* LXVIII (Nov. 1954), 503–534.

[10] See G. L. S. Shackle, "A Non-additive Measure of Uncertainty," *Review of Economic Studies,* XVII (1949–1950), 70–74; Keirstead, *op. cit.,* pp. 18–21.

predict the behavior of enough of these, they may arrive at a close approximation of the outcome of an innovation. It seems useful, therefore, not to view the uncertainty of an innovation in terms of its formal uniqueness, but rather in terms of the predictability of its component factors.

A priori, many factors might adversely affect a novel manufacturing method and, if not foreseen, constitute a risk. First, there are the mechanical, hydraulic, thermic, electromagnetic, and chemical principles relevant to the functioning of a piece of equipment. If these are not known, enigmatic "bugs" are likely to impede or prevent the functioning of the producers' good in question. A related risk may be due to inability to predict the availability of labor and raw materials. Thus a process might function technically as predicted, but the types of labor and raw materials needed might be too costly or too scarce physically, regardless of cost, to allow commercial success.

A third reason for losses could be a rate of obsolescence of unforeseen rapidity. An innovating businessman might lose income and capital by being rapidly outstripped by some other businessman with a superior innovation in the same line. Moreover, one part of an industry may render another obsolete. Electric steel furnace improvements may leave the most ingenious innovations in steel crucibles unprofitable. On a still larger scale, the entire industry in which the innovation occurs may become unexpectedly obsolete because of innovations in other industries. Electric light may replace gas or kerosene, for example. Schumpeter apparently considered obsolescence on this scale, that is, by "creative destruction," the greatest risk for innovations.[11]

The danger of unexpected obsolescence rises when entry into an industry is easy for newcomers willing to initiate technological changes. Conversely, the risk of obsolescence is reduced by

[11] Joseph A. Schumpeter, *Capitalism, Socialism, and Democracy* (2d ed.; New York: Harper and Brothers, 1947), pp. 87 ff.

barriers to entry—large capital requirements, difficulties of acquiring complex experience, a strong patent position, or control
of market outlets or essential supplies. On the other hand, if
established firms are not progressive and innovations *must* be
introduced by newcomers, then barriers to entry increase the
apparent riskiness of innovation because the difficulties of organizing a business are necessarily added to those of innovation.

But developments outside any particular innovator's branch
of an industry might also render an innovation more profitable
than anticipated. The innovator might act without knowing
that technological changes elsewhere are about to raise the
demand for his own product. Or it might be that his very innovation, by improving quality or reducing price, creates the opportunity for other innovations whose success then raises his
own sales unexpectedly. Conceivably he might have expected
to increase profits by selling more at a lower price; but as it
turned out, he might finally have sold the larger quantity without lowering his price; or he might have sold far more at the
low price than seemed reasonable at the time of innovation.

The risks just described could be called "production risks"
because they involve inability to predict the functioning of
machinery—including fuel, raw material, labor costs, and obsolescence—in terms of the changing level of production skills
and resources of the economy. These "production risks" shade
over into others which involve forecasting the specific responses of individuals and social groups to the innovation. The
possibility that new machines, or the output of new machines,
though technically satisfactory, will not be adopted by individuals for reasons of inertia or prejudice may be called "customer risk." Insofar as prejudice is the result of publicity by
groups adversely affected by the innovation, "customer risks"
merge with "interference risks." These latter involve inability
to predict the reactions of groups that may thwart an innova-

tion, not because of blind prejudice against the new technique per se, but because of strategic considerations with respect to the group's social and economic status. It is the organization of society that in these cases provides both the incentive and the means for thwarting an innovation. Interference risks include the possibility of strikes, boycotts, vandalism, slander, business conspiracies, patent suits, tariff changes, and a variety of adverse government decisions.

Finally, there is a risk of "timing," the danger of launching an innovation too close to a business depression. Since this risk affects all ventures, it should be counted a risk of innovation only insofar as poor timing is likely to cause greater or more frequent losses among innovating organizations than among other new or expanding firms. For example, if the innovation consists of using a relatively greater proportion of fixed capital in a production process, it is likely to mean less liquidity and greater exposure to crises. Timing may also be more important for an innovating venture because the peroid of adjustment, of "ironing out the bugs," may require that, to have much chance of survival, it be launched at least five years before a crisis, compared with fewer years for other new firms. It is interesting to note that reasoning which applies to timing with respect to depressions applies equally well to timing with respect to floods and fire in the absence of insurance.

All of these factors are risks—possible causes of loss—only when their behavior cannot be effectively predicted. Thus a large, ironclad government contract for muskets might relieve an Eli Whitney of most "customer," "interference," and "timing" risks relevant to machine-tool innovation. But saying that risks involve inability to predict does not say that anything unpredictable must be a risk and might therefore cause a loss. The mere fact that an innovator believes some development might occur and threaten his innovation does not mean that such a development is a real possibility. It is lack of knowledge that makes the behavior of a factor seem unpredictable to an innovator, but lack of knowledge may also mean that a factor is not sufficiently known to be considered relevant or irrelevant on compelling grounds. The innovator is most ignorant of the factors which he considers the most unpredictable threats to his innovation (as well as of those which are really the greatest threat—if these two are not the same), and he is in no position to estimate how great the chance of loss on account of these factors actually is. He may correctly regard an attempt at innovation to be almost certain of failure or success; but if he considers the attempt risky (uncertain), he must lack the means of determining whether the attempt really is very risky in an actuarial sense and, if so, for what reasons.

Before pursuing this line of reasoning further, it should be noted that a historical study may shed light on the innovator himself as a possible determinant of losses. Predictability and chance of loss cannot be considered apart from the innovator's capability and procedures. As Charles O. Hardy once put it:

In a sense all risks are due to ignorance for if all the conditions of any situation were known there would be no risk involved in it for anyone. There is, however, a distinction worth maintaining between risks due to the limitations of human knowledge and risks which are due to the failure or inability of individuals to take advantage of the knowledge which is accessible to themselves.[12]

The quality of the risk takers is part of the total situation and influences the outcome as much as the predictability of technical and interference factors. Unlike roulette, and far more than in real estate or security speculation, the risk-taking innovator plays an important part in determining his own chance of success. The entrepreneur and his advisers do not just decide that a certain sum of money will be staked on an innovation. They

[12] Charles O. Hardy, *Risk and Risk-Bearing* (Chicago: University of Chicago Press, 1923), p. 2.

decide precisely how the venture is to proceed, how much preliminary exploration will be tried, what the criteria for changing plans will be, who is to be consulted, and how fast one
step is to succeed another. They decide whether the path of
innovation will be cautious or bold. It is noteworthy that Professor Usher has given particular importance, not to caution,
but to the entrepreneur's willingness to exercise good judgment.
According to Usher, if good judgment is exercised, risks of loss
in attempting innovations need not exceed the risks of common
routines in established industries.[13]

The cautiousness or boldness of the innovator are determined
by the general mores of the community and by relatively pe-
culiar experiences that make his own personality differ from
the general code. In a specific situation the apparent cautiousness or boldness of his behavior is determined by his view of
the factors that he considers strategic.

Whenever caution leads to the acquisition of knowledge increasing the predictability of strategic factors, it should lower
risks. The chance of loss could thus be reduced because the
course of action is likely to be in closer accord with the material, psychological, and organizational requirements of the innovation. This result is probable, but, of course, not inevitable.
Caution may lead to knowledge of the wrong factors, which,
wrongly interpreted, will change action in a wrong direction.
It is even possible that correct knowledge may indicate a course
of action that would not be right if knowledge of other, more
important, factors were available.

The proportion of losses that actually occurred may be used
to estimate the extent to which unpredictable factors threatened
a large group of innovations. This procedure raises one enormous problem: Is there an adequate record of losses, particularly of firms that failed? Can one overcome the success bias
of the literature which, of course, consists largely of tributes to

[13] Usher, *op. cit.*, p. 534.

inventors, industrialists, and firms that succeeded? The validity of the entire study hinges on this point.

It should be frankly admitted that the difficulty could not be entirely eliminated. Although it was not insuperable, it remained a skeleton in the closet. Many unsuccessful attempts at innovation probably did vanish without telling their tale. Conceivably, some of these might even have been important attempts in the sense of much having been risked and lost in the hope of great gains. But if the proportion of failures had been uniform throughout all industries and all periods, or varying at random, one would expect such records as did survive to indicate a fairly uniform incidence of failure. One would not ordinarily expect the failures of one decade to be well remembered and those of the next decade to be forgotten. One would not expect the failures in blast-furnace innovation of the 1830's to be recorded and the memory of failures in electric power innovation during the 1890's to be buried with the men who made the attempts. And yet if one tried to maintain that innovation was always very risky, one would have to make that kind of assumption.

All the dead men and their tales have not vanished: In certain industries during certain periods, the tales of technological and other failures are well known and well documented. In other industries, or in the same industries during other periods, records of failures as a result of attempted innovation are rare. Above all, however, the recurrence of failures here and the absence of records of failures there make an interesting pattern: Where the objective conditions made the occurrence of failures likely, a record of failures exists. Where objective conditions made failures highly unlikely, the records suggest an almost unbroken series of successful innovations. In one sense this study is an exploration of these objective conditions.

In general, it will be shown that the social, political, and economic structure was conducive to innovation and that the unexpected dovetailing of technological innovations in separate industries tended to enhance the profitability of innovations beyond the expectations of the innovators. A combination of vast and multiplying opportunities and cautious exploitation made failure at innovation a rare occurrence in most categories.

Throughout the study, it is assumed that when a large number of innovations is considered, rarity of loss in the presence of great risk must be a contradiction in terms. If hypothetical innovations, as well as those actually attempted, were to be included, the statement might not hold; but it is hard to see what point there might be in such a study. For example, if innovations were invariably undertaken with great caution, it is hypothetical and futile to speak of losses that might have occurred if innovators had been unthinking and rash. The relevant question is whether a cautious approach could lead to knowledge of predictive value. Would it show the role of possible impurities in the furnace or give a better estimate of prospective sales? If techniques for acquiring information about key variables were lacking, innovations were necessarily gambles in spite of all caution.

Finally, does the absence of losses (and therefore of risk) in connection with a long series of innovations necessarily reflect on the daring of innovators? Does it not take just as much boldness to expose yourself to illusory as to real dangers if you have no means of determining which is which? No doubt there is some truth in the position implied by these questions. But this study is not an appraisal of the moral qualities of innovators. No attempt is made to determine whether innovators "deserved" the incomes they received, or something higher or lower. It will simply be shown that the vast majority of innovations which seemed hazardous to people at the time were not, in fact, risky and that for most sweeping changes in manufacturing methods the process of innovation was already a safe and even predictable routine.

II

Iron and Steel

INTENSE power could be harnessed, controlled, and applied only by mechanisms made of a substance that was both tough and capable of being shaped with precision The larger use of power in the technological transformation called the Industrial Revolution therefore involved the progressive substitution of first iron, then steel, for wood. Iron was the cheapest material that was both tough and malleable, and it was toughest and most malleable as steel. In the United States, pig iron production increased from about 15 pounds per inhabitant in 1810[1] to 380 pounds in 1900.[2] Steel production increased from about

[1] James M. Swank, *History of the Manufacture of Iron in All Ages and Particularly in the United States from Colonial Times to 1891,* hereafter to be cited as *Iron in All Ages* (Philadelphia: American Iron and Steel Association, 1892), p. 376.

[2] U.S. Bureau of the Census, *Census of Manufactures, 1905* (Washington, 1907), Bull. 78, p. 37.

5 ounces [3] per inhabitant to 285 pounds.[4] Thus pig iron production expanded from 55,000 tons to 14,452,000 tons; and the proportion further refined into steel increased from 2 per cent to 74 per cent.[5] By 1900 the total value added by manufacturing in blast furnaces and steel mills amounted to 282 million dollars.[6]

This tremendous expansion had a purely quantitative side. The greater volume was in part due to the use of more men, more ore, more fuel, and more equipment of unchanged design. In larger part, however, it was due to the introduction of better equipment which could be operated by less skilled workers, consume ore and fuel of lower quality, and nevertheless increase both quality and quantity of output per worker. Few innovations had more than one or two of these effects. Usually they either increased quality by such means as a novel chemical process, or they decreased unit costs by reducing the expense on either labor, capital, fuel, or iron ore. In blast furnaces, for example, labor costs were reduced by increasing capacity with stronger blast engines and hotter blast ovens. Fuel costs were reduced by substituting anthracite and coke for charcoal and by re-using furnace gas. Quality was improved by chemical analysis and selection of ores and fuels.

In refining, the introduction of puddling furnaces for making wrought iron and the use of crucibles for making cast steel reduced fuel costs by allowing the substitution of coal for charcoal.[7] The Bessemer process sharply reduced all refining costs,

[3] Victor S. Clark, *History of Manufactures in the United States* (Washington: Carnegie Institution, 1929), I, 516.

[4] U.S. Census Bureau, *op. cit.*, Bull. 78, p. 69.

[5] Steel production in 1900 amounted to 10.7 million tons. Of this amount 3.0 million were produced in open-hearth furnaces. Since many of these were using some scrap, a corresponding downward adjustment in the percentage would be necessary for strict accuracy.

[6] U.S. Census Office, *Twelfth Census: Manufactures* (Washington, 1902), X, 4.

[7] Timber was abundant in the United States, but the cost of converting

but the quality of Bessemer steel could not be controlled with precision. Quality control came with the open-hearth process and with nickel, tungsten, and chromium alloys.

In shaping, forges with trip hammers gave way to trains of grooved rolls. Unit labor costs were then further reduced by specializing these rolls and mechanizing auxiliary operations. Unit capital costs were reduced by improving this specialized equipment and at times by making it again more versatile. Fuel costs were reduced by integrating operations to avoid reheating, by cold rolling, and by substituting electricity for direct steam power. As stated in the introduction, by 1900 the iron and steel industry was so mechanized that moving a lever or turning a wheel was practically the only manual labor needed from the time the raw materials arrived at a plant until the finished steel products were loaded on freight cars.

All these innovations together allowed steel production to grow from hundreds of tons a year to millions of tons. They played the largest part in reducing the price of pig iron from $38 a ton in 1810 to $14 a ton in 1900 and in reducing the price of steel from about $200 a ton to $19 a ton.[8]

Innovation from 1817 through the Civil War

The effect of the Civil War on the demand for iron, particularly for rails, machinery, and munitions, and on the supply of iron by raising tariffs made the decade of the 1860's pivotal for the iron and steel industry. It was pivotal not only for the rate of expansion, but also for the pace and manner of techno-

---

it into charcoal was greater than the cost of mining coal and making coke (Louis C. Hunter, "Influence of the Market upon Technique in the Iron Industry in Western Pennsylvania Up to 1860," *Journal of Economic and Business History*, Feb. 1929, pp. 241–281.

[8] These prices, to be sure, applied to steel of different average qualities. See Clark, *op. cit.*, I, 139, III, 387; U.S. Census Office, *Twelfth Census*, X, 47; U.S. Census Bureau, *op. cit.*, Bull. 78, pp. 73–74.

logical innovation. Before 1860 rule-of-thumb methods prevailed in making iron and steel, and even leading manufacturers did not keep track of the exact cost of each process. At times, when books were balanced and stock was taken at the end of a year, ironmasters who thought they were making profits showed losses, and vice versa.[9] Being unfamiliar with the scientific principles on which their methods were based and unprepared to compare costs in detail, ironmasters were necessarily reluctant to abandon old and proved ways. Most changes in production methods were suggested by immigrant workers who claimed knowledge of superior practice abroad. The claims of these workers were treated with skepticism, and a lag of eight to twenty years commonly occurred before a successful British or German innovation was first attempted in America.[10]

After 1870 production costs were more closely observed, and innovations were introduced by engineers on the basis of metallurgical knowledge or experiments. Moreover, innovations moved across the Atlantic in both directions. Fundamentally new methods continued to originate in Europe, but innovations that made established methods more large scale, integrated, and automatic were generally American. By 1900 American iron and steel workers surpassed the best Europeans in productivity by as much as 200 per cent.[11]

The first major innovation introduced from Europe in the nineteenth century was the process of refining pig iron by puddling and then shaping the resulting bar iron with trains of rolls instead of trip hammers. This process had been patented in England by Henry Cort in 1784, but it was not

[9] Andrew Carnegie, *Autobiography of Andrew Carnegie,* posthumously arranged for publication by John C. Van Dyke (Boston: Houghton Mifflin Co., 1920), p. 135.

[10] Stephen L. Goodale, *Chronology of Iron and Steel* (2d ed.; Cleveland: Penton Publishing Co., 1931), pp. 106–164.

[11] Clark, *op. cit.,* III, 74.

brought to America until 1816. The Welsh ironworker, Thomas C. Lewis, who introduced the process, had landed in New York in 1815; but a year had passed before he found an iron-master willing to build a puddling furnace and a rolling mill. The ironmaster who finally agreed was Isaac Meason of western Pennsylvania. His puddling furnace and rolling mill were located at Plumsock in Fayette County and operated successfully from 1816 until 1831. The works were then partially destroyed by a spring flood.[12]

Less successful were attempts to smelt ore with coke, as had been done in England for a century. One of the earliest American attempts, a furnace at Bear Creek, Armstrong County, Pennsylvania, was supervised in 1819 by the same Thomas C. Lewis. It failed primarily because Lewis could not talk its penny-wise owners into financing an installation with a strong blast. But a number of other attempts failed even with adequate equipment, including one with the very best apparatus, imported from Glasgow. This last attempt was the greatest failure of all, a venture at Farrandsville, Pennsylvania, which cost a group of Boston financiers $500,000. In 1835 the Franklin Institute still offered a gold medal to the person who would smelt the greatest amount of iron with coal or coke alone, and the Institute even considered it necessary to specify that the amount should not be less than twenty tons during the year. The reasons given for various failures included primarily miscalculation of transportation costs and the poor quality of the pig iron due to impurities in the coal. The Farrandsville attempt had the additional misfortune of beginning operations in the depression year of 1837.

The first successful coke-smelting furnaces were finally built near Lonaconing, Maryland, in 1839 by the George's Creek Company and by the Mount Savage Iron Company. The iron

[12] Swank, *Iron in All Ages*, pp. 214–217.

produced was not sufficiently strong or malleable, when both hot and cold, to meet the requirements of blacksmiths, farmers, and small millowners; but it was good enough for a rapidly growing new market, rails.[13]

Because anthracite does not burn as easily as coke or charcoal, it was not until James Neilson had developed the hot blast in Scotland in 1828 that anthracite furnaces made progress. Anthracite had two advantages. It was a "natural" fuel that did not require expensive processing, and it was more transportable than some kinds of coke because it did not crumble. Moreover, its behavior in a furnace was fairly uniform and predictable. These advantages of anthracite for decades outweighed the fact that coke would lend itself more readily to intense, large-scale blasting.

The first American experiments with a hot blast were conducted by Frederick Geissenhainer, a wealthy New York clergyman, born in Germany. Geissenhainer claimed to have succeeded in smelting with anthracite on a commercial scale near Pottsville, Pennsylvania, in 1836; but, as he explained to the Commissioner of Patents, an accident to his machinery ended operations; and he was too ill to straighten things out. After Geissenhainer's death in 1838, his patents were sold to George Crane, who had definitely succeeded at anthracite smelting near Yniscedwyn, Wales, in 1836 and 1837. Final success at smelting with anthracite on a commercial scale in the United States was achieved in October 1839 at Pottsville under the direction of Benjamin Perry, the same English ironworker who had supervised the large coke-smelting failure at Farrandsville. This furnace, built for Burd Patterson of Pottsville, was operated for thirteen months, was then idle for four years, and was

[13] Hunter, *op. cit.*, pp. 255–272; James M. Swank, *Cambria County Pioneers* (Philadelphia: Allen, Lane, and Scott, 1910), pp. 55–70, and *Iron in All Ages*, pp. 367–370.

again in operation for two. Whether or not it was a net gain, financially, is uncertain.

More important in many respects were the anthracite furnaces of the Lehigh Crane Iron Company of Catasauqua, Pennsylvania, completed in 1840 and 1842. The machinery of these furnaces was ordered under the direction of George Crane, the Welsh inventor mentioned above, and one of these furnaces remained in operation for over thirty years. The owners of the Lehigh Crane Iron Company had financed what was apparently the first commercial (unsuccessful) attempt to smelt exclusively with anthracite in 1826. Other furnaces had failed in the same way, but some had had considerable success at smelting with mixtures of anthracite and charcoal. Anthracite smelting spread more rapidly than coke smelting in America from 1840 until 1870. By 1855 more pig iron was smelted with anthracite than with charcoal, and six times as much as was smelted with coke.[14]

Between 1828 and 1849 there were several unsuccessful attempts to make cast steel in the United States. Cast steel was made from low-grade steel further refined in closed crucibles at high temperatures. The crucible process reduced the cost of high-quality steel by allowing the use of mineral fuel and by speeding operations. The early failures in the United States were primarily due to inability to find a clay like English Stourbridge clay that could withstand high temperatures. In 1832 a suitable clay was found by Dr. William Garrard, an English immigrant, who then organized the Cincinnati Steel Works. This firm operated successfully on a small scale until

[14] Fritz Redlich, *History of American Business Leaders* (Ann Arbor, Mich.: Edwards Brothers, Inc., 1940), pp. 70–73; Swank, *Iron in All Ages,* pp. 356–364, 376–377; William Firmstone, "Sketch of Early Anthracite Furnaces," *Transactions of the American Institute of Mining Engineers,* III (1874–1875), 152–156; *Bulletin of the American Iron and Steel Association,* hereafter cited as *A.I.S.A. Bulletin,* XXIII (March 6 and 13, 1889), 65.

the panic of 1837. Later failures such as that of George and J. H. Shoenberger of Pittsburgh resulted from ignorance of the role if impurities, like phosphorus, in determining the quality of steel. After Joseph Dixon of the Adirondack Iron and Steel Company of Jersey City perfected plumbago crucibles in 1849, the problem of heat-resistant melting pots was no longer serious, but the problem of quality and reputation for poor quality remained. In 1850 Springfield Armory technicians found the Adirondack Company's steel equal to the best imported English steel, but the superintendent and other manufacturers made no attempt to use it. Complete technical and financial success at making cast steel was not attained by any firm before 1860 when Hussey, Wells and Company of Pittsburgh finally began regular prodution of high-quality tool steel. Two years later James Park, Jr., and Company, also of Pittsburgh, entered the field. Park's firm became one of the world's largest cast steel producers, and Park himself took the lead at introducing a number of other European innovations, which will be described later.[15]

The introduction of European innovations that did not involve chemical difficulties proceeded more smoothly. No business failures are recorded in the adoption of German devices for drawing off unburned furnace gas as fuel for other uses. The processes of iron boiling and steel puddling were also commercially successful the first time they were attempted in America.[16]

Equally successful were the earliest American innovations,

[15] Swank, *Iron in All Ages,* pp. 309, 385–392; Redlich, *American Business Leaders,* pp. 91–93; Felicia J. Deyrup, *Arms Makers of the Connecticut Valley* (Smith College Studies in History, vol. XXXIII; Northhampton, Mass., 1948), pp. 139, 192; Harrison Gilmer, "Birth of the American Crucible Steel Industry," *Western Pennsylvania Historical Magazine,* XXXVI (March 1953), 17–36.

[16] Swank, *Iron in All Ages,* pp. 453–455; Goodale, *op. cit.,* pp. 112–125; Redlich, *American Business Leaders,* pp. 77–79, 91.

most of which involved the conservation of heat and mechanical energy. One of these was Henry Burden's rotary concentric
squeezer for working puddled iron free of slag. The Commissioner of Patents considered it the first important American invention in the making of iron. Burden introduced the device in
1840 at his own ironworks near Troy, New York, and it quickly
spread to other states and to Europe. Another successful innovation was John Griffin's method of conserving fuel by placing
steam boilers over the puddling furnace of the Moore and
Hooven works at Norristown, Pennsylvania, in 1846. David
Thomas of the Lehigh Crane Iron Company radically increased
the power of blowing engines with immediate success in 1852.
This practice was not adopted in Britain until many years
later. About the same time a number of casting innovations
were made, such as drop-bottom melting cupolas, improved
molding machinery, and better handling and pickling methods.[17]

Between 1845 and 1853 three large firms that pioneered innovations both before and after the Civil War were founded:
the Trenton Iron Works, the Cambria Iron Works, and Jones
and Laughlin. The Trenton Iron Works were financed by Peter
Cooper and mainly operated by his son-in-law, Abram S.
Hewitt. The works were built to roll rails, but reductions in
the tariff and the British practice of selling rails for bonds
forced the firm into other lines—wire, rivets, and spikes. In
1852 the works pioneered the rolling of wrought iron beams
for buildings, the first ones being intended for Cooper Union.
To roll these beams the Trenton works introduced "three-high"
mills, in which a third roll could shape the beams again as
they were being returned over the top roll, thus saving labor,
capital, and fuel. Another innovation was a "universal" mill

[17] Margaret Burden Proudfit, *Henry Burden: His Life* (Troy, N.Y.:
Pafraets Press, 1904), pp. 66, 67; Swank, *Iron in All Ages,* p. 455; Goodale,
op. cit., pp. 119–135; Clark, *op. cit.,* I, 416–417.

which saved labor by adding rolls that trimmed edges. It was apparently developed without knowledge of similar German equipment. Hewitt was one of the first ironmasters to subscribe to British iron journals, and he was therefore not dependent on immigrant workers for reports of foreign technological progress. As soon as he heard of Bessemer's Cheltenham paper on the manufacture of malleable iron and steel by blowing air through molten pig iron, he took steps to obtain the American rights. But, like many British ironmasters, he used pig iron that was too phosphoric, and after two months, in January 1857, he abandoned the experiment.[18]

Hewitt's innovations in iron rolling were not patented, and because contemporary iron trade journals in America were little more than hardware catalogues, they received no attention in western Pennsylvania. As a result, several innovations were reinvented and reintroduced by such men as John Fritz of the Cambria Iron Works. These works had been founded at Johnstown, Pennsylvania, in 1851. Among Fritz's innovations were the three-high mill, lifting plates, "live" or driven rollers, and the use of heavy cast guide rails. From the Cambria works these innovations spread to other mills, and Benjamin Franklin Jones of Jones and Laughlin later told Fritz that "Cambria was the cradle in which the great improvements in rolling mill practice were rocked." [19]

During 1857–1858 the Cambria works experimented with refining by means of blowing air through molten pig iron. These experiments at Cambria were made by William Kelly, a Kentucky ironmaster, who had developed the idea some eight

[18] Allan Nevins, *Abram S. Hewitt, with Some Account of Peter Cooper* (New York: Harper and Brothers, 1935), pp. 74–133; Swank, *Iron in All Ages,* pp. 400–404, 435.

[19] John Fritz, *The Autobiography of John Fritz* (New York: John Wiley and Sons, 1912), pp. 113–135; Swank, *Iron in All Ages,* pp. 397–399; Clark, *op. cit.,* I, 415; B. F. Fackenthal, "John Fritz, the Ironmaster," *Pennsylvania German Society,* XXXIV (Oct. 1923), 95–112.

years earlier than Bessemer. Between 1847 and 1857 Kelly had
experimented with air blasts at his own works and had successfully applied the results to purposes other than refining. His
experiments and results do not appear to have been of sufficient
scale to be considered either a cause or a meliorating factor in
his bankruptcy in the panic of 1857. In any case, Kelly had no
knowledge of the chemistry involved in his process, and his
methods were not suitable for mass production.[20] Two years

[20] The significance of Kelly's experiment can be evaluated by considering his own account as prepared in the 1880's for Swank's *Iron in
All Ages*. It should be remembered that molten metal and air blasts had
always been in close proximity at blast furnaces.

"I devised several plans for testing this idea of forcing into the
fluid metal powerful blasts of air; and, after making drawings of the
same, showed them to my forgemen, not one of whom could agree with
me, all believing that I would chill the metal, and that my experiment
would end in failure. I finally fixed on a plan of furnace . . . about 12
feet high having a hearth and bosh like a common blast furnace . . .
the lower [tuyère] was fixed in the hearth near the bottom, and intended
to conduct the air-blast into the metal . . . I began my experiments
with this furnace in October, 1847, but found it impossible to give it
sufficient attention [until] 1851 . . . After numerous trials of this furnace I found that . . . when the blast was continued for a longer period,
the iron would occasionally be somewhat malleable . . . The variability
of results in the working of my experimental furnace was then a mystery
which is now explained. . .

"I now decided that, if I could not succeed in making malleable iron,
I could turn my invention to practical account by . . . supplying a cheap
method of making run-out metal, and, after trying it a few days, we entirely dispensed with the old and troublesome run-out fires.

". . . In 1857 I applied for a patent, as soon as I heard that other
men were following the same line of experiments in England; and, although Mr. Bessemer was a few days before me in obtaining a patent,
I was granted an interference, and the case was heard by the Commissioner of Patents, who decided that I was the first inventor of this
process, now known as the Bessemer process, and a patent was granted
me over Mr. Bessemer" (William Kelly quoted in Swank, *Iron in All
Ages*, pp. 397–399).

Victor S. Clark points out that Kelly and his associates had "no knowledge of the chemical reactions which their process involved; conse-

after these experiments were abandoned, in 1860, the Cambria works hired a chemist, Captain Robert W. Hunt, probably the first at an American ironworks.

The Jones and Laughlin works of Benjamin Franklin Jones and James Laughlin were founded at Pittsburgh in 1853 and were third in adopting three-high mills. A partner of this firm, Bernard Lauth, an Alsatian engineer, developed machinery that could lower fuel costs by rolling iron cold. During the Civil War, Lauth applied the three-high principle to plate rolling. These works also led in the substitution of belts for gears. Like the Trenton and Cambria works, Jones and Laughlin took steps toward vertical integration of mine, furnace, and rolling mill. They were particularly noted for pioneering the use of Lake Superior ores.[21]

By the end of the Civil War, iron and steel makers in the United States had by no means caught up with European technology. At Sheffield, England, twenty-ton plates, twelve inches thick, were rolled as early as 1863; in the same year the best American mills could roll armor no more than one and a half inches thick.[22] Tungsten steel and other alloys were made commercially in Germany years before American works made them experimentally.[23] Abram S. Hewitt became a United States Commissioner to the Paris Exposition of 1867 and reported "a prevailing willingness and practice in the European works to handle iron in larger masses for every purpose than we do in the United States."[24] It should be noted that such

---

quently they were unable to control the quality of their product . . . and they did not develop the details of their method in the direction which eventually gave it importance" (Clark, *op. cit.*, I, 415–416).

[21] Ben Morrell, *"J. & L.": The Growth of an American Business* (New York: Newcomen Society, 1953); Goodale, *op. cit.*, pp. 136, 150, 160; Clark, *op. cit.*, II, 79; Redlich, *American Business Leaders*, pp. 80, 87–88.

[22] Clark, *op. cit.*, II, 18.   [23] *Ibid.*, II, 20, 78.

[24] *Reports of the United States Commissioners to the Paris Exposition, 1867* (Washington: Government Printing Office, 1870), II, 4.

large-scale handling was precisely the skill at which American works later outstripped the Europeans. In his official capacity as Commissioner, Hewitt soberly noted European progress in cast steel, in precise quality control, in the application of the Siemens regenerative furnaces, and in the Bessemer process.[25] To his partner at the Trenton works, he wrote with more enthusiasm. Of English steelworks, he said, "the new rolling mills beat us to death by the use of hydraulic cranes everywhere to lift and carry the iron. They do not employ half the men we do for the same work." Of French steelworks, he said, "They roll one inch round iron in lengths of 100 feet . . . but I cannot begin to make you see the progress. You must come for yourself." And Krupp's processes in Germany struck him as "the most difficult ever attempted by human ingenuity." [26] Before leaving Europe, Hewitt obtained the American rights to use and license the Siemens-Martin open-hearth process.[27]

The Bessemer Process

That summer, 1867, the first commercial American Bessemer steel plant, the Pennsylvania Steel Works, began operations at Steelton, Pennsylvania. Like no other innovation, the Bessemer process revolutionized the iron and steel industry; and like no other metallurgical innovation, its introduction in the United States has been described as risky. One historian speaks of "the catastrophes that attended the Bessemer converter in the United States" [28]; another writes, "Bessemer steel makers encountered the difficulties which usually face pioneers [and] earned little or no profits." [29] And a third speaks of "many dis-

[25] *Ibid.*, pp. 4–84.
[26] Letters to Edward Cooper, written in July 1867, quoted in Nevins, *op. cit.*, pp. 240, 246.
[27] *Ibid.*, pp. 243–246.
[28] Burton J. Hendrick, *The Life of Andrew Carnegie* (Garden City, N.Y.: Doubleday, Doran & Co., 1932), p. 178.
[29] Clark, *op. cit.*, II, 71.

couraging vicissitudes." [30] These catastrophes and vicissitudes are said to have occurred in spite of the fact that the chemical difficulties in Bessemer's original process had been solved by 1858. The role of phosphoric and sulfuric impurities had been discovered, and Robert Mushet had introduced his process of adding spiegeleisen to the converter to remove excess oxygen and to add the proper amount of carbon. G. F. Göransson in Sweden had developed an alternate process of using manganiferous ores, and he had discovered the advantage of blowing in larger amounts of air at lower pressure.

In 1864 and 1865 Bessemer steel was successfully produced at two experimental works at Wyandotte, Michigan, and at Troy, New York. The engineers in charge of these works wrote that the apparatus used was built "as cheaply and as simply as it could be made for purposes of experiment only." [31] Nevertheless, both plants were later counted as commercial failures by some writers. The returns from these experiments were, however, to be derived from patent control, not from production. The Wyandotte group, led by E. B. Ward,[32] Z. S. Durfee,

[30] James M. Swank, "Losses of American Bessemer Steel Manufacturers," *A.I.S.A. Bulletin,* vol. XVI, Dec. 6, 1882.

[31] William F. Durfee, "The First Bessemer Steel Works in the United States," *Transactions of the American Institute of Mechanical Engineers,* Nov. 1884, reprinted in the *A.I.S.A. Bulletin,* XVIII (Nov. 12, 1884), 291. See also Robert W. Hunt, "History of the Bessemer Manufacture in America," *Transactions of the American Institute of Mining Engineers,* V (June 1876), 201–207. Hunt had been the first chemist at the Cambria works and was later superintendent at Wyandotte and Troy.

[32] E. B. Ward (1811–1875) owned the largest merchant fleet on the Great Lakes, was president of the Flint and Pere Marquette Railroad and of the Burlington and Iowa Railroad, and had extensive interests in shipbuilding, lumber, real estate, and other industries.

He was president of the Eureka Iron Company and the Wyandotte Rolling Mill Company, founded in 1853 and 1855. The Wyandotte Bessemer experiments were carried on at the blast furnace of the Eureka Iron Company of Wyandotte, but Ward's associates in these steel experiments were primarily Pennsylvania ironmen. When steel was successfully

Daniel J. Morrell, and James Park, Jr., held Kelly's and Mushet's patents; and the Troy group, led by A. L. Holley, John F. Winslow, and John A. Griswold, held Bessemer's patents. Each had made steel only by infringing on the other's patents. Their interests were consolidated in 1866, and the Pennsylvania Steel Company's plant was ready for operation the following year. This plant was designed by A. L. Holley, who had built the Troy works. The patent holders received five dollars a ton royalty for rails and ten dollars a ton for other steel.

But the Pennsylvania Steel Company did not have to worry about prices and sales. Its stockholders were also its customers. They included Samuel M. Felton, president of the Philadelphia, Wilmington, and Baltimore Railroad; J. Edgar Thomson, president of the Pennsylvania Railroad; the leading Philadelphia machine-tool builders, William Sellers and Company and Bement and Daugherty; the locomotive works of M. W. Baldwin and Company; Morris, Tasker and Company; and others. During the early years profits were plowed back and dividends were paid in stock, but beginning with the depression year 1873, liberal dividends were paid annually. In 1873, 1874, 1875, and later, the company's output of steel rails increased annually. The first commercial Bessemer steel works in America were a solid success.[33]

---

produced in Sept. 1864, Ward's Michigan associates refused to adapt their rolling mill to steel rolling. Ward shipped the steel to his North Chicago Rolling Mill, which he had founded in 1857, and there the first Bessemer steel rails made in the United States were rolled on May 24, 1865. See *A.I.S.A. Bulletin*, VIII (Jan. 15, 1875), 4; *Michigan Pioneer and Historical Collection* (Lansing, Mich., 1877–1929), VII, 491–514, XX, 302, XXI, 340–346; John S. Van Alstyne, "The Iron Industry: Its Rise, Progress, and Decline in Wyandotte Graphically Set Forth," *Wyandotte Herald*, Feb. 18, 1901 (a copy of this article has been deposited in the Michigan State Library, Local History Division, Lansing, Mich.).

[33] Hunt, *op. cit.*, pp. 207–208; *A.I.S.A. Bulletin*, VII (Oct. 29, 1874), 325, IX (Oct. 15, Oct. 22, 1875), 308, 316; Swank, *Iron in All Ages*, pp. 409–410; Clark, *op. cit.*, II, 231; Redlich, *American Business Leaders*, pp. 94–101.

All other Bessemer steel works that began operations between 1867 and 1873 were commercially successful and survived the depression, with one exception—the Freedom Iron and Steel Works at Lewistown, Pennsylvania. These works had been added in 1868 to a successful iron company, the product of which did not, however, meet Bessemer requirements. The machinery was therefore dismantled after a year and sold.[34] This machinery, unlike that used at most other American works, had been imported. Such works used equipment designed by A. L. Holley, who had made a number of changes from British practice. He did away with the deep pit and raised the converter to get working space underneath, substituted cupolas for reverberatory furnaces, and used different types of cranes.[35]

In the light of this successful record, how did the late American introduction of the Bessemer process acquire its reputation for riskiness? One explanation might be that accounts of businessmen like Carnegie and James M. Swank have received more attention than accounts of engineers like Durfee, Hunt, and Holley. Carnegie was often (rather unfairly) criticized for having resisted technological progress. The primary support for this criticism was his failure to adopt the Bessemer process until 1872.[36]

Carnegie's later claims that the Bessemer process was experimental even in the 1870's and that transferring it to the United States was still an experiment "certain to be long and costly" [37] may have been in response to such criticism. Other claims of riskiness, that is, of many early losses, may have been intended as justification for a continued high tariff on steel in the face of the high profits earned by the few large steelmakers who had brought the patent-holding company. Thus James M. Swank,

[34] Hunt, *op. cit.*, p. 209.   [35] *Ibid.*, p. 214.
[36] James Howard Bridge, *The Inside History of the Carnegie Steel Company* (New York: Aldine Book Co., 1903), pp. 72–74, 268.
[37] Carnegie, *op. cit.*, p. 185.

on whose books and articles later histories (by Victor S. Clark, Stephen L. Goodale, etc.) appear largely based, was also secretary of the American Iron and Steel Association and editor of its *Bulletin*. As secretary and editor he fought for the tariff and defended the Bessemer steel makers from charges of monopoly from the 1870's until the 1890's. Some of his earliest historical articles were excerpts from his letters to Representative William D. Kelley, chairman of the tariff-making House Ways and Means Committee from 1881 to 1883. These letters claimed that steelmaking involved losses, low prices, and unprofitableness all around.[38] They would mention losses that had occurred years before a company had thought of making steel and would bring in all later failures to pay cash dividends; but they did not mention profits plowed back, stock dividends, and expansion of earnings and output.

From the Open Hearth to the Duquesne Revolution

Between the Civil War and the end of the century many other major and innumerable small innovations occurred in iron and steel making. Several attempts to innovate were unsuccessful and resulted in losses, some in business failure. But attempts to innovate led to fewer losses than total refusal either to innovate or to imitate.[39]

One of the great European innovations of the 1860's was the gas regenerative furnace developed by William and Friederich Siemens. With its extremely high temperatures generated under conditions that nevertheless allowed chemical control, this furnace created opportunities in a number of industries. James Park, Jr., of Pittsburgh, who had helped finance the Wyandotte experimental Bessemer works, first introduced the Siemens regenerative furnace to the United States, though without legal

[38] *A.I.S.A. Bulletin*, XVI (Dec. 6, 1882), 325.
[39] Even the use of obsolete equipment was generally not as detrimental as the use of an obsolete location.

permission and without Siemens' assistance. One furnace for smelting and refining copper worked well, but another for heating steel failed. Almost all the furnaces regularly introduced by others, beginning in 1867, were satisfactory and led to large fuel savings. Around 1875 an iron-rail mill rolling 40,000 tons a year could save at least $70,000 a year by substituting a Siemens regenerative furnace for the old reverberatory type, an amount equal to half the annual labor cost or to one-fifth of the capital cost.[40]

The most important use of the Siemens regenerative furnace was in conjunction with an open-hearth bath of molten pig iron and scrap to make steel. This process allowed the use of cheaper raw materials and cheaper apparatus to make steel of a higher and more uniform quality. Unlike Bessemer steel, open-hearth steel had sufficient quality to compete with crucible steel. By 1900 it was replacing Bessemer steel for tin-plate and structural beams, and it had replaced crucible steel altogether except for use in fine springs, high-grade tools, and cutlery. Its production was rising eight times as fast as crucible steel production after 1886–1890, and almost four times as fast as Bessemer steel production, surpassing it in 1908.[41]

Abram S. Hewitt, as mentioned above, had acquired the right to use and license the open-hearth process in America, while sharing royalties equally with the Martin brothers of Sireuil, France. Hewitt's attempt to use the process was unsuccessful, but his right to license was highly lucrative. He tried to use an eight-ton converter in 1868 and 1869 but failed, according to his own later opinion, because of inability to determine and control the quality of the pig iron and scrap used.

[40] A. L. Holley, "Some Pressing Needs of Our Iron and Steel Manufacturers," *Transactions of the American Institute of Mining Engineers,* IV (Oct. 1875), 82–83; Swank, *Iron in All Ages,* pp. 421–422; Redlich, *American Business Leaders,* pp. 55–56.

[41] U.S. Census Office, *Twelfth Census,* X, 23; U.S. Census Bureau, *op. cit.,* Bull. 78, p. 69; Clark, *op. cit.,* II, 248–249, III, 67–79.

The steel made was uneconomical because it could be rolled only at extremely high temperatures. Hewitt therefore returned to using the Mushet-Heath process of fusing wrought iron with certain types of carburized iron, which he himself had introduced in 1866. Meanwhile, his Trenton Iron Works and New Jersey Steel and Iron Company were declining because of geographical disadvantages and because Peter Cooper, the largest stockholder, opposed Hewitt's plans for moving west.[42]

There were other unsuccessful attempts to introduce the open-hearth process in America. One of these occurred at the William Butcher Steel Works near Philadelphia. Butcher had originally come from England to introduce the Bessemer process at the Pennsylvania Steel Works. When the owners of these works adopted A. L. Holley's plans instead, Butcher went to Philadelphia, and with the capital of Philip S. Justice, a Philadelphia iron wholesaler, he organized a steelworks for making weldless steel tires. Butcher's tires competed unsuccessfully with British imports, and he changed to making cast steel frogs, switches, and car wheels. In 1870 he contracted to make the first large tonnage of alloy steel in America for the Eads Bridge across the Mississippi at St. Louis. This contract proved troublesome to fill. Butcher had built a 3.5-ton open-hearth furnace in 1869–1870, and he began testing it in January 1871. He made ninety-two attempts to use the furnace but finally gave up in September 1871. Shortly afterwards he went bankrupt, and his plant came into the hands of the machine-tool pioneer, William Sellers, and others. In 1872 the name of the plant was changed to Midvale Steel Works. William F. Durfee, who had been superintendent at the Wyandotte experimental Bessemer works and who had first applied the Siemens furnace to puddling, took charge and was assisted by Charles F. Brinley, who had three years of postgraduate university training in metallurgical chem-

[42] Nevins, *op. cit.*, pp. 243–250, 256–262; U.S. Census Office, *Twelfth Census*, X, 68.

istry at Yale. The two men analyzed the plant's raw materials, rebuilt equipment where necessary, kept accurate records of trial runs, and made the open-hearth furnace a success. The Eads Bridge was formally opened in 1874.[43]

Meanwhile, the open-hearth process had been successfully introduced by the Bay State Iron Works at South Boston in 1870 under the supervision of Samuel T. Wellman, who had acquired experience in the course of Hewitt's unsuccessful attempt. This furnace produced good steel from the start and operated night and day for several years.

In 1873–1874 Wellman supervised the building of the first steelworks using the open-hearth process exclusively, the plant of the Otis Iron and Steel Company of Cleveland. This firm was organized by Charles Augustus Otis, who had been in the iron business in Cleveland for over twenty years and who had seen European open hearths in operation. In 1886 the Otis company pioneered the use of basic linings in the open-hearth furnace, a method which Wellman had observed in Europe the year before. These experiments were abandoned, however, when the pressing demand for steel in 1886 made the use of the faster acid process in all the company's open-hearth equipment more profitable. Wellman later invented a charging machine, which in addition to the open hearth's other advantages made it more economical of labor than the Bessemer process. In the meantime Hewitt retained A. L. Holley to recommend and install the open hearth at the works of the other major steel companies.[44]

In England, William Siemens tried to combine the steps of smelting and refining by using ores directly in the open hearth,

[43] Hunt, *op. cit.*, p. 207; Richard T. Nalle, *Midvale—and Its Pioneers* (New York: Newcomen Society, 1948), pp. 10–13.

[44] *The Otis Steel Company—Pioneer, Cleveland, Ohio* (Cambridge, Mass.: privately printed, 1929); Redlich, *American Business Leaders,* pp. 99–100; U.S. Census Office, *Twelfth Census,* X, 68; Clark, *op. cit.,* III, 69; Nevins, *op. cit.,* p. 442.

and he achieved some experimental success. Two American steel men, James Park, Jr., and Robert J. Anderson, organized separate works at Pittsburgh for using the new Siemens process in 1877 and 1881, but both failed.[45] Somewhat earlier, about 1868, Shoenberger and Company of Pittsburgh had experimented with the Ellershausen process of refining pig iron by agitation in contact with ore but had failed to make it a commercial success.[46]

Other failures before 1900 involved modifications of the Bessemer process. Thus in 1882 Henry W. Oliver attempted to use the Clapp-Griffiths process from Wales in which a much lighter blast was introduced at the side of the converter, instead of at the bottom, thus reducing blowing-engine costs and allowing better manipulation during manufacture. He hoped to economize by using high-phosphorous iron and dephosphorizing it in the converter. The plant was closed and the equipment scrapped in the following year, 1883. By 1886 eight other firms were using the Clapp-Griffiths process, without attempting to dephosphorize, and all of these gave up before 1900. The Tropenas process from England and the Ropert-Bessemer and Walrand-Legenisel process from France had the same measure of success.[47] It should be noted that, as before the Civil War, all these failures involved attempts to introduce European processes that involved basic chemical rather than mechanical or other changes.

Post-Civil War innovations in blast furnaces involved no basic chemical changes and no comparable failures. Nevertheless, the increases in productivity were spectacular. From 1860 to 1875 the daily output of the largest furnaces increased from 40 to 100 tons of pig iron. By 1900 the record was above 800 tons,

[45] Swank, *Iron in All Ages*, p. 423.   [46] Goodale, *op. cit.*, p. 170.

[47] Henry Oliver Evans, *Iron Pioneer: Henry W. Oliver, 1840–1904* (New York: E. P. Dutton, 1942), pp. 100–107; U.S. Census Office, *Twelfth Census*, X, 66; Clark, *op. cit.*, III, 65–66, 70, 77–78.

and the national average was 500 tons per furnace. The large Pittsburgh furnaces were smelting as much daily as charcoal furnaces had made yearly around 1850. The output of American furnaces was almost twice as great per furnace as that of German furnaces and three times as great as that of English and French furnaces. At the best American furnaces, workers were more than three times as productive as workers at the best German furnaces, though partly through the use of better ores and more fuel. By 1900 British and German ironmasters were studying and imitating American furnace construction and practice.[48]

This rise in productivity was the result of larger and hotter furnaces operated with more and better auxiliary equipment. New types of hot-blast ovens, stronger blowing engines, steam blasts, water jackets for cooling, mechanical loaders, automatic pig-casting machines, and other changes in technique were all introduced by engineers who knew how to experiment with caution. Their experiments depended on better thermometers, on new types of refractory materials, and, in the case of blowing engines, on the development of light, corrosion-resistant steel alloys. The Etna Iron Works at Ironton, Ohio, the Isabella Furnaces near Pittsburgh, and a number of furnaces at Andrew Carnegie's plants were outstanding in making these innovations.[49]

Generally, fuel-saving innovations were introduced without much difficulty. During the 1880's a number of works began using petroleum and natural gas for raising steam, for puddling, and for reheating ingots. By the end of 1885 practically every iron and steel mill near Pittsburgh was using natural gas. When

[48] Clark, *op. cit.*, II, 76, III, 73–75.
[49] Holley, "Some Pressing Needs of Our Iron and Steel Manufacturers," pp. 77–99; Charles M. White, *Blast Furnace Blowing Engines, Past, Present—and Future* (New York: Newcomen Society, 1947), p. 18; Clark, *op. cit.*, II, 252–256.

the demand for gas by households raised prices around 1890, ironworks and steel mills shifted back to coal.[50] Fuel was also saved by avoiding reheating between smelting and rolling. The North Chicago Rolling Mills of E. B. Ward, who had given the greatest financial support to the Wyandotte Bessemer experiments, were outstanding in this respect. During the 1880's [51] these works pioneered in taking molten iron directly from the blast furnace to the puddling furnace or Bessemer converter and then rolling the ingots without reheating. The North Chicago Rolling Mills were the world's largest three-converter plant, but they dispensed with so much reheating equipment that they looked remarkably small to Eastern and European visitors.[52]

Domestic and foreign rolling-mill innovations were also introduced with little trouble. As significant as any were those of John Fritz, since 1860 superintendent at the Bethlehem Iron Company, and those of his brother George, who had taken John's place at the Cambria works. The Cambria works were the second to roll steel rails in America.[53] George Fritz introduced a new type of blooming mill; and when reversing engines of great power appeared in England, he was first in replacing the three-high rolling mills, which his brother had invented, with two-high reversing mills. At the Bethlehem works, John Fritz introduced many blast-furnace and rolling-mill changes and pioneered the use of British hydraulic presses in place of steam hammers. The Bethlehem Iron Company, later the Bethlehem Steel Company, shared the lead in experimenting with alloys in America, and at the turn of the century introduced high-speed tool steel.[54]

[50] Clark, *op. cit.*, II, 250–252.   [51] Ward had died on Jan. 2, 1875.
[52] Clark, *op. cit.*, II, 260, 266.
[53] These were rolled with the first Bessemer ingots of the Pennsylvania Steel Company.
[54] Clark, *op. cit.*, II, 261, III, 84–86; Goodale, *op. cit.*, p. 177; Fritz, *op. cit.*, pp. 139 ff.; Frank Barkley Copley, *Frederick W. Taylor, Father*

The greatest number of innovations between 1870 and 1900 were introduced at the various plants of Andrew Carnegie and his associates, particularly at the Lucy Furnaces, the Edgar Thomson Works, the Homestead Works, and the Duquesne Works. Through acquisition of competing plants, expansion, and technological progress the Carnegie enterprises also experienced the highest rate of growth in the iron and steel industry during these decades. By 1900 they had the capacity to make one-fifth of the pig iron and more than one quarter of the steel in America. Willingness to innovate and rapid growth were interrelated, and this was recognized by officials of the firm. As Charles Schwab wrote in a memorandum intended for private use within the company, "The great success with which we have always met in our business has been largely due to the fact that we have anticipated our competitors in manufacturing better and cheaper than they do." [55]

Carnegie himself was not a technical expert, but he excelled in the ability of selecting subordinates. This ability was reinforced by his willingness to pay unprecedented salaries and to give talented men substantial fractions of the firm's capital stock. Moreover, he never regarded booms and depressions as permanent but rather thought in terms of long-run growth. He avoided speculation in the early 1870's and 1890's; and when the depressions came, he took advantage of his unimpaired credit and of low prices to scrap, rebuild, and expand plant and equipment.

In blast-furnace construction, the Carnegie works helped launch "new eras" in the 1870's and again in the 1890's. Simul-

---

of *Scientific Management* (New York: Harper and Brothers, 1923), II, 4 ff.

[55] Memorandum quoted in full in the minutes of the July 6, 1897, meeting of the board of directors of the Carnegie Steel Co., Papers of Andrew Carnegie, Manuscript Division, Library of Congress, vol. XLIII, item 8358; Clark, *op. cit.*, III, p. 44; Henrick, *op. cit.*, I, 196–199, 208, 297, II, 356; Bridge, *op. cit.*, p. 297; Goodale, *op. cit.*, p. 212.

taneously with the Isabella Furnaces of John W. Chalfant, Henry W. Oliver, and others, Carnegie's Lucy Furnaces near Pittsburgh were the first large (75-foot) American blast furnaces. Among other innovations, the Lucy Furnaces introduced a machine for cooling slag, stronger blasting engines, and better linings. They were among the first to employ a chemist.[56]

In 1896 the Carnegie works introduced machines that automatically loaded blast furnaces and machines that automatically cast pigs and loaded them into freight cars, thus permitting furnaces to rise to one hundred feet and a saving of one-half of the direct labor cost in smelting iron, a development called the "Duquesne Revolution." [57] Andrew Carnegie personally bought the rights to the Thomas-Gilchrist basic process that allowed the use of phosphoric irons in making steel, and he assigned these rights to the Bessemer patent pool in 1881. After much controversy with a rival American inventor, Jacob Reese, Carnegie's Homestead Works were first in applying the process to the open hearth in regular commercial production in 1888. The Pennsylvania Steel Works had previously applied the basic lining to the Bessemer converter, but this combination did not play an important part in American industry and was not copied by anyone for fifteen years.[58]

Another steelmaking innovation at a Carnegie plant was the Jones mixer, which combined metal from different furnaces before introducing it into a Bessemer converter. Other innovations included the use of high-pressure steam to keep ingots

[56] Clark, *op. cit.*, II, 77; Bridge, *op. cit.*, pp. 54–64; Redlich, *American Business Leaders*, pp. 80–81; C. M. White, *op. cit.*, p. 18.

[57] Goodale, *op. cit.*, pp. 225–226; Evans, *op. cit.*, pp. 284–286; Bridge, *op. cit.*, p. 181.

[58] Jacob Reese, "The Basic Steel Process and Its Possibilities in the United States," *A.I.S.A. Bulletin*, XXIII (July 3, 1889), 177; Hendrick, *op. cit.*, II, 39; Bridge, *op. cit.*, p. 164; Swank, *Iron in All Ages*, p. 424; Clark, *op. cit.*, III, 77.

under pressure while cooling, and later the use of soaking pits for bringing ingots to a uniform temperature.[59] It was Carnegie's Keystone Bridge Company, moreover, that had contracted for the first large-scale use of alloy steel for the Eads Bridge in 1870. By 1891 the Carnegie works were rolling nickel steel ingots of the unprecedented weight of fifty tons. Finally, during the 1890's the Carnegie works, together with Westinghouse Electric, pioneered in converting steelworks to electric power.[60]

All these innovations, and others, made production costs at the Carnegie works the lowest in the industry. As a result, Carnegie could usually afford to be the last to join a pool and the first to withdraw. Once he told Abram Hewitt:

Hewitt, I am tired of this beam pool and I'm going to get out of it. . . . I can make steel cheaper than any of you and undersell you. The market is mine whenever I want to take it. I see no reason why I should present you with all my profits.[61]

His statement was no bluff, for Carnegie withdrew in fact, and his earnings on beams increased 400 per cent the following year. While his competitors were suffering losses in the depth of the depression from 1893 to 1895, Carnegie expanded his steel production 69.6 per cent and his profits 66.7 per cent.[62]

The reactions of his competitors were ambivalent. Willis L. King of Jones and Laughlin, for example, believed Carnegie had done more than any other man to improve "the art, science, and practice of steel making [and had] increased tonnage and reduced costs years before it would otherwise have been brought about," but he felt that his "unreasonable competition

[59] Clark, *op. cit.*, II, 265–275.
[60] *Ibid.*, II, 313; Goodale, *op. cit.*, pp. 225–226; Malcolm MacLaren, *The Rise of the Electrical Industry during the Nineteenth Century* (Princeton: Princeton University Press, 1943), p. 96.
[61] Quoted by Hendrick, *op. cit.*, II, 51.
[62] Bridge, *op. cit.*, pp. 295–297.

was childish and against public policy" because it encouraged industrial wars and demoralized the industry.[63]

It is significant that the greatest innovating firm apparently suffered the fewest losses in these wars. As Carnegie once cabled Charles M. Schwab:

If we get a small profit per ton, well; if we cannot get a profit per ton, well also, though not so well. If we have to take orders at a slight loss, as we have in the past, I would take them. For many months I saw red marks across certain sales which denoted they were taken at a loss, but I always said to myself, "this loss is gain." [64]

Progressiveness and Freedom of Entry

The American iron and steel industry in general was old, dating back to early Colonial times, and slow growing until around 1840. It gained considerable momentum before the Civil War and reached its period of most rapid growth in the 1880's.[65] Technologically, it was not progressive until around 1850 when fairly large, vertically integrated firms became prominent. The industry lagged behind European practice by ten years or more until the decade following the Civil War, and then it took the lead along many, but not all, lines. Patents and other devices were not generally used to restrict entry; but by 1900 entry was limited by enormous capital requirements for all but a few specialized firms.

The progressiveness of a large industry depends more on willingness to imitate than to innovate. Ignorance was the chief obstacle to imitation before the time of technical journals, trained engineers, and thorough accounting. Ignorance explains

[63] Willis L. King, "Recollections and Conclusions from a Long Business Life," *Western Pennsylvania Historical Magazine,* XXIII (Dec. 1, 1940), 229–230, 326.

[64] Cable to Schwab, July 31, 1900, quoted by Hendrick, *op. cit.,* II, 118.

[65] American Iron and Steel Association figures on pig iron production cited by Swank, *Iron in All Ages,* pp. 376–377.

the delays in adopting puddling and rolling and other innovations before 1860. It may also explain the pronounced antagonism and outspoken opposition of many influential persons against such activities as Durfee's Bessemer experiments at Wyandotte and Frederick W. Taylor's various experiments at Midvale. As a matter of fact, Durfee himself had "very little knowledge of an exact character as to what had been done by others," only "a very clear idea of the rationale of the new process." His experiments were based on copies of Bessemer's American patents and Fairbairn's *History of the Manufacture of Iron.*[66]

To the uninformed, technological change meant trouble and confusion. According to one writer in the 1870's:

The dying out of old furnaces, the building of new ones, the alternate stagnation and activity of every branch of the wrought iron business, the constant and increasing activity of every branch of the steel trade, the substitution of iron for wood, and of steel for iron, the multitude of new types of iron and steel furnaces, direct processes, etc., all struggling for existence at once, furnish a problem for the ironmaster the like of which has not been seen in this generation.[67]

Long before Carnegie started "industrial wars," there was widespread suspicion and fear of technological change. In 1876 A. L. Holley felt that

the world has a right to complain of their narrowness of observation, of their stolid incomprehension of the results of science, of that pride of ignorance, of that bigotry, of that positive fear of the diffusion of knowledge, which is the normal condition of . . . a large number of managers of metallurgical enterprises.[68]

[66] Durfee, *op. cit.*, p. 291; Copley, *op. cit.*, I, 239.

[67] *A.I.S.A. Bulletin,* XII (Nov. 13, 1878), 269. A slightly altered version is quoted by Clark, *op. cit.*, II, 291.

[68] A. L. Holley, "The Inadequate Union of Engineering Science and Art," *Transactions of the American Institute of Mining Engineers,* IV (Feb. 1876), 198.

These fears rarely led to organized hostile action, but there was a general reluctance to scrap obsolete equipment if the product, regardless of fuel and labor costs, was satisfactory. In the late 1860's, the Player hot-blast stove led to such increases in productivity that old furnaces could have been abandoned and the loss of fixed capital recouped in two years. But abandoning and rebuilding occurred rarely.[69] The Siemens gas regenerative furnace likewise allowed spectacular savings, and again ironmasters were reluctant to scrap old equipment that was still in working condition.[70] Holley believed that accepting the lowest bids for steam engines before building a blast furnace or steel mill was the basic cause of many breakdowns. He noted a great temptation to "save the heavy cost of radical change" by patching up inferior engines with new valves, condensers, and gears when the "way to get the greatest possible profit out of an engine of bad type is to melt it down in a cupola." [71]

Some owners of the Bethlehem Steel Company may serve as an illustration of unwillingness to imitate or innovate because of a conflict of interest. In the late 1890's these owners objected to Frederick W. Taylor's labor-saving changes because "they did not wish me, as they said, to depopulate South Bethlehem. They owned all the houses in South Bethlehem and the company stores, and when they saw we were cutting the labor force down to about one fourth, they did not want it." [72]

In short, the progressiveness of the innovating firms should not be taken as that of the industry as a whole. It should be remembered that rolling mills, introduced in 1817, did not generally replace forges and bloomeries until the 1850's and that in 1896 nine bloomeries were still active. In 1890, 43 per cent of the rolled iron and steel was iron. Although a ton of

[69] Clark, *op. cit.*, II, 77.

[70] Holley, "Some Pressing Needs of Our Iron and Steel Manufacturers," pp. 82–83.

[71] *Ibid.*, p. 81.   [72] Quoted by Copley, *op. cit.*, II, 46.

puddled iron required twenty times as much labor as a ton of Bessemer steel—and more skilled labor at that—4,715 puddling furnaces were still active in 1894.[73] Coke smelting did not exceed all other forms combined until 1883, forty-four years after it had been introduced.[74] Even then charcoal smelting continued to expand. More iron was smelted with charcoal in 1905 than in 1880.[75] The explanation lies partly in quality differences; but the point is that the "gale of creative destruction" did not blow very hard.

By contrast, there was a sporting interest in production records among the owners and managers of Bessemer steel works and large blast furnaces. The desire to surpass rivals in daily tonnage, as well as yearly profits, led to the rapid adoption of minor technological changes and even to concessions to labor.[76] Moreover, most of the successful innovating firms employed able engineers and metallurgists who, in one way or another, prodded their superiors into allowing innovation after innovation, often over a period of decades. These firms and their leading personalities will be considered in a later section.

With the primary exception of the Bessemer process, patents were used more for collecting royalties than for hampering a competitor or restricting entry. This policy was inevitable because the industry was not serviced by large-scale equipment makers and because even great innovations, again excluding the Bessemer process, were not sufficiently radical to allow domination of the industry or of any significant segment. The discovery of a scientific principle was generally more important than the particular device used to apply the principle. Many important blowing-engine and rolling-mill innovations were not

[73] Clark, *op. cit.*, III, 82.   [74] Swank, *Iron in All Ages*, pp. 376–377.
[75] U.S. Census Bureau, *Manufactures, 1905*, pp. 37, 46. Capacity and production reached their maximum around 1890. Crucible steel production expanded until around 1900 (*ibid.*, p. 70).
[76] Clark, *op. cit.*, II, 264–265.

patented at all. Such ironmasters as Abram Hewitt and John Fritz often allowed others to inspect their plants and even lent original castings to visitors who wanted to copy machinery.[77] Among the engineers and superintendents of the big works there was a kind of co-operation that differed from the business-man's co-operation in making pools. According to John Fritz:

Mr. Holley, Captain Hunt, my brother George, and Captain Jones would frequently come to Bethlehem to talk over our troubles—not high finance, but the difficulties we daily met, which at times seemed almost insuperable. We did not meet as diplomats, to find out what each other wanted, but we met as a band of loving brother engineers trained by arduous experience, young, able, energetic, and deter-mined to make a success. I doubt if ever five natural brothers were more loyal to each other than the five brother engineers above named. What each of us knew was common to all.[78]

There can be little doubt, however, that capital requirements restricted entry in the last two decades of the century. This restriction applied more to the established sectors of the in-dustry than to new sectors because firms making well-known products could meet aggressive competition only if they were large enough to own rolling mills, steel mills, blast furnaces, and, eventually, railroads, mines, and ships. As early as 1883 the Columbus Rolling Mills, built to roll rails, found that they could not compete with integrated firms making their own steel. The mills were therefore remodeled to roll structural shapes. But by the end of the century mills rolling structural shapes also had to be part of integrated concerns.[79] In addition to this handicap, small firms were hampered by inability to secure favorable railroad rebates and to weather price wars in other

[77] Fackenthal, *op. cit.*, pp. 102–103; Swank, *Iron in All Ages*, p. 414; Nevins, *op. cit.*, p. 262.

[78] Fritz, *op. cit.*, p. 160.   [79] Clark, *op. cit.*, II, 334.

ways. Many ideas, to be tried at all, therefore had to be brought to the attention of large established firms.

Risks

Did actual losses in iron and steel making innovations occur most frequently as a result of inability to predict the fluctuations of the economic system? Or was inability to predict the functioning of machinery, including operating costs and obsolescence, the greatest handicap? Or was neither factor important?

From the first attempts to smelt with anthracite to the Siemens direct process and the Clapp-Griffiths process, inability to foresee what a piece of apparatus would do to a mass of raw material caused losses, at times heavy losses. These losses were generally borne by the firms that used the apparatus because, if not constructed in a machine shop on the premises, the apparatus was usually built to order by special engineering and contracting firms. The losses were often heavy because the infancy of metallurgical, chemical, and thermodynamic science did not allow the experimental, and therefore inexpensive, testing of all relevant factors under laboratory conditions. At times favorable results in the laboratory could not be reproduced on a commercial scale because the larger scale involved factors ignored, consciously or not, in the laboratory. One could make a model train of rolls of new design, but it took the passing of real metal, under actual heat and pressure, to determine whether flanges would tear or rails would split. As a matter of fact, rolling-mill innovations generally differed less from existing rule-of-thumb knowledge than changes in smelting and refining, and losses were proportionately smaller. The more an innovation made purely mechanical changes, the less likely was failure. Even the difficulties that did occur when mechanical changes were made should perhaps not be attributed altogether to innovation, because in the first half of the century breakdowns were frequent and serious with any kind of equipment.[80]

The greatest problem was lack of chemical knowledge. It was not until 1838 that the first chemical analysis of the blast-furnace process was attempted. In that year Robert Bunsen of Kassel, Germany, studied samples of gases taken from different levels in a furnace.[81] American iron and steel makers employed their first chemists in the 1860's and 1870's. The unsuccessful attempts to smelt with coke or anthracite; to make crucible, Bessemer, or open-hearth steel before 1870; or to apply the Siemens Direct, Ellershausen, or Clapp-Griffiths processes after 1870—all involved chemical properties and processes that were not fully understood. Lack of chemical knowledge also introduced uncertainties into the use of old equipment. Before the era of chemistry, in the fall of 1851, Abram Hewitt had to write a customer:

For twelve months we did not make a ton of iron that was not superior to any other iron we have ever seen. Now the reverse is true. It occurred once before, under similar circumstances, and afterwards the iron recovered its regular quality. We have no doubt that this will now be the case.[82]

When chemical knowledge finally became available and was applied to metallurgical industries, the effect was sweeping. Before 1870 Carnegie believed smelting gave him more anxiety than any other part of his business.[83] Then a chemist, trained in Germany, was hired, and

iron stone from mines that had high reputation was now found to contain ten, fifteen, and even twenty per cent less iron than it had

[80] Fritz, *op. cit.*, p. 54; Robert Allison in "The Old and the New," *Transactions of the American Society of Mechanical Engineers*, XVI (1895), 760.

[81] Goodale, *op. cit.*, p. 117.   [82] Quoted by Nevins, *op. cit.*, p. 139.

[83] Carnegie, *op. cit.*, p. 179.

been credited with. Mines that hitherto had a poor reputation were found to be now yielding superior ore. The good was bad and the bad was good, and everything was topsy-turvy. Nine-tenths of all the uncertainties of pig-iron making were dispelled under the burning sun of chemical knowledge.[84]

It was ignorance of chemistry that led to the failure of William Butcher's open-hearth furnace in 1871 and knowledge of chemistry by his successors, William F. Durfee and Charles A. Brinley, that led to the successful operation of the same furnace the following year.[85] The United States Government soon took the lead in the development of metallurgical knowledge when, on March 3, 1875, Congress appropriated money for a United States Commission on the Tests of Iron, Steel, and Other Metals. This Commission acquired a large number of samples of metal products and tested the effects of variations in chemical composition and temperature on toughness, tensile strength, elasticity, and other qualities. Its experimental work was supplemented by an integration of reports by managers of rolling mills and railroads and by engineers and scientists in many fields. As a result of the Commission's work, national standards of quality were established, and countless manufacturers were persuaded to adopt scientific testing procedures in their own plants.[86]

Serious losses nevertheless continued to occur for chemical reasons until the end of the century, indicating in some cases that metallurgical science was not yet equal to all problems and in others that scientific theories were not yet considered authoritative. On the other hand, beginning with the Thomas-Gilchrist process in the 1870's, more and more innovations in iron and steel making were originated by chemists and metallurgists with academic training. The lag in chemical knowledge behind the needs of industry and the resulting losses were

[84] *Ibid.*, p. 182. [85] *Supra*, pp. 38–39.
[86] *Iron Age*, XVI, July 1, 1875, 1; Oct. 14, 1875, 11; Dec. 23, 1875, 23.

rather unique in nineteenth-century producers' goods innovation, and this lag will be referred to again.

Less important than losses on account of the undeveloped state of chemistry were losses on account of excessive material or labor costs or obsolescence. Innovators were faced with relatively fewer uncertainties with respect to the quantitative than the qualitative availability of ore, flux, coke, and the like. The records also suggest that they knew enough about the availability of labor, trained or untrained, native or immigrant, to avoid gambling on this factor. Occasionally, however, there were losses because one innovation was rapidly superseded by another. Thus in 1893 the Bethlehem Iron Company designed and built the world's largest steam hammer, one that could deliver a blow of 125 tons. Within two or three years it was supplanted by hydraulic presses that allowed greater precision and easier maintenance. The hammer stood idle for about seven years and was finally scrapped.[87] But even such losses were not as heavy as they might have been had a specialized producers' goods maker tooled up for making the equipment on a large scale. As a matter of fact, fear of obsolescence was often so great that it led to losses in the sense of unrealized gains. Dank's puddling machine, a rotary mechanism that dispensed with much manual puddling, was developed by a Cincinnati manufacturer between 1868 and 1870. The machine involved a high initial investment, but it reduced operating costs by some four dollars a ton. Even after it was perfected, it was not adopted by all puddling furnaces because the process of refining by means of puddling furnaces rather than Bessemer converters was considered obsolescent. As it turned out, however, twenty years elapsed before the number of puddling furnaces began a permanent decline.[88] It was the open-hearth furnace that slowly made puddling obsolete.

[87] *A.I.S.A. Bulletin*, XXXVI (May 10, 1902), 65.
[88] Clark, *op. cit.*, II, 79, 260–261.

In addition to these "production risks" there were the "customer risks" that groups might refuse to adopt a new process, or the product of a new process, against their own apparent economic interest. But since new processes were almost never introduced by specialized equipment builders, producer conservatism with respect to machines and the like, though pervasive, was not a threat to firms attempting to innovate.[89] The innovators made novel equipment only for their own use, not for sale. The problem was more serious if the innovation was product-changing as well as process-changing. There was, for example, the prejudice against American crucible steel.[90] Nevertheless, after the Civil War the demand for new products was usually sufficient, in spite of prejudice, to guarantee the success of innovations that were otherwise adequate. Even when prejudice could have been reinforced by depression, as in the 1870's, the new Bessemer steel works operated at full capacity, and the new large-scale blast furnaces were running profitably.[91] Similarly, in the depression of the 1890's the new alloy steel works were running full time.[92]

"Interference risks," the possibility that an innovation might be thwarted by social friction of one kind or another, did not appear very serious in the American iron and steel industry. Labor unions were not strong enough to resist technological change. The great strikes and lockouts at Carnegie's Edgar Thomson Works and Homestead Works in 1887, 1889, and 1892

[89] In the Pittsburgh area there was only one firm specializing in the construction of blast furnaces and steel mills as a whole, that of James P. Witherow, founded in 1876. Witherow held a number of patents for iron making and steelmaking appliances, but none of these involved drastic changes. The firm was primarily engaged in building furnaces and mills for enterprises outside the Pittsburgh area, in Alabama and New York, on Lake Superior, etc. See George H. Thurston, *Pittsburgh's Progress, Industries, and Resources* (Pittsburgh: A. A. Anderson and Son, 1886), pp. 70–71.

[90] *Supra*, p. 27.   [91] *Supra*, pp. 34–35; Clark, *op. cit.*, II, 222.

[92] Clark, *op. cit.*, III, 80.

involved primarily labor's unsuccessful resistance to longer hours and lower wages per ton and finally recognition of the union itself. Technological change was often related to these disputes because the management was inclined to reduce wages per ton after installing more efficient equipment. In other words, it demanded an ever larger share of increases in production when these increases were due to technological improvement. In the light of daily wages paid by competitors, it could present these claims as reasonable. The point is, however, that although the distribution of gains from technological change was challenged by labor, change itself was not.[93]

It has already been said that, with the exception of the Bessemer process, patents were used more for collecting royalties than for restricting the operations of competitors.[94] With respect to innovations this means that anyone was free to improve on another's invention, provided he paid the royalty.

A greater interference uncertainty was the level of tariffs, though here again one must distinguish the threat to innovation of a lower tariff from the threat to iron and steel making in general. It would seem reasonable to consider tariff risks relevant to innovation only insofar as a particular innovation involved a greater commitment of capital relative to output than previously common in the industry—provided, of course, that such capital could not readily be converted to other uses. Other things being equal, tariff risks would therefore be highest in the manufacture of products new to the economy, but not to the world.

But if the possibility of tariff reduction was a risk and therefore a factor inhibiting innovation, actual tariff reductions often stimulated innovation. When the tariff reduction of 1846 made competition with British rails impossible, American rolling mills

[93] Hendrick, *op. cit.*, I, 366 ff.; Bridge, *op. cit.*, 199–200.
[94] *Supra*, pp. 49–50.

turned to other products; and a number of innovations in the rolling and use of structural beams and wire for building telegraphs, fences, and bridges followed.[95] On another occasion, in 1881, the tariff on wire rods was reduced from 1.2 to 0.3 cents per pound, and every American wire rod mill but one was forced to close. The exception was the Cleveland Rolling Mill Company where Henry Chisholm, in response to the competition, integrated his works and eliminated much reheating in converting ingots to billets and billets to wire.[96]

Occasionally production risks and interference risks with respect to innovations were compounded by certain specific risks incidental to the founding of any new business. For example, in 1886 a group of Pittsburgh iron and steel manufacturers organized the Duquesne Steel Company to give Carnegie some competition in steel rails in that area. The plant was designed to be as up to date as possible, and it incorporated several novel features, including the method of rolling ingots without reheating after soaking. But before various mechanical difficulties were eliminated, the owners, primarily William G. and D. E. Park of the Black Diamond Steel Works, were forced to sell out to Carnegie. The latter had responded to their challenge by sending a circular to various railroads warning them against rails made by the new method. He claimed, perhaps with some justice, that the Duquesne rails were defective because of lack of homogeneity. One of Carnegie's officials is reported to have said that "if they had made rails by our method we would have recognized them as legitimate competitors." As it was, the members of the rail pool refused to relinquish any desirable orders to the Duquesne Steel Company. In any case the company encountered a number of other difficulties.

[95] Swank, *Iron in All Ages*, p. 435; Goodale, *op. cit.*, p. 127; Nevins, *op. cit.*, pp. 103–108.
[96] Goodale, *op. cit.*, pp. 197–198.

There was labor trouble because, unlike Carnegie's plants, the Duquesne works tried to operate on a completely nonunion basis. Moreover, the capital originally subscribed in 1886, $350,000, proved inadequate; and within two years the company had to be reorganized as the Allegheny Bessemer Steel Company with a capitalization of $700,000. Before 1890 William G. Park had to provide an additional $300,000, raising the capitalization to $1,000,000. This same amount, $1,000,000, was the amount paid by Carnegie for the plant, plus an additional sum for material on hand. Within a year, however, the earnings of the plant had themselves reached $1,000,000; and Carnegie's other plants, Homestead and Edgar Thomson, adopted a number of the devices first introduced at Duquesne.[97]

The importance of "timing risks" is not easily appraised. It can seldom be established beyond doubt that an unsuccessful attempt to innovate might have succeeded if it had been undertaken a few years earlier or later. A later successful attempt usually differed in manner as well as timing; and it is hard to prove that the change in manner was not the more strategic change. Kelly's attempts to refine pig iron with air blasts came to an end with the depression of 1857, but his approach differed so much from Bessemer's, especially with respect to the possibility of mass production, that it is not comparable with later attempts. Kelly's failure was not due to lack of time to "iron out bugs" or to an increased scale of operations with increased illiquidity. It was his basic small-scale approach, with its attendant variations in quality, that precluded commercial success.[98] Similarly, a large-scale, low-cost approach was the key to the Bessemer works' success. Their output thus met the requirements of long-term growth factors in the economy, and they were therefore relatively immune to even great cyclical variations. From the Civil War until the 1890's, steel output increased every year, except for 1883 and 1884 and even then it

[97] Bridge, *op. cit.*, pp. 174–180.   [98] *Supra*, pp. 29–31.

fell only to the approximate level of 1881.[99] In the depression of the 1890's, scale- and output-increasing innovations were likewise profitable for Carnegie and the alloy steel makers.[100]

There were a number of other attempts to innovate that failed in years of crisis or shortly afterwards, but it appears unlikely that a mere change in timing might have transformed many of these failures into success. The $500,000 attempt to smelt with coke at Farrandsville [101] had the misfortune of coinciding with the depression of 1837, but it was not finally abandoned until 1839, the same year that two other firms achieved commercial success. Impurities in the coal and poor location appear to have been more important than unlucky timing. Henry W. Oliver's attempt to use the small-scale Clapp-Griffiths process in 1882 allowed him little time to experiment before the crisis of 1883.[102] After the depression, however, eight other establishments tried to make the process pay, but success was limited.

Technological Insight, Business Authority, and Caution

Among the innovating firms, technological insight was combined with busines authority in varying degrees. Before 1850 most ironmasters were both technicians and businessmen; but understanding neither business nor technics with precision, they were not well equipped to originate or import great changes. Most basic changes had to be suggested to them by immigrant workers or by the representatives of foreign patent holders. Outstanding among the rare exceptions were Frederick Geissenhainer and anthracite smelting, William Garrard and crucible steel making, and Henry Burden and his concentric squeezer. But of these three "engineer-entrepreneurs" only Burden had acquired his early technical training in America.

[99] Statistics of the American Iron and Steel Association, reproduced by Swank, *Iron in All Ages*, p. 511.

[100] *Supra*, pp. 45, 55.   [101] *Supra*, p. 24.   [102] *Supra*, p. 40.

After 1850 technician-presidents, inventor-owners, and similar combinations became more unusual. Such innovating firms as the Cambria Iron Works, Jones and Laughlin, the Bethlehem Iron Company, the North Chicago Rolling Mills, the Otis Iron and Steel Company, the Midvale Steel Company (after 1887), and the various Carnegie concerns (before Charles M. Schwab became president in 1897) were neither controlled nor owned to any significant extent by their leading technicians. Nevertheless, there were exceptions and, among the nontechnical business leaders, there were gradations in the amount of enthusiasm or tolerance for technological innovation.

One step in which technicians exercised considerable authority involved the introduction of the Bessemer process to America. The active promoter at Wyandotte was Z. S. Durfee, a blacksmith, and at Troy, A. L. Holley, an engineer. Both gained the support of wealthy iron manufacturers, and both remained influential partners in the experimental and patent-holding companies that were subsequently formed. When the two groups combined, Durfee became general agent and Holley took charge of almost all the early installations. The first commercial installation in America was the one supervised by Holley for the Pennsylvania Steel Company. Samuel M. Felton, a civil engineer and Harvard graduate, appears to have been the leading promoter, as well as first president, of this firm. Among the firm's chief owners, besides Felton himself, were William Sellers and William B. Bement, two outstanding inventors and engineer-entrepreneurs in machine tools, and J. Edgar Thomson, an engineer who was also president of the Pennsylvania Railroad. Felton hired John Barnard Swett Pearse as chemist in 1868 and made him general manager in 1870. A later manager was Felton's son-in-law, Luther S. Bent, who also succeeded Felton as president. Under all these men with technical training, the Pennsylvania Steel Company introduced the acid Bessemer process in 1867, the basic Bessemer process in 1884, and in 1889 the tilting open-hearth furnace and the duplex method of beginning the refining process in an acid Bessemer converter and completing it in a basic open hearth.[103]

The second commercially successful Bessemer plant in America, the Cleveland Rolling Mills, began operations in 1868 under Henry Chisholm, another engineer-entrepreneur who contributed several important innovations, among them a process for making wire from steel scrap.[104]

Whom one considers "the" innovator in firms without engineer-entrepreneurs is a matter of definition. It may be the owner or his agent, who hires an able technician as superintendent, who ponders technological changes with this man, and who then allows him to proceed in his own way or orders him to follow a particular plan. Conversely it may be the superintendent, who, with more or less difficulty, manages to persuade the owners to finance a new process or machine. It may be that the two are considered to perform the innovating function jointly. If the innovation is to be a success, businessmen and engineers must each have an adequate grasp of effects on plant and markets. Whichever point of view one chooses, however, is far less interesting than the fact that in most iron and steel works technical originality and final responsibility were in different hands.

Whether or not technological change was initiated tentatively and cautiously or, by contrast, in a speculative, perhaps even reckless, way cannot be easily determined or reduced to a simple answer. On this question one must evaluate contradictory statements from contemporary technicians and business managers, from those inside and outside a firm, and from the same person at the time of innovation and in retrospect years

[103] *A.I.S.A. Bulletin*, XXIII (Jan. 30, 1889), 28; Redlich, *American Business Leaders*, pp. 94–101; Goodale, *op. cit.*, pp. 204–205. For other sources, *supra*, pp. 32–36.

[104] Redlich, *American Business Leaders*, pp. 97–98. Also *supra*, p. 57.

later. Thus Henry Clay Frick, chairman of the Carnegie Steel Company, said of Henry W. Oliver that "if he is allowed to run loose, he will soon wreck the credit of any concern that he attempts to do business for." [105] Yet Oliver's failure in promoting Clapp-Griffiths converters does not seem to have involved negligence. In experimenting with high phosphoric iron in the converters, he was following the advice of Captain Robert Hunt, one of the country's most experienced metallurgists. Oliver further had the misfortune of beginning operations shortly before the depression of the 1880's.[106] Later owners described William Butcher's management of his steelworks at Midvale as "reckless and utterly wanting in system." [107] But ignorance and recklessness are easily confused, and it is often popular to attribute failure to moral flaws. Conversely success is often attributed to moral excellence. In speaking of Charles J. Harrah, Jr., president of the Midvale Steel Company for twenty-five years, a writer said, "To his courage and willingness to take what appeared to be great risks, the later success of the Company is largely due." [108] The same Harrah, however, refused to let Frederick W. Taylor experiment with tungsten alloys during the 1880's because the company was not producing such alloys. Taylor resigned and ultimately developed high-speed tool steel at the Bethlehem Steel Company.[109]

In general, it appears that investors were more willing to stake their funds on innovations that had been successfully tried abroad than on original American suggestions. Personally seeing financial success abroad in coke smelting, crucible refining, and open-hearth steelmaking was a greater stimulus to nontechnical men such as James Park, Jr., Charles A. Otis, Henry W. Oliver, and even Andrew Carnegie than the recom-

[105] Minutes of the Carnegie Steel Company quoted in Hendrick, *op. cit.*, II, 13.

[106] Evans, *op. cit.*, pp. 100–104.

[107] Quoted by Nalle, *op. cit.*, p. 11.

[108] *Ibid.*, p. 16.   [109] Copley, *op. cit.*, II, 4.

mendations of local technicians by themselves. At times little
or no effort was made to determine if foreign processes were
apt for American raw materials and markets, and losses resulted.[110]

With respect to the introduction of American inventions, it
appears that the closer an account was written to the time of
innovation the more cautious the innovating procedures appear.
When reminiscing, the great superintendents had a tendency
to speak of almost insuperable difficulties, surprises, disap-
pointments, and doubts, of severe strain, and of bitter oppo-
nents who invariably scolded them for being "visionary." Insofar as such words indicate that innovation required effort and
persistence, the appraisals seem warranted. But insofar as they
indicate a venturesome readiness to gamble against great odds,
they seem misleading and even contradictory to statements
made near the time of innovation. For example, John Fritz,
when reminiscing in his eighties, used nearly all the expres-
sions mentioned above; [111] and yet he had been one of the
most cautious innovators. When a friend had asked if failure
of his three-high mill might not ruin his reputation, Fritz had
said:

It is my rule not to make a move in any new thing until I have
thought it over, not only as a whole, but also in all of its details,
and I assure you this is no exception, and I now feel that success is
assured.[112]

The old mill was dismantled, the new mill installed, and the
first pile of metal drawn. It went through the rolls without the
least hitch of any kind, making a perfect rail.[113]

[110] *Supra,* pp. 24–27, 36–40.
[111] Fritz, *op. cit.,* pp. 110, 132–134, 158, 160–161, 205.
[112] *Ibid.,* p. 113.
[113] *Ibid.,* p. 114. Two days later, however, through an accidental fire,
the wooden mill building burned to the ground. It was rebuilt at once
(*ibid.,* pp. 116–120).

Fritz was so cautious that for more than five years after the Pennsylvania Steel Company had begun making Bessemer steel he delayed adoption of the process at Bethlehem, and even after that he doubted if it would be a financial success in the long run.[114] He remained dubious about the open-hearth process until he personally saw it in operation at Le Creusot, France.

It should be noted, however, that Fritz's employers at the Cambria works and later at the Bethlehem Iron Company were even more conservative. His innovations were accepted only after repeated bluffs, threats, and stratagems.[115] Even the introduction from England in the 1880's of Whitworth's hydraulic forging presses—a revolutionary development which allowed the first heavy steel forgings and which the United States Navy Gun Foundry Board sponsored as a guaranteed customer—required him "to make the fight of my life to carry it through." The Bethlehem board of directors felt that the Navy did not understand practical steelmaking, that the plant would be too costly, that the process was too different and would require too much training of labor, and that the company was earning profits and there was no need to change. All these fears proved unwarranted.[116]

If the word "visionary" in its derogatory sense of ambitious delusions does not suit John Fritz, it is also inappropriate for A. L. Holley and other creative engineers. The men who introduced the most radical technological changes of American origin preached extreme caution. They insisted that, whenever possible, innovations should be no more than secondary and supplementary to the regular operations of a firm. These views were not only expressed while trying to persuade business leaders to finance an untried novelty but were often pointed out at the height of a successful career to fellow engineers. In

[114] *Ibid.*, pp. 160–161. [115] *Ibid.*, pp. 110, 132, 134, 185–186.
[116] *Ibid.*, pp. 183–188.

his presidential address to the American Institute of Mining Engineers in 1876, A. L. Holley said:

The lowest functions, as in the case of poor humanity, must first be considered; that the conditions of maintenance and regular working, which constant familiarity with objects and phenomena alone can provide, are earliest in order. Conservation first and improvement afterwards. . . .

The trained scholar . . . might disorganize a whole establishment. As there must be one final authority, judgment founded on experience almost universally ranks the wider and more fruitful culture of the school . . . Plodding, practical economics must sit in judgment upon theory and limit the reaches of the imagination.[117]

Frederick W. Taylor, who was employed by the Midvale Steel Company and later the Bethlehem Steel Company and whose innovations were outstanding in machine tools, steelmaking, and time-and-motion studies, gave engineering students the following key to success:

Legitimate invention should be always preceded by a complete study of the field to see what other people have already done. Then some one or more defects should be clearly recognized and analyzed, and then it is entirely legitimate for the engineer to use his ingenuity and his inventive faculty in remedying these defects, and in adding his remedy to the existing elements of the machine or the process which have already been found to work well. Any other invention than this should be looked upon as illegitimate, since it is almost sure to waste the money of your employer, as well as your own, and to result in partial, if not complete disaster. Throughout the manufacturing world there exists a proper and legitimate suspicion and dislike for the man who is forever coming forward with new and radical improvements.[118]

Perhaps these quotations, and others that could be added, suggest no more than that outstanding engineers were cautious

[117] Holley, "The Inadequate Union of Engineering Science and Art," pp. 195–196.

[118] Quoted by Copley, *op. cit.*, I, 195.

or that caution may have been essential to achieve outstanding results. No doubt, men have a greater inclination to record successes than failures, and all journals and biographies have a success bias. But even if all failures had been forgotten, the knowledge that successful engineers were generally cautious would still be significant. It would indicate that cautious procedures could yield success and that in many lines of advance wild gambles were not essential.

The success bias of the records nevertheles makes it hard to prove that excessively bold and incautious engineers did not often cause business losses. Indeed, as described above, it happened now and then. But it does not seem to have been vital to technological development. Even successful engineers, in spite of all their caution and prestige, had difficulty in persuading employers to finance innovations. Fritz, Holley, Taylor, and others time and again insisted that the problem of convincing employers was "the greatest difficulty," [119] "the principal hindrance," [120] or required "the fight of my life." [121] Now if engineers of the highest reputation encountered such resistance from businessmen who had personally experienced the profitability of successful innovation, how likely was it that other engineers with less reputation would have met with less resistance and therefore might have precipitated failures? In an industry as large as the manufacture of iron and steel in America, there was bound to be an example of almost everything; but by and large, engineers without reputation, or with a reputation for bold fiascoes, were in a poor position to make themselves heard. Original innovation, in contrast with imported innovation, was in the hands of the cautious, but even cautious procedures had to overcome strong entrepreneurial misgivings.

[119] Taylor quoted in Copley, *op. cit.*, I, 247.
[120] Holley, "The Inadequate Union of Engineering Science and Art," p. 198.
[121] Fritz, *op. cit.*, p. 184.

To the last statement Abram S. Hewitt, Benjamin Franklin Jones, and Andrew Carnegie appeared to be exceptions. It was Carnegie who in the last three decades of the century allowed his managers and engineers to set the technological pace in blast furnaces and steel mills. Whether Carnegie was a rash or cautious gambler, or no gambler at all, is therefore of interest, and his attitude toward innovation and creative subordinates should be considered at some length.

His competitors certainly considered him some kind of gambler. Willis L. King of Jones and Laughlin believed that the Carnegie Steel Company succeeded because

Carnegie had the courage to go into debt to enlarge and improve his mill at times of great business depression, and profited greatly by the timidity of his competitors who were unwilling to assume the risk.[122]

Moreover, according to his favorably disposed biographer, Burton J. Hendrick, Carnegie was the "least analytical of mortals," a man who arrived at decisions by an intuitive process that led to exclamations of "I've got the flash!" or "I don't get the flash." Indeed, "the process of conscious logic played little part in his conclusions," and his method of choosing subordinates was comparable only to the unerring instinct of homing pigeons, a trait "beyond the realm of definition." [123]

Certain evidence, some of it cited by Hendrick himself, appears at variance with this portrait. Wherever he was, Carnegie insisted on receiving complete weekly reports of the company's operations, and his detailed comments on these reports indicate that he studied them carefully. He sometimes grumbled about too much detail and repetition; nevertheless, general statements angered him. "What we have a right to ask is figures," he once wrote to Charles M. Schwab. "You must have arrived at this opinion from some data. You have not founded it upon

[122] King, *op. cit.*, p. 229.   [123] Hendrick, *op. cit.*, I, 203–204.

nothing. Why do you keep this data from your Board and partners? . . . Really you do not do yourself justice in the apparent 'slap-dash' manner in which you recommend this to the
Board." [124]

He did not appraise subordinates by sheer intuition, but demanded a thorough account of all their actions and opinions:

We want every motion to show who voted for it, and who against it.
. . . The Minutes should, in addition to this, record every reason or
explanation which a member desires to give for his vote. If this were
properly done, then any of us looking over the Minutes would be
able to judge of the judgment displayed by the voter, which of
course would affect his standing with his colleagues. It would
bring responsibility home to him direct, and I do not see any other
way that will enable us to judge whether any of our partners has
good judgment or not. . . . The Minutes cannot err in being too full,
the fuller the better. They can err in being too much curtailed.[125]

Carnegie's investment in expansion and innovation in the
depressions of the 1870's and 1890's appeared highly speculative to contemporaries, but this appearance does not prove that
Carnegie should be regarded as a speculator, that he viewed
the ultimate profitability of his outlay as uncertain. It has been
suggested above that he thought in terms of long-run American
growth. This tendency may have been first inspired by the
contrast between torpid Dunfermline, Scotland, and booming
Pittsburgh around 1850, which gave him his first and basic
image of America. In 1853, when he was seventeen years old,
he wrote back to Dunfermline:

[124] Letter to Charles M. Schwab, Oct. 1, 1897, Papers of Andrew
Carnegie, vol. XLV, items 8828–8830.

[125] Letter to F. T. F. Lovejoy, Dec. 9, 1895, Papers of Andrew Carnegie,
vol. XXXV, items 6760–6762, quoted inaccurately by Hendrick, *op. cit.*,
II, 44. Partners who did not perform adequately could be bought out
at book value by others representing three-fourths of the Carnegie firm's
stock according to the famous "Iron Clad Rule." Fifteen men were
bought out in this manner. Carnegie himself usually retained between
50 and 60 per cent of the stock.

Our public lands, of almost unlimited extent, are becoming settled
with an enterprising people. Our dense forests are falling under the
axe of the hardy backwoodsman. The Wolf and the Buffalo are
startled by the shrill scream of the Iron Horse, where a few years
ago they roamed undisturbed. Towns and cities spring up as if by
magic. Cincinnati, Ohio, was settled in 1817 and now contains a
population of 165,000. Pittsburgh in 1840 had 40 and now numbers
93,000. Nor are these cases remarkable, everywhere throughout the
Northern states show like results. . . . Our Railroads extend 13,000
miles. You cannot supply iron fast enough to keep us going. Our
Telegraphs embrace 21,000 miles. The country is completely cut
up with Railroad Tracks, Telegraphs and Canals. . . . Hundreds of
labor saving devices are patented yearly. . . . Everything around
us is in motion.[126]

Others thought of America in a similar vein in times of prosperity; but insofar as they had access to funds when sales and
prices fell, their actions do not show a confidence as deeply in-
grained as Carnegie's. In the summer of 1895 when steel prices
had not yet reached the low point of the depression, he wrote,
"Now is the time to buy mills. . . . The country has been
economizing for nearly three years, and a boom is the natural
result." [127]

Carnegie's early business experience involved many general
areas of business—manufacturing, transportation, extraction,
communication, and finance. This wider experience as compared with that of other iron and steel executives must have
contributed to his superior grasp of the potential growth of
the American economy, the interdependence and complementarity of opportunities, and their relation to the demand for
steel. His extensive reading and long absences from Pittsburgh,
especially his long periods of residence in Europe, further dis-

[126] Letter to George Lauder, Jr., Aug. 18, 1853, quoted in full by
Hendrick, *op. cit.*, I, 72–77.
[127] Letter to John A. Leishman, July 2, 1895, Papers of Andrew
Carnegie, vol. XXXII, items 6179–6183.

tinguished him from other iron and steel executives and further broadened his outlook.

In any case, when he considered something a gamble, such as the Bessemer process in its early years or Minnesota ores in the 1890's,[128] he did not invest readily. He had an aversion to speculation in any form, and this attitude grew more pronounced as he grew older.[129] On one occasion he wrote, "We can stand the loss, and it will teach those responsible for it a lesson. What we cannot well stand is to have our name blazoned all through the country as associates of a speculating failure [Henry W. Oliver]." [130] He opposed buying stock on margin or with bank credit and dealt harshly with any associate or subordinate whom he found speculating.[131] A typical expression of his feelings occurs in a letter to President John A. Leishman:

It appears you speculated for ore, in Minnesota ore stock, which you bought when already in debt, simply because you thought it would rise in value. . . . You do not realize what the Presidency means. . . . You say it was not "a speculation." We can't see what it was but that. No conservative businessman can have any other name for it. . . . [I] ask you if it be possible for you to make a full statement and tell the whole truth.[132]

Of himself he said:

I found that when I opened my paper in the morning I was tempted to look first at the quotations of the stock market. As I had determined to sell all my interests in every outside concern and concentrate my attention upon our manufacturing concerns in Pittsburgh, I further resolved not even to own any stock that was bought and sold upon

[128] Hendrick, *op. cit.*, I, 164; letter to Charles M. Schwab, Oct. 8, 1897, Papers of Andrew Carnegie, vol. XLV, items 8900–8901; Bridge, *op. cit.*, p. 259.

[129] Hendrick, *op. cit.*, I, 299.

[130] Letter to John A. Leishman, Feb. 28, 1895, Papers of Andrew Carnegie, vol. XXXI.

[131] Hendrick, *op. cit.*, I, 196, 218–219.

[132] Letter to John A. Leishman, Jan. 4, 1896, Papers of Andrew Carnegie, vol. XXXV, items 6913–6914.

any stock exchange. . . . Nothing tells in the long run like good
judgment, and no sound judgment can remain with the man whose
mind is disturbed by the mercurial changes of the Stock Exchange.
. . . He cannot judge of the relative values or get the true perspective
of things. . . . His mind is upon the stock quotations and not upon
the points that require calm thought.[133]

Carnegie expected technological change and, whenever he
thought risks were not involved, welcomed and supported it.
He urged his managers to visit competing plants to look for
promising men and new ideas. He allowed the introduction of
many technological improvements as a matter of routine. Even
expensive and novel equipment that channeled waste gas from
blast furnaces to steel mills required no previous consent.[134]
Once Henry Clay Frick, his board chairman, sought approval
for replacing a set of obsolete pumps, and Carnegie replied,
"This seems wholly unnecessary. . . . No absent partner wants
to consider such trifling but highly important advances. The
pumps, of course, should be ordered at once." [135] At other times
he urged his men to keep up with European advances and to
adopt them without delay. "The true plan is to build the new
furnaces upon the most approved system. . . . Even if we save
half a dollar per ton by the change it would justify a large additional expenditure now. Before any decision is made against
the improved plan I should like to have an opportunity to con-
sult with you fully." [136]

But Carnegie's enthusiam for technological change did not
extend to proposals with an uncertain chance of success. According to the firm's bylaws, a major "change in methods or

[133] Carnegie, *op. cit.*, p. 153.

[134] Letter to John A. Leishman, July 2, 1895, Papers of Andrew Carnegie, vol. XXXII, items 6179–6183; letter to Charles M. Schwab, Sept.
11, 1897, *ibid.*, vol. XLIV, items 8689–8691.

[135] "Thoughts on Minutes," Sept. 28, 1897, sent to Carnegie Steel
Co., Oct. 8, 1897, Papers of Andrew Carnegie, items 8900–8901.

[136] Letter to William L. Abbott, Oct. 28, 1888, Papers of Andrew
Carnegie, vol. X, item 1681.

products" required a two-thirds majority of the board of directors. Carnegie warned his men against "gimcracks," agreed to
experiments with nickel alloys only if patents would be "unas-
sailable," and generally considered risky novelties not worth
the trouble of experimentation.[137] On acquiring a new plant,
his orders were typically that "a first class mechanical manager
. . . should be selected and given full charge. But before any
change is made a full report should be made upon the works.
. . . We do not wish to spend any more money than necessary,
and above all *we do not wish to make any mistakes mechani-
cally* [italics are Carnegie's]." [138]

During the 1880's and 1890's the leading technician of the
Carnegie firm was Charles M. Schwab. After a brief time at
St. Francis College, Schwab entered the firm as a stake driver
at the age of seventeen. He had "virtually a photographic
mind" [139] and a determination to educate himself in mathematics, chemistry, metallurgy, and engineering. Carnegie's
partner, Henry Phipps, supported Schwab's efforts with a loan
of one thousand dollars for a home laboratory and books.
Schwab was rapidly promoted, and soon his knowledge of
chemistry made him indispensable to Captain "Bill" Jones,
superintendent of the Edgar Thomson Works. In 1881 he was
appointed chief engineer. Six years later, at the age of twenty-
five, he became superintendent of the newly acquired Homestead Works; and ten years after that Carnegie made him
president of the company.

[137] Letter to William L. Abbott, Oct. 28, 1889, Papers of Andrew
Carnegie, vol. X, item 1745; letter to F. Rey, June 26, 1890, *ibid.*, vol. XI,
items 1853–1854.
[138] Letter to Carnegie Brothers and Co., Oct. 23, 1888, Papers of
Andrew Carnegie, vol. X, item 1679.
[139] E. G. Grace, *Charles M. Schwab* (privately printed, 1947), p. 23.
Schwab could quote from cost sheets years after he had seen them. He
kept no files in his office, saying that he did not need them since he remembered their contents.

In his first year as president, Schwab proposed a program of expansion, remodeling, and technological improvement costing one million dollars. Carnegie did not find the proposal convincing and, as soon as he heard of the board's approval of Schwab's plan, sent a cable from Scotland ordering the work suspended. A series of critical, almost belligerent, letters followed the cable although "I am not to be considered as deciding the proposed changes are not desirable." "We are in business to make money. Why is it that no figures were given showing what increased profits might be expected from investing. . . ?"[140]

To these messages Schwab replied:

I appeal to you, in all the years connected with your firm, and having recommended the principal improvements that we have made in these years, can you point to a single error? It has, indeed, been most discouraging at times to have been unduly criticized for a certain piece of work . . . before the thing has been practically tested and tried, but I submit . . . whether in all these improvements made at Homestead and Braddock, and recommended at Duquesne and other works, they have not been fully justified. . . .

The faculty which I possessed of devising new methods, etc., and which was given such free play at the works . . . [now yields] many more ideas, better ones, and much broader ideas with reference to improvements in machinery and methods than I ever had at the works, and I find great delight in having the details of such schemes and improvements worked out and solved by the superintendents of the works. . . .

We are now far ahead of any of our competitors [in production economies].[141]

[140] "Thoughts on Minutes," Sept. 14, 1897, quoted in the minutes of the Sept. 25, 1897, meeting of the board of directors of the Carnegie Steel Co., Papers of Andrew Carnegie, vol. XLV, items 8772–8773; "Further Thoughts upon Minutes of August 31st 1897," Sept. 18, 1897, *ibid.*, vol. XLIV, items 8715–8717.

[141] Letter to Andrew Carnegie, Oct. 5, 1897, Papers of Andrew Carnegie, vol. XLV, items 8871–8883.

Carnegie answered: "What frightens me is proposed changes in products or methods. . . . [But] I am thorough [sic] converted. . . . Believe me, I am rejoicing equally with yourself at your brilliant success and at the improvements which I am sure you are going to make." [142]

In short, even leading American innovators sponsored improved production methods in a spirit of caution. The factors which determined the outcome of most original American attempts to innovate were sufficiently known so that sweeping, even revolutionary, changes could be introduced by a cautious approach without loss. On the other hand, many foreign innovations, to be successfully imported, required a knowledge of chemistry that had as yet not been attained. In these attempts caution was of little use in reducing the chance of loss because the technique for replacing uncertainty with knowledge was undeveloped. Especially in the early years, it was not known what impurities to avoid or, if this had been known, how to detect and eliminate such impurities. For all other kinds of iron- and steel-making innovations, cautious procedures reduced the chance of serious loss to insignificant proportions.

Summary

Between 1800 and 1900 iron and steel production increased from thousands of tons to millions of tons. Charcoal furnaces and water-powered trip hammers were superseded and slowly eliminated by enormously complex steam- and electric-powered mills that smelted, refined, and shaped vast masses of metal in a single, entirely mechanical, operation. The innovations that made this transformation possible originated primarily in Europe; but, especially after 1870, auxiliary American innovations doubled and tripled efficiency. Although there were many firms

[142] Letter to Charles M. Schwab, Oct. 18, 1897, Papers of Andrew Carnegie, vol. XLVI, items 8977–8979.

that at one time or another attempted innovations, most owners of ironworks and steel mills were not enthusiastic about experimenting with technological changes. A significant handful of outstanding firms, however, contributed innovations over a period of three or more decades. Even in these firms technical originality and final business authority were rarely combined in the same person.

Unsuccessful attempts at innovation generally involved a gamble on the chemical suitability of new raw materials in a familiar process, the suitability of familiar raw materials in a new process, or both new materials and a new process. These gambles were necessary if some innovations were to be attempted at all, since inexpensive laboratory techniques for eliminating chemical uncertainty were either unknown or considered inconclusive. Almost all other innovations involved small commitments of capital or were introduced with such caution that serious losses rarely occurred. Occasionally a piece of equipment became obsolete with unexpected rapidity; but usually caution led to knowledge that eliminated all but the general business risks of tariff reduction and depression, or it inhibited action altogether. Compared with the losses due to chemical uncertainty, losses due to tariff reduction occurred rarely, but then tariffs were only rarely reduced. It is doubtful whether a significant number of failures at innovation which involve poor timing alone can be found and proved to be such in the iron and steel industry.

III

Textiles

IN most manufacturing industries the use of inanimate power for driving machines can be traced back to the Middle Ages, and in some industries to Classical Antiquity. The classic Industrial Revolution, therefore, did not mean the initial use of inanimate power any more than it meant the initial use of iron. Rather it consisted of the accelerated introduction of an ever greater variety of power-driven machines.

In America, as in Britain, this acceleration occurred first in the textile industry. The manufacture of yarn and cloth was taken out of households and harnessed to the same water wheels that had long been used in fulling cloth. The machines that replaced spinners and weavers grew rapidly in size, efficiency, and precision; and by 1820 Americans had taken the lead in devising innovations. By 1850 the transition from small wooden to large-scale metal machines was almost complete. Around the middle of the nineteenth century, however, just when the great acceleration in machinery production began in other industries, the rate of expansion in textiles declined. Production never again doubled in one decade or tripled in two. Technological leadership meanwhile reverted almost wholly to the Europeans.

From 1850 to 1900 further innovations, both domestic and imported, increased the weight of cotton that the average workers processed annually by 75 per cent and the weight of wool by about 105 per cent.[1] Quality also improved during these decades, especially with the introduction of worsted machinery and of looms that could weave more intricate patterns. All these innovations led to the use of about 20 per cent more capital per dollar of output in cotton textiles and some 30 per cent more in wool textiles.[2] During the last three decades of the century, larger capital expenditures helped increase the mechanical horsepower per worker from 1.1 to 2.7 in cotton manufacturing and from 1.0 to 1.8 in wool manufacturing.[3]

Throughout the century textile manufacturing remained one of the most important industries in the United States. In 1900, value added by manufacturing cotton and wool yarn and cloth ($275 million) still approached the combined value added by blast furnaces, steelworks, and rolling mills ($282 million); [4] and the total value added in the manufacture of textiles and clothing ($1,082 million) exceeded the total added in the manufacture of iron and steel and all their finished products ($984 million).[5]

[1] U.S. Bureau of the Census, *Census of Manufactures, 1905* (Washington, 1907), Bull. 74, pp. 15, 17.

[2] *Ibid.*

[3] U.S. Census Office, *Twelfth Census: Manufactures* (Washington, 1902), VII, cccxxx; U.S. Census Bureau, *op. cit.*, Bull. 74, pp. 121–122.

[4] U.S. Census Bureau, *op. cit.*, Bull. 74, p. 14; U.S. Census Office, *Twelfth Census*, X, 4. This chapter is concerned with these two parts of the textile industry, ignoring silk, flax, hemp, and jute. Value added in the manufacture of all products primarily using these other fibers amounted to only $60 million in 1900.

[5] U.S. Census Office, *Twelfth Census*, VII, clxiv.

The innovations in textile manufacturing methods involved two basic steps on a commercial level: the construction of new equipment and its actual introduction in yarn and cloth manufacturing. In the early decades, as will be described in more detail, these steps were often integrated—the machine shop being a part of the textile mill. As early as 1806, however, Arthur Scholfield devoted himself exclusively to making wool-carding machines for sale.[6] By 1821 the machine shop of the Boston Manufacturing Company had turned out equipment for nine other mills.[7] From these beginnings, textile machinery building became a separate industry. Between 1845 and 1865 the last machine builders separated their organizational connections with textile mills.

Throughout most of the century, innovations involved both these industries, textile making and textile machinery building. But the interests of the two did not always coincide. Depression, cutthroat competition, rapid obsolescence, and competition from new areas sometimes meant losses to machinery users and handsome profits to machinery builders.

The risks of innovation should therefore be seen from the point of view of both these industries. For example, what appears as a customer risk to the machine builder may seem like a production risk to the millowner. The innovator in either case is the person (or group) who thinks that he sees the commercial possibilities of a textile machinery invention and who backs the development of that invention with funds and reputation, regardless of whether he owns the shop that builds the machine or whether he plans to use or sell the machine.

[6] Arthur H. Cole, *The American Wool Manufacture* (Cambridge: Harvard University Press, 1926), I, 92.

[7] Caroline F. Ware, *The Early New England Cotton Manufacture: A Study in Industrial Beginnings* (Cambridge: Riverside Press, 1931), p. 82.

Widespread Innovation before 1835

The initial attempts to establish yarn and cloth factories in America failed. Outstanding among these early failures were a cotton factory at Beverly, Massachusetts, set up in 1787,[8] and a wool factory at Hartford, Connecticut, established in 1788.[9] Both of these began on an ambitious scale and attempted to mechanize all processes from carding to weaving. Both had public support in the form of subsidies, income from lotteries, tax exemptions, and testimonials from Alexander Hamilton or George Washington. Yet both were abandoned in the middle 1790's. Like other similar factories, they had encountered a number of difficulties. British export and emigration restrictions had meant gaps in vital technological information, and thus the factories found themselves making an inferior product on inferior machines that were only partly water- or horse-powered. With respect to wool, the poor quality of domestic fleece was a further handicap. In the case of cotton, according to George Cabot, one of the partners at Beverly wrote: "A want of skill in constructing the machinery and of dexterity in using it, added to our want of a general knowledge of the business we had undertaken, have proved the principal impediments to its success." [10]

The arrival of Samuel Slater in America in 1789 and of John and Arthur Scholfield in 1793 did much to close this gap in technological knowledge. Slater had memorized the construction of the spinning frame in Richard Arkwright's and Jedediah Strutt's works, and the Scholfields understood the proper way of building wool-carding machines. These latter machines reduced from hours to minutes the time needed to untangle and

[8] See Ware, *op. cit.*, p. 20.
[9] Cole, *American Wool Manufacture*, I, 64–69.
[10] Letter to Alexander Hamilton, Sept. 6, 1791. See Alexander Hamilton, *Industrial and Commercial Correspondence*, Arthur H. Cole, ed. (Chicago: A. W. Shaw, 1928), p. 62.

straighten wool fibers before spinning.[11] Like the cotton-spinning frame and Eli Whitney's gin of 1793, they eliminated a major bottleneck at a strategic time. Nevertheless, proper construction of these and other machines was not in itself enough to guarantee commercial success.

A fundamental reorientation was needed. To be most profitable, the new power-driven machines had to be fitted into the American economy in ways that avoided competition with the seasoned quality of British cloth. Thus Slater's business associate, Moses Brown, learned first to exploit a shortage of cotton yarn in America [12] and then, when he undertook weaving, to stress the greater weight of his product as a sign of durability suited for the frontier.[13]

In wool manufacturing the lesson was not as readily seen. The Scholfields first became associated with a venture, the Newburyport Woolen Manufactory, that tried to make broadcloth and flannel in competition with imports. Within two years this factory needed public assistance, and after ten, in 1803, it was sold and converted into a cotton mill.[14] The Scholfields then successfully promoted power carding as a service to household spinners, much as power fulling had long been provided for household weavers. As early as 1803, however, Arthur Scholfield had wanted to add machine building to carding; and in 1806 he sold the carding business altogether. Many Scholfield machines were sold to fulling mills which then gradually absorbed the processes of spinning and weaving to become regular factories. Some of the earliest wool mills processed wool to any extent desired by a customer—through carding, spinning, or weaving.[15] Because of the inferiority of American

[11] Cole, *American Wool Manufacture*, I, 95–96.
[12] Ware, *op. cit.*, pp. 25, 31–32.   [13] *Ibid.*, pp. 49–50.
[14] Cole, *American Wool Manufacture*, I, 88–89.
[15] *Ibid.*, I, 91–93, 219–226.

fleece, these mills could not compete with British cloth in quality until economic conditions under the Embargo and Nonintercourse Acts in 1807–1809 finally led to large-scale imports of merino sheep.[16]

By 1807 there were at least a dozen cotton mills in the United States.[17] Nearly all of these were built by Slater or by mechanics who had helped Slater build his early machinery and who had then gone into business for themselves.[18] These mechanics were men with limited means, and they remained in the general vicinity of Providence. Slater's first mill was operated by nine children and had only 72 spindles, compared with the 636 spindles in the unsuccessful Beverly venture.[19]

Itinerant mechanics built in local blacksmith shops much of the machinery for other early mills. A few settled down and established machine shops of their own, manufacturing first one or two specialized machines and then expanding their line.[20] Between 1807 and 1810 these mechanics equipped about sixty new mills within thirty miles of Providence.[21] After twenty-five years, less than a third of these were still in operation, whereas, by contrast, most of Slater's own mills, built before 1807, survived. Since almost no record remains of the mills that failed, their disappearance must remain a matter of speculation. One writer suggests that they may have been built more hurriedly, with jennies and the crudest arrangements for the

[16] *Ibid.*, I, 15–16.

[17] Clive Day, "The Early Development of the American Cotton Manufacture," *Quarterly Journal of Economics*, XXXIX (May 1925), 450–461.

[18] George S. White, *Memoir of Samuel Slater: The Father of American Manufactures* (2d ed.; Philadelphia, 1836), pp. 106–107.

[19] William R. Bagnall, *The Textile Industries of the United States* (Cambridge: Riverside Press, 1893), I, 96, 159.

[20] Thomas R. Navin, Jr., "Innovation and Management Policies, The Textile Machinery Industry: Influence of the Market on Management," *Bulletin of the Business Historical Society*, XXIV (March 1950), 19–20

[21] G. S. White, *op. cit.*, p. 258.

application of power, and that they were therefore not worth salvaging when the original owners failed.[22]

When Robert and Alexander Barr were brought to America by the arms maker Hugh Orr in 1786 to build spinning frames, nothing could be done to remedy lapses in their memory or understanding.[23] The spinning frame had to be introduced by a man like Smauel Slater who had trained his memory for years on Arkwright's best machines and who had left almost nothing to chance.

On the other hand, the introduction of power weaving from England around 1813 found America already far more skilled and experienced in technological matters. The power loom could thus be developed by local mechanics with little more to go on than the impressions of a businessman, Francis Cabot Lowell, who had been allowed to visit British cotton mills in 1810 and 1811. Although Lowell had tried to learn every possible secret, he could not duplicate what he had seen. The Boston Manufacturing Company was organized nevertheless, and about a year after the capital was fully subscribed, in 1814, the company's mechanic, Paul Moody, had constructed a working power loom.[24] The difference was not that weaving was easier to mechanize than spinning. On the contrary, the drawing out and twisting of spinning can be performed by simple and safe rotary motions, whereas the opening and closing and back and forth movements of looms necessarily mean a great danger of thread breakage. The difference between 1786 and 1813 was

[22] Day, *op. cit.*, pp. 452, 465; information based on G. S. White, *op. cit.*, and on Louis McLane, *Report of the Secretary of the Treasury, 1832: Documents Relative to the Manufactures in the United States* (House Executive Documents, 22d Congress, First Session, no. 308; Washington, 1833).

[23] Bagnall, *op. cit.*, pp. 85–86.

[24] See Nathan Appleton, *Introduction of the Power Loom and Origin of Lowell* (Lowell: B. H. Penhallow, 1858); George Sweet Gibb, *The Saco-Lowell Shops: Textile Machinery Building in New England, 1813–1949* (Cambridge: Harvard University Press, 1950), pp. 7–14.

that the growth of spinning and carding mills had led a generation of carpenters and blacksmiths to train themselves as potential machine builders and inventors.

From the standpoint of organization, the founding of the Boston Manufacturing Company's $100,000 cotton mill at Waltham was the beginning of a new era. From the standpoint of technology, however, Moody's adaptation of the power loom and his other inventions—an improved warp dresser for looms, the double speeder roving frame, the use of high-speed dead spindles, and the practice of spinning directly on shuttle bobbins [25]—were no more than a few important innovations among many. Between 1790 and 1835 American innovations were so numerous in both cotton and wool manufacturing that in some lines it was possible to claim that England had lost her leadership.

With respect to looms, for example, an American power loom had been patented by Amos Whittemore in 1796, and other looms had been built in New Hampshire in 1809 and Rhode Island in 1812.[26] Two years after Moody finished his cam loom, William Gilmour introduced a successful crank-type loom in Rhode Island.[27] The same year, 1816, Ira Draper of Weston, Massachusetts, patented self-acting loom temples for holding and guiding the cloth in weaving. These temples were adopted in England many years after they were in general use in America.[28] Amos Whittemore had patented in 1797 a card-setting machine that compared in originality with Whitney's cotton gin.[29] Further originality was shown in mechanizing the process of opening the cotton fibers and picking out impurities. A number of opening and picking inventions occurred in the

[25] Gibb, *op. cit.*, pp. 33–39.

[26] G. S. White, *op. cit.*, pp. 385–389; Gibb, *op. cit.*, pp. 13–14.

[27] Bagnall, *op. cit.*, pp. 546–550.

[28] Melvin Thomas Copeland, *The Cotton Manufacturing Industry of the United States* (Cambridge: Harvard University Press, 1912), p. 83.

[29] Gibb, *op. cit.*, p. 28.

1820's, and these were synthesized and improved around 1832 by Benjamin Innis, an employee of the cotton manufacturers, P. Whitin and Sons.[30] Two other American inventions that rapidly found their way to England were Asa Arnold's compound gear for regulating the varying velocity for winding filaments of cotton, invented in 1823, and Charles Danforth's cap spinner for improving the weft, invented in 1828.[31]

A highly original American innovation was the ring spinning process invented in 1828 by John Thorp of Providence. In this system, a ring is placed around each spindle, and a twist is imparted to the yarn by making it pass somewhat more slowly around the ring than around the bobbin on the spindle. In contrast with the alternate twisting and winding of the mule, ring spinning machines had all the advantages of a continuous process. They required less power; they could be driven at a higher speed; and they spun yarn of better quality. Thorp's first machines, however, were so clumsy that they created a prejudice against the process among millowners. This prejudice retarded the later introduction of improved ring spinning machines by William Mason around 1835.[32] At this time Mason was superintendent of the machine shop of the Crocker and Richmond textile mill at Taunton, Massachusetts. After Crocker and Richmond failed in 1839, Mason acquired control of the machine shop and founded the Mason Machine Works. In a few years Mason shifted his attention from ring to mule spinning machines, and around 1845 he allowed Fales and Jenks of Pawtucket, Rhode Island, and P. Whitin and Sons of Northbridge, Massachusetts, to take the lead in the manufacture of

[30] Thomas R. Navin, Jr., *The Whitin Machine Works since 1831: A Textile Machinery Company in an Industrial Village* (Cambridge: Harvard University Press, 1950), pp. 28–32.

[31] Howard Rockey, "From Plantation to Loom," in Waldemar Kaempffert, ed., *A Popular History of American Invention* (New York: Charles Scribner's Sons, 1924), pp. 233–234.

[32] Copeland, *op. cit.*, p. 66; Navin, *The Whitin Machine Works*, pp. 34–35.

ring spinning machines. Among American textile machinery innovations, only the automatic loom can compare in originality and importance with ring spinning.

In the technique of wool manufacturing, between 1790 and 1835 Americans made important innovations in gigging, shearing, and fulling; they revolutionized carding; and they independently harnessed spinning and weaving to power. Even before the Scholfields had arrived in America in 1792, Samuel G. Dorr of Albany had invented the first nap-cutting apparatus that used blades on a revolving cylinder resembling a lawn mower. This innovation was not brought to England until 1815.[33] In 1797 Walter Burt of Wilbraham, Massachusetts, patented a modern gig mill for raising the nap before shearing, and, modified by others, it was later introduced in England.[34] Power looms appeared shortly after 1815, and by 1830 there was a strong trend toward their general use.[35] In England, meanwhile, another twenty years were to pass before power looms gained the upper hand. Perhaps most important of all innovations in wool manufacturing was John Goulding's carding machine of 1826 that combined a number of devices invented by others in such a way that the process of roping or "slubbing" with its machinery could be eliminated. The wool now left the carding machine ready for immediate spinning. Twenty-five years elapsed before this innovation found its way to England.[36]

From a British point of view, American technical skill left much to be desired. Thus British textile men often conceded that Americans were ingenious at devising novel machines, but they pointed out that these same machines were usually brought to greater efficiency as soon as they were introduced in Britain. James Montgomery, who had managed cotton mills in both countries, wrote in 1840:

[33] Cole, *American Wool Manufacture*, I, 130–131.
[34] *Ibid.*, I, 128–130.   [35] *Ibid.*, I, 123.   [36] *Ibid.*, I, 102–107.

The number of machines taken from America, for which patents have been obtained in Great Britain, have led many to suppose that the Americans must have obtained to considerable perfection in labour-saving machinery. This, however, is not the case; nor do I think that, in this respect, they are at all equal to the British; and, indeed, most of those machines that have been taken from this country, are in a much higher state of perfection in Britain, than any of the same kind I have seen here [where machine makers] seem to proceed on the supposition that their machinery is already perfect. The machines are calculated for one kind of goods, and only one system of working. . . . [In Great Britain] every machine is so constructed, that all its parts can be adjusted with the greatest accuracy, to suit the various qualities of cotton, or whatever kind of goods may be wanted.[37]

What such observers failed to see was that the American willingness to accept minor imperfections and to specialize in a single type of yarn or cloth was precisely the factor that in this early period encouraged highly original innovations. As others noted about American industry as a whole:

The willingness on the part of the American public to buy what is offered them, if it in any way answers the purpose, has given a great advantage to the North American manufacturer over his European competitor. . . . In the United States they overlook defects more than in Europe, and are satisfied if a machine intended to supersede domestic labour will work even imperfectly, while we insist on its being thoroughly well made and efficient.[38]

But during this early period, before 1840, many novel machines proved to be so imperfect that they were failures after they were installed in a mill. Some, like Thorp's ring spindles,

[37] James Montgomery, *A Practical Detail of the Cotton Manufacture of the United States* (Glasgow: John Niven, Jr., 1840), pp. 109–110.

[38] *Reports of Juries*, London Exhibition of 1862, class XXXI, pp. 2–3, quoted by D. L. Burn, "The Genesis of American Engineering Competition, 1850–1870," *Economic History*, II (Jan. 1931), 306.

are remembered only because they introduced a method that later became important. Many others left no trace outside the records of the Patent Office, which, of course, do not indicate whether they were tried at all and, if so, the extent of failures. Even some moderately successful inventions of the period have been all but forgotten. One was Brewster's spinning machine. Between 1813 and 1824 Gilbert Brewster of Norwich, Connecticut, developed a self-operating spinning machine that in many ways anticipated Roberts' self-acting mule.[39] It appears that Brewster was able to sell a considerable number of his machines to wool and cotton manufacturers but that most of these found them suited only for warp yarn and likely to get out of repair. After 1828 mention of this machine in contemporary sources virtually disappears.[40] By the 1820's so many inventions had failed under manufacturing conditions that new inventions were at times specifically advertised as being different from all these failures.[41]

The number of successful innovations was sufficiently great, however, to cause a rapid rate of obsolescence; and Secretary of the Treasury Louis McLane reported in 1832 that most textile mills owned quantities of discarded equipment. One Rhode Island cotton mill built in 1813 had by 1827 scrapped and replaced every original machine.[42] The need for replacement tended to give an advantage to large mills, such as the Boston Manufacturing Company, because these mills, founded by bankers and wealthy merchants, had greater financial resources. It was common for small mills to use 85 per cent or more of the initial capital for buildings, land, and machinery; and at times the initial capital subscription did not even cover

[39] Patented in 1825 in England, made practical around 1832, but not introduced in America until about 1840.

[40] Cole, *American Wool Manufacture,* pp. 117–118; Joseph L. Bishop, *A History of American Manufactures from 1608 to 1860* (3d ed.; Philadelphia: Edward Young and Co., 1868), II, 297.

[41] Ware, *op. cit.,* p. 26.   [42] McLane, *op. cit.,* I, 956.

these expenses.[43] By contrast, the owners of the Waltham venture planned to keep at least a third of their capital liquid and actually limited their investment in plant and equipment to about 40 per cent.[44] In small mills lack of liquidity meant more failures in depression years like 1829–1830, and a tardy replacement rate led to relatively lower returns in good years.[45]

The importance of larger machine shops increased simultaneously with the importance of larger mills. Indeed, construction of the earliest large mills often began with the building of a large machine shop, because existing American shops were unable to supply conveniently the type of equipment needed and also because machinery exports from Britain were still prohibited. Once established, the auxiliary machine shops of large mills were available for building the machinery for other new mills. As long as the secular trend in prices continued downward, however, and as long as cost-cutting inventions continued to be devised and eagerly sought, the small machine shops fared better than small mills. Their survival nevertheless depended on their location in the Blackstone Valley north of Providence or some other textile manufacturing area to which machinery could not be shipped economically from the large shops.[46]

Technological Conservatism, 1835–1900

After 1835 a number of interrelated developments led to the decline of the small machine shop even in the Providence area and to a much slower rate of innovation. One such development was the substitution of iron for wood in the construction of machinery. Wool-carding machines had been constructed wholly of iron as early as 1822,[47] but this trend did not gather

[43] Ware, *op. cit.*, p. 139.

[44] Appleton, *op. cit.*, p. 30; Ware, *op. cit.*, p. 139.

[45] McLane, *op. cit.*, I, 929–969.

[46] Gibb, *op. cit.*, pp. 44–46, 172; Navin, "Innovation and Management Policies," pp. 19–20.

[47] Cole, *American Wool Manufacture*, I, 99.

momentum until the 1830's when large-scale machine tools became more readily available and when textile machinery designs of larger proportions were developed. At the same time railroads began to decrease, but not to eliminate, the localized character of some machinery markets. Although there were important variations in size, timing, and degree of specialization, the machine shops of a few textile mills acquired more and more outside customers and independence between 1830 and 1860. The capital and experience required in the building of textile machinery eventually grew to the point that mechanics with original ideas could rarely develop these independently. Outstanding among the cotton machinery firms that emerged were the Lowell Machine Shop (successor to the Waltham shop); the Saco Water Power Machine Shop at Biddeford, Maine; [48] the Amoskeag Manufacturing Company at Manchester, New Hampshire; the Whitin Machine Works at Northbridge, Massachusetts; [49] the Mason Machine Works of Taunton, Massachusetts; the Matteawan Machine Shop of New York; and the Bridesburg Machine Works near Philadelphia. Davis and Furber of North Andover, Massachusetts, and the Smith Woolen Machinery Company of Philadelphia became the outstanding producers of woolen machinery.

For a variety of reasons the rise of these shops, and of others that were more specialized, was associated with a decline in the rate of innovation. This decline began in the 1830's—before the growth of cotton manufacturing had reached its maximum rate, that of 1844–1846.[50] But the rate of expansion of textile

[48] The rise of these two shops as well as that of the Pettee Machine Works at Newton Upper Falls, Mass., has been traced in detail by Gibb, *op. cit.*

[49] See Navin, *The Whitin Machine Works.*

[50] Ware, *op. cit.*, p. 108. Wool manufacturing reached its maximum rate of growth during the Civil War decade, which led to an actual decline in cotton manufacturing. From 1870 to 1900, however, the rate of growth of wool manufacturing, including worsteds, was less than half that of cotton manufacturing.

manufacturing was no longer a certain stimulus to innovations in machinery. As a matter of fact, with entry into the textile machinery building industry now inhibited by the difficulty of acquiring complex experience, innovation was retarded in boom years by the presure to fill blacklogs of orders with a minimum of delay.[51]

Lack of growth and fierce price competition during the 1870's, by contrast, encouraged rather than discouraged technological change. Most ideas were again imported from Britain and copied rather than adapted; but the large machine shops prospered during the depression. The value of shares of the Lowell Machine Shop actually increased every year from 1873 through 1877.[52]

Limited competition for replacements, among other reasons, kept the large shops from developing and promoting original innovations.[53] Superintendents of textile mills preferred to have all machines of a given type made by a single manufacturer in order to keep labor-training and maintenance standardized.[54] A machine builder would therefore hesitate to introduce a basic change in machine design for fear of losing his special advantage with old customers. Each machine shop thus came to have its own group of traditional customers; and if an innovation became necessary, the machine builder would generally wait until his customers requested it. Since the mills were constantly interested in lowering costs and marketing novel fabrics, these customers did provide a steady flow of suggestions, which are reflected in the large number of patents

[51] See Navin, "Innovation and Management," p. 24.

[52] Gibb, *op. cit.,* pp. 199–210.

[53] On the other hand, intense competition did occur in the process of equipping Southern mills between 1880 and 1905, but this competition was a matter of price rather than quality. See Navin, *The Whitin Machine Works,* pp. 204–259; Gibb, *op. cit.,* pp. 241–255, 272–276, 318–320, 351–355.

[54] Navin, "Innovation and Management," p. 23.

granted for modifications and attachments to existing machines. Some of the resulting innovations were then licensed for use by other mills and even for manufacture by other machine shops for their special customers; yet by and large each mill had to initiate changes in its own production methods.[55] But since mill technicians were not engineers [56] who could develop fundamentally different but still practical machines without full-scale trial and error and since full-scale trial and error had in fact become inaccessible to these men, the range of innovation was limited to minor elaborations and simplifications. That fundamental innovations continued to appear in Europe and that American machine builders could also innovate when they tried—as in the development of the Northrop automatic bobbin-changing loom in the 1890's and wool ring spinning in the 1920's—suggest that the decline in American originality was partly due to organizational factors.

By contrast, English machine builders in the late nineteenth century mechanized the textile industries of several countries and seldom viewed themselves as job-order shops for individual customers. They produced standardized lines of equipment, introduced changes when they saw fit, and cared little if their old customers had problems in keeping up with the times. Moreover, from about 1840 to 1880 the customers, both old and new, of English machine builders were more receptive to innovations than the customers of American shops. They were less likely to insist that innovations be incorporated in high-speed equipment because power (coal instead of water) was more expensive and British labor was cheaper. Cheaper labor

[55] *Ibid.*, pp. 20–21.

[56] Engineers first appeared in the textile industry in the 1870's to assist in the selection of site and machinery for new mills. They pressed machine shops for cheaper and better machines and may have accelerated a few innovations, but they generally discouraged uniformity and therefore delayed interchangeability in machine building (Navin, *The Whitin Machine Works*, pp. 122–123).

costs also made possible the mechanization of part of a process while leaving other parts in the hands of craftsmen. Thus it appears that the initial necessity for continued hand combing played an important part in delaying the introduction of worsted machinery in the United States.[57] It was easier to make a change in an English specialized small-scale mill than in an integrated, and therefore less flexible, large-scale American mill. The small scale was itself justified because English textile mills continued working for countries with custom-made rather than ready-made clothing industries and were thus confronted by a demand that did not require uniformity. Compared with the United States, English and other European machine builders found it more profitable to introduce fundamental quality-improving innovations because they were not at the same time required to adapt these innovations to the largest and most rapid scale of production possible. Nevertheless, as will be seen below, some of the most significant American imports of British innovations were changes to more rapid, large-scale operation.

The textile industry in the middle of the nineteenth century provides a curious instance of American manufacturers paying "the penalty of taking the lead." Introducing a novel machine in an American mill might involve not only the scrapping of a relatively larger existing machine but additional expenses in adjusting and possibly scrapping various complementary machines in an integrated mill.[58] Eventually, however, innovations were developed that took the form of large machines requiring simultaneous changes in vertically related stages of production. By that time, around 1900, it was Britain, where spinning and weaving continued as separate industries and

[57] Cole, *American Wool Manufacture*, I, 334–335.

[58] For a theoretical analysis of this phenomenon, see Marvin Frankel, "Obsolescence and Technological Change in a Maturing Economy," *American Economic Review*, XLV (June 1955), 296–319.

where factory buildings were too small and weak for the largest machines, that was at a disadvantage. The Northrop bobbin-changing loom was such an innovation:[59] by 1939 only 5 per cent of British cotton looms were automatic, compared with 95 per cent of American looms.[60]

The outstanding British innovations after 1840 came to America with a lag of decades. Their adoption was often inspired by American mill engineers who, after the 1870's, supervised the construction of new mills. The first novel machines were usually British imports. Then years passed before American machine shops decided to exploit their tariff advantage to copy these machines. The machines produced often were openly promoted as close copies of British machines.

When it came to changing the design of machines, the attitude of all the principal American machine shops, as Dr. Navin has pointed out, was "merely accepting whatever changes were forced upon them from the outside." [61] This attitude was displayed in the introduction of carding machines with revolving instead of stationary flat cards, of mechanical combing machines, of fly frames, of slashers, and of all kinds of worsted machinery. In the case of the revolving flat card machines, not only the patent rights but also patterns and special tools were purchased in England in 1886 by the first manufacturer, the Pettee Machine Works.[62] When the Lowell Machine Shop undertook the building of worsted drawing and spinning machinery in 1898, it first purchased Prince-Smith

[59] *Infra*, pp. 104–106.

[60] See *Equipment and Labour Utilization in the Cotton Industry* (Manchester: Cotton Board Labour Department, 1947). No doubt the resistance of British Trade Unions and the inflexibility of their organizations, particularly the wage lists, contributed substantially to this lag. See Roland Gibson, *Cotton Textile Wages in the United States and Great Britain: A Comparison of Trends, 1860–1945* (New York: King's Crown Press, 1948), pp. 68–92.

[61] Navin, *The Whitin Machine Works*, p. 111.

[62] Gibb, *op. cit.*, p. 345.

and Stells machines through a third party, the Massachusetts Mohair Plush Company, and then brought English mechanics to Lowell for setting up production to copy minutely these machines.[63]

There were, however, some important American innovations between 1835 and 1900 that should not go unnoticed. One of these was the pattern power loom, invented by William Crompton in 1837, one year after he came to the United States from England. His invention consisted basically of a pattern chain that activated a series of mechanisms for raising and lowering various harnesses at predetermined intervals. The pattern loom itself was not new; what the innovation achieved was automatic synchronizing of the harness changes with other motions of the loom, so that more complicated patterns could be woven and so that changing from one pattern to another would be inexpensive.

Crompton invented his device while superintendent of the cotton machinery department of the Crocker and Richmond cotton mill of Taunton, Massachusetts. This firm actively encouraged Compton, but as previously mentioned, it failed in the depression of 1839. Crompton returned to England and there equipped one cotton mill with about 150 looms using his device. Back in the United States, later in 1839, he found no American cotton mills interested in his loom, but the following year he adapted his device to wool weaving for the looms of the Middlesex Mills of Lowell, Massachusetts. The machine shop of Phelps and Bickford of Worcester was licensed to build Crompton looms on a royalty basis and eventually became the Crompton Loom Company. Crompton's son, George, in 1857 broadened the loom in size and redesigned it for faster operation. Around 1863 Lucius J. Knowles developed a modification that allowed some harnesses to remain raised for several picks, thus easing the strain on warp yarns. Knowles organized his own Knowles Loom Works and competed successfully with

[63] *Ibid.*, p. 292.

the Crompton Loom Company. In 1897 the two firms merged to form the Crompton and Knowles Loom Works.[64]

An example of rapid obsolescence resulting from the American preference for modification by means of attachments instead of fundamental redesign occurred in wool spinning around 1870. Before the 1870's wool had been spun on power-driven spinning jacks, which differed from jennies primarily in having the spindles carried on that part of the machine that moved back and forth and having the roving placed on the stationary part of the machine, rather than the reverse. As a matter of fact, it was this arrangement that had facilitated the application of power. The back and forth movement, however, was still under manual control. Between 1869 and 1871 four different American inventions appeared that made the spinning wholly automatic by means of attachments, called "operators." Had the introduction of automatic woolen mules from England not been gathering momentum in the years immediately following, a great patent controversy and perhaps a consolidation might have occurred. As it was, however, the mule quickly made the operators obsolete. The woolen mule, which should not be confused with the cotton mule, involved substantially the same mechanisms as the operators but integrated them into a single structure with the rest of the machine. It was thus capable of carrying a larger number of spindles and operating at a variety of speeds.[65]

Costly patent controversies did attend the introduction and spread of two other American modifications of textile machinery. One of these was the Wellman "self-stripper" for cleaning

[64] George Crompton, *The Crompton Loom* (Worcester: privately printed, 1949), pp. 32–73; Cole, *American Wool Manufacture*, I, 306–309, 363–366; Copeland, *op. cit.*, pp. 83–89; Jonathan Thayer Lincoln, "The Cotton Textile Machine Industry—American Loom Builders," *Harvard Business Review*, XII (Oct. 1933), 94–105.

[65] Cole, *American Wool Manufacture*, II, 88–91. The first mules had been installed in American mills as early as 1865, but for some reason did not attract much attention.

the cards of pre-1887 carding machines, and the other the light-weight, high-speed spindle, which was developed between 1870 and 1883. These controversies were not, however, costly in the sense that one of the litigants might have found his heavy expenditures on manufacturing facilities a total loss. The patent holders were generally willing to license manufacture by any interested machine shop in order to gain the most rapid spread and quickest returns on their inventions. What the controversies involved was largely who should get the royalties and who should pay the court costs, not who could produce or who could use a new device.

The Wellman card self-stripper was an inexpensive attach-ment, patented in 1853 by George Wellman, a cotton-mill employee. This attachment cost about $60 per machine and saved about $300 worth of hand cleaning annually. In 1854 Horace Woodman of Biddeford, Maine, challenged Wellman's patent, but the Circuit Court of Washington, D.C., decided in favor of Wellman. In 1866, two years after Wellman's death, the administrator of the will concluded an agreement with Woodman to avoid a renewal of the dispute. As a result, the royalty, which had risen from $7 in 1861 to $13 in 1865, was in-creased by an additional $5, all of which was to accrue to Woodman and his partners. It has been estimated that during the following ten years this agreement earned roughly $400,000 for Woodman and his partners, whereas Wellman's estate earned an additional $1,100,000. It did not affect the competi-tive position of machine makers and cotton mills among them-selves, except insofar as large mills had to pay a relatively smaller back royalty to Woodman, compared with other mills, for strippers already installed.[66]

The spindle controversy was far more complicated but essentially similar. The introduction of the light-weight, high-

[66] Thomas R. Navin, Jr., "The Wellman-Woodman Patent Controversy in the Cotton Textile Machinery Industry," *Bulletin of the Business His-torical Society*, XXI (Nov. 1947), 144–152.

speed spindles was probably the most important innovation between 1835 and 1880.[67] The lighter spindle weight allowed great fuel savings for steam mills; and the higher speeds allowed additional increases in output compared with costs. Both lighter weight and higher speed were made possible by redesigning spindles to avoid vibration. The initial step involved extension of the bolster of the spindle to provide support at the spindle's center of gravity. This type of spindle was patented rather vaguely in 1870 by Oliver Pearl and specifically in 1871 by Jacob Sawyer, who then acquired the backing of George Draper and Son, of Hopedale, Massachusetts. The Draper firm had been manufacturing twisters, spoolers, warpers, and various loom attachments. Both groups were eager to license their patents to as many machine shops as possible. A complicated series of patent-infringement suits, alternative inventions, and mergers of interest followed with results that were particularly favorable to the Drapers.[68] The sums involved in these maneuvers can be suggested by the fact that the Whitin Machine

[67] Gibb, *op. cit.*, p. 211.

[68] Oliver Pearl sued two Lowell mills that had bought Sawyer spindles, but the court ruled that infringement had not occurred. Meanwhile Francis Rabbeth developed a spindle in which the shaft was allowed considerable play and which increased maximum speed from about 6,500 to 10,000 revolutions per minute. Rabbeth's patents were partly owned by the Fales and Jenks Machine Company of Pawtucket, which in 1879 pooled its spindle interests with George Draper and Sons. Fales and Jenks, however, insisted on being the exclusive manufacturers of the new spindle. The Whitin Machine Works of Northbridge, Mass., which, among others, was placed at a disadvantage by this agreement, now proceeded to develop a different light-weight spindle in which play was limited to vertical adjustment, somewhat along the principle of a gyroscope. The Whitin company in turn reached an agreement with George Draper and Sons in 1885, acquiring an exclusive right to equip new frames with its "gravity" spindles in exchange for assigning its patents to the Sawyer Spindle Company and allowing George Draper and Sons to equip old spindles. The Whitin Machine Works had the advantage of paying only 18.5 cents royalty per spindle to the Drapers, instead of the 45 cents which other machine makers paid on their spindles; but this advantage was lost in a further suit in 1893.

Works alone paid $2,080,000 in royalties to the Draper subsidiary, the Sawyer Spindle Company.[69]

The Draper firm was something unique in the American textile machinery industry—a firm that for three generations actively developed and promoted innovations. Ira Draper invented the self-acting loom temple in 1817. George Draper further developed the temples, merged interests with Warren Dutcher's alternative approach in 1854, and took the lead in promoting high-speed spindles in the 1870's. Finally, William F. Draper supported the most notable of all American textile innovations since the ring spindle, the automatic bobbin-changing loom, generally known as the Northrop automatic loom. The new loom did not have to be stopped every five minutes when the shuttle ran out of yarn, and it was therefore possible to double the number of looms per worker. A Northrop loom cost three times as much as a common power loom, increasing the equipment cost of a new mill by about 13 per cent, but it saved one-quarter of the labor cost of making cloth. The unique circumstances of its development have been aptly summarized by Navin:

Probably the most exceptional of all devices invented between the 1850's and the 1920's was the Draper automatic loom, an innovation that would be considered of the first order in any industry. But the Draper loom was as exceptional in origin as in its design. The Drapers had the advantage of an established position in the textile industry; they were no mere upstarts. They had made their money from the royalties on a patent pool which they controlled. Having need of only a small plant, they had no need to reinvest their earnings in fixed assets; their capital was large and it was liquid. As they saw their key patents about to expire they turned every effort toward inventing a satisfactory automatic loom. What

[69] For a detailed account of this controversy, see Navin, *The Whitin Machine Works*, chap. x, "The Spindle Controversy, 1871–1893," pp. 180–203.

they achieved was unusual indeed, but no more unusual than the special set of circumstances that drove them to risk such large sums on developmental work. Similar risks could never have been taken by other manufacturers in the industry; others had neither so much to lose nor so much liquid capital to risk. It is worth noting that the Drapers, upon becoming large-scale manufacturers themselves, did not take such risks again.[70]

The contrast with other companies was not too much overstated by George Draper himself in 1878:

I find in all cases, almost without exception, that all of the principal machine shops are opposed to the introduction of improvements for the reason that it is costly for them to make the necessary changes, and it takes the personal attention of the leading men to the details that are required, and every point has to be considered, while in order to duplicate machines they have only to give the order; the patterns and the drawings and everything being ready for it and their hands being accustomed to do it.[71]

The Draper company first showed an interest in an automatic shuttle-changer in July 1888 when a member of the firm heard that such a device had been invented at Providence. It was inspected and found impractical. To overcome its defects, $10,000 was placed at the disposal of Alonzo E. Rhoades. A year later the Drapers began financing the alternative approach suggested by James H. Northrop, and this device was experimentally attached to looms in the Seaconnett Mills at Fall River. After these experiments, the conclusion was reached that an entire new loom would have to be designed to encompass the new device properly and that automatically changing the bobbin in the shuttle would be a superior approach to changing both shuttle and bobbin. Four years and sixty patents

[70] Navin, "Innovation and Management," p. 18, note 3.

[71] Deposition of George Draper, Aug. 6, 1878, in the case of *Oliver Pearl et al.* v. *Appleton Co. et al.*, II, 1297, quoted by Gibb, *op. cit.*, p. 215.

later the looms were tried in the mills of the Queen City Cotton Company of Burlington, Vermont, which were built specifically for the trial.

When the successful results were announced in 1895, orders for automatic looms poured in. As had been their practice with spindles, the Drapers licensed a number of machine shops to manufacture the looms. Sales went well enough among the new mills in the South but lagged in the largest potential market, the old mills of the North. The Drapers accordingly decided in 1899 that if these mills were to scrap their old looms aggressive promotion was needed and that therefore the Draper company itself should organize both the manufacturing and the selling of machinery. With this beginning the Drapers eliminated virtually all competition from the manufacture of plain-goods looms.[72]

It should be noted, however, that around the turn of the century some other machine shops adopted a more positive attitude toward innovation. In a dozen years of competition, Northern mills had found that they could not meet Southern prices for coarse textiles and had therefore turned increasingly toward the production of quality goods. Moreover, with rising per capita real incomes the American market for quality goods had become attractive. Imports of British machinery, primarily for the making of high-quality cloth, doubled from 1883 to 1893.[73] American machine makers began copying the British machines but found it difficult to meet British prices in spite of the high tariff. They therefore attempted to apply their experience with rapid large-scale production to quality machines.

[72] William F. Draper, *Recollections of a Varied Career* (Boston: Little Brown and Co., 1908); *Textile World,* May 1895, pp. 30–35, Sept. 1900, pp. 431–434; *Proceedings of the Association of New England Cotton Manufacturers,* LIX (1895), 88–104; Rockey, *op. cit.,* pp. 240–245; Navin, *The Whitin Machine Works,* pp. 273–279; Copeland, *op. cit.,* pp. 83–90.

[73] Gibb, *op cit.,* p. 259.

Among the results were the Whitin high-speed comber of 1905 [74] and the Lowell high-speed worsted spinning machines of 1904. [75]

Characteristics of the Innovators

It is easier to generalize about innovators in American textile making before 1835 than later. In the early period some innovators were well-to-do merchants such as George Cabot, Hugh Orr, Moses Brown, and Francis Cabot Lowell, who believed that factory methods of processing cotton and wool could be profitable in the United States. They were therefore ready to finance mechanics such as Robert Barr, Samuel Slater, Paul Moody, and others, who claimed they could duplicate British machinery. These innovators unquestionably took risks because they had no way of knowing whether the mechanics hired could fulfill their claims and whether the cost and quality of any resultant yarn or cloth would appeal to the American market. The would-be innovators were certain only of the enormous profitability of factory methods in England. Indeed, the large scale of some failures in the 1780's suggests that some early innovators might not have realized that unpredictable factors were involved.

Later ventures were attempted on a smaller scale, and efforts were made to concentrate on peripheral American needs that were not aptly covered by imports. Even these beginnings involved hardships and frustration, and those who finally succeeded in making an innovation were not likely to be enthusiastic about trying again. For example, William Gilmour first placed his knowledge of the crank-type power loom at the disposal of Samuel Slater, but Slater declined the offer against the advice of his younger brother John, who had not come to America until 1803 and had therefore missed the hardest

[74] Navin, *The Whitin Machine Works,* pp. 265–268.
[75] Gibb, *op. cit.,* pp. 293–295.

years.[76] As a matter of fact, Slater waited another eight years, until 1823, before installing his first power looms and did not finally abandon hand weaving until 1827.[77]

By the time a large-scale enterprise, the Waltham venture, was again attempted, the characteristics of the American market were far better understood and a remarkable spread in machine-building skills had occurred. War with Britain, moreover, made the venture appear still more favorable, although actually introducing a new element of uncertainty. The Boston Manufacturing Company spared no expense to benefit from the knowledge of such men as Nathaniel Bowditch in mathematics, Jacob Perkins and Loammi Baldwin in engineering, and Daniel Webster in law.[78] Its care in controlling expenses amounted to a pioneer adaptation of mercantile accounting to manufacturing.[79] It even pioneered in Congressional lobbying, and its success in obtaining a minimum duty of 25 cents per yard on sheeting gave it tariff protection of 83.5 per cent, compared with the general level of 25 per cent.[80]

Another type of early innovator was the mechanic who, with funds of his own, or perhaps with partners, placed a novel machine on the market. The first such machines were usually made to order and guaranteed for satisfactory performance. If these proved a success, a specialized machine shop would be organized. Arthur Scholfield and his carding machines were in this category, and so was a large proportion of other innovations before 1835.

The mills in which many of these mechanics had their inspirations generally specified in their contracts something like, "Should I be fortunate enough to make or suggest any improvement for which it might be thought proper to obtain a

---

[76] G. S. White, *op. cit.*, p. 389; Bagnall, *op. cit.*, p. 546.
[77] Ware, *op. cit.*, p. 74.   [78] Gibb, *op. cit.*, p. 61.
[79] *Ibid.*, p. 60.   [80] Ware, *op. cit.*, p. 71.

patent, such patents are to be the property of the Company." [81]
Moreover, such contracts prohibited disclosing the details of
machinery to outsiders for seven years or so, a stipulation that
required the mechanic to place himself under bond.[82] It does
not appear, however, that these regulations greatly retarded
the rate of innovation. After 1835 the founding of new textile
machinery works by inventors become expensive and therefore
difficult; and with the possible exception of the loom works
of Lucius Knowles, inventors now had to persuade the existing
machine shops to adopt their ideas.

The advent of large-scale metal machines led to conservatism
among both machine builders and machine users. The users
wanted to keep the machinery in their mills uniform, and they
also wanted to avoid what they considered unprofitable scrapping. The builders wished to keep their replacement market
with old customers. Technical changes were therefore limited
to attachments, most of which were not sufficiently expensive
to jeopardize the solvency of mill or shop. But many shops were
not even enthusiastic about novel attachments. Thus the Lowell
Machine Shop, the largest of all, refused to buy the exclusive
rights to Wellman's card self-stripper for a mere $3,000.[83] Nor
can the imports and duplication of British machinery in the
later nineteenth century be considered hazardous innovation.
By this time information about sales of imported cloth, the level
of the tariff, and the technical performance of British machinery was readily available, and the remaining uncertainties for
the mill manager were hardly more than the usual uncertainties
confronting an enterprise in a competitive economy.

By and large, it can be said that after 1845 the little in-

[81] Boston Manufacturing Company Papers, Memorandum Book, Nov.
24, 1820, preserved at the library of the Harvard School of Business Administration and quoted by Ware, *op. cit.*, p. 26.

[82] *Ibid.*

[83] Navin, "The Wellman-Woodman Patent Controversy," p. 148.

novating that went on was attempted in a spirit of caution that bordered on disaste. In this connection, one might note the reactions of machine builders to the activities of George Draper. The superintendent of the Lowell Shop expressed it this way:

I recollect that George Draper at that meeting, or the one following it, made very impertinent remarks. I think he did convey fully to that meeting that machine builders had not at that time made good spindles; I think he considered they were not competent to make good spindles. . . . I believe the day is not distant when Mr. Draper will give his reasons for thus outraging machine builders. I do not know that my passion was so aroused by that occasion that then, or about then, I commenced thinking of different ways spindles might be made.[84]

The firm of George Draper and Sons was indeed, as Navin has suggested, *sui generis*.[85] It cannot now be determined whether there was room for only one such firm in the textile machinery industry, but it should be noted that this one firm was extraordinarily successful. Moreover, it should be noted that, when innovating, George Draper and Sons proceeded with extreme caution. After the company became interested in automatic looms in 1888, it first made an "exhaustive investigation, both in this country and in Europe to determine just what had been accomplished by all the inventors of record who had formerly tried to solve the problem of automatic weaving." [86] It was found that, beginning with John Patterson Reid and Thomas Johnson in 1834, about sixty inventors had worked on the problem and that some of their looms could operate after a fashion, though not sufficiently well to merit commercial introduction. The patent claims of these inventors were studied with

[84] Testimony of George Richardson in *Oliver Pearl et al.* v. *Appleton Co. et al.*, July 12, 1878, quoted by Gibb, *op. cit.*, p. 648.

[85] Navin, *The Whitin Machine Works*, pp. 115–116.

[86] George Otis Draper, *Labor-saving Looms*, 3d ed. (Hopedale, Mass.: Draper Co., 1907), p. 35.

care by the Drapers' lawyers. Only when these investigations proved encouraging were comparatively small sums placed at the disposal of the firm's inventors, Alonzo E. Rhoades, James H. Northrop, J. W. Keeley, E. S. Stimson, C. F. Roper, and others. Whenever a subsidiary device, such as a warp stop-motion, was required, previous inventions and the current patent situation were investigated with equal care. Before adopting a new mechanism as a basis for further development, it was tested for months under actual operating conditions. According to William F. Draper:

Our routine has been, firstly, to run a number of looms experimentally in a room in our shop and by means of special observers, in addition to the weavers, to note results in detail. These results are collated in daily reports, which are preserved for study and reference. Notes are made of everything outside of perfect weaving, the breakage, wear or slipping of parts, the failure of mechanism to act every time as intended, imperfections in the cloth, like thick or thin places, the number of warp and filling threads broken and why the break, if it can be known. After studying these reports in connection with personal observation of the running looms, changes are made, with a view to improvement if possible. Pieces that break are strengthened, or strains are removed; parts that slip are more securely fastened; and wear is obviated where it seems possible.

New devices are suggested to obviate cloth imperfections, or breakage of warp or filling, of bobbins or shuttles. The new parts are made and tested in comparison with the old ones, and nine times out of ten they don't work as well. Perhaps they don't overcome the difficulty; perhaps in overcoming it they introduce new ones. After one failure comes another attempt, and as a rule another failure, but something is learned from each trial and the general course is toward improvement.[87]

[87] William F. Draper, "Continued Development of the Northrop Loom," *Proceedings of the Association of New England Cotton Manufacturers,* LXXIV (1903), 159.

Like most other great innovations, the development of the Northrop loom thus proceeded in a step-by-step fashion that at all times kept the venture from becoming a gamble. If the total funds ultimately spent had been committed irrevocably in 1888, the development of the loom could well be described as a bold risk. But such a commitment was hardly necessary, and it would indeed have been rather odd. Only after five years, after the step-by-step approach had led to a loom that was almost flawless, were large sums invested in a final drive for perfection.

When the Draper company began taking orders in June 1894, the economy was still deep in the depression that began in 1893; nevertheless sales, particularly in the South, were large.[88] A half-dozen imitations appeared on the market, but only one survived, and that on the basis of an inferior principle.[89] The Northrop loom was an unparalleled success.

Risks

During the early decades of the American textile industry, knowledge of technical principles was so limited that the performance of a proposed machine could hardly be predicted even as a rough approximation. As George Cabot wrote Alexander Hamilton, the innovator was "subject to be misled by every pretender to knowledge." [90] Frequent technical failures therefore made the production risks of innovation high. At times, as in the case of the Barr brothers' spinning frame, a machine would not function at all. But the costs of such total fail-

[88] G. O. Draper, *op. cit.*, p. 36.

[89] The Harriman automatic loom stopped weaving altogether while a system of cams and levers substituted a full shuttle for an empty one (Henry I. Harriman, "The Harriman Automatic Loom," *Proceedings of the Association of New England Cotton Manufacturers*, LXVIII [1900], 318–320).

[90] Letter to Alexander Hamilton, Sept. 6, 1791, in Alexander Hamilton, *Industrial and Commercial Correspondence*, p. 62.

ures were usually borne by would-be inventors who did not themselves plan to install the machines in actual production. When technical failures resulted in losses to innovators, it was usually because a machine would not function well enough. The quality would be too poor or the machine would break down too often. Such was the case with Cabot's Beverly factory, with power looms before 1814, with the Brewster spinning machine, with Thorp's ring spindles, and with many others. After 1835, however, the spread of technical knowledge and the inevitable intervention of many experts in connection with the innovations actually attempted almost eliminated this risk.

Another production risk could involve unexpected shortages of the right kinds of labor and raw materials. Indeed, the shortage of labor caused much concern to potential promoters of early factories, but this concern seems to have been excessive. As Alexander Hamilton pointed out in 1791, the possibility of exploiting the unused time of women and children was the essence of the early innovations in textile production.[91] The employees of Slater's first mill were nine children between the ages of seven and twelve, and by 1801 Almy and Brown were employing over one hundred children between the ages of four and ten.[92] The only adults needed were overseers and repair mechanics. Eventually, the employing of entire families became common in southern New England, and the hiring of unskilled farmers' daughters (the boardinghouse system) was the rule in northern New England. Skill was required primarily in dyeing and finishing, in the making and repairing of machines, and, later, in mule spinning.[93] It should, however, be remembered that, as Gibb has put it, "the Industrial Revolution in its infancy produced surprisingly few basic technical skills

[91] Alexander Hamilton, "Report on the Subject of Manufactures," Dec. 5, 1791, *American State Papers, Finance*, I, 126.

[92] Ware, *op. cit.*, p. 23.

[93] *Ibid.*, pp. 198–235.

not already familiar to American mechanics." [94] The American blacksmiths, carpenters, and millwrights did not need to be trained by Samuel Slater in the use of their tools; they primarily needed accurate specifications. These native skills were augmented by a steady flow of skilled immigrants. Although labor remained relatively scarce in America compared with Europe, it does not appear that unexpected shortages or rises in wages provided a serious threat to innovations actually attempted.

Production risks due to shortages of raw materials likewise appear to have been of little significance as a threat to innovation. An important early exception was the shortage of high-quality wool, which was not appreciated by the promoters of the woolen factories at Hartford and Newburyport and which contributed to their failures.

Another kind of production risk is a rate of obsolescence of unforeseen rapidity. After the first decades, such unexpected obsolescence was probably the most serious of all production risks. It should be noted that not all losses due to obsolescence are losses to innovators. In fact, the last imitator usually has far less time to recoup his investment than the original innovator. It is, moreover, possible for innovations to be invariably profitable to their first promoters and at the same time to impose a heavy cost of obsolescence on an industry as a whole. Therefore, as previously described, obsolescence was a serious problem for textile mills in certain periods, but its incidence does not seem to have been sufficiently rapid to threaten innovators themselves. In the cases of the cam versus the crank power loom, ring spindles versus the self-acting mule, and the like, when two inventions appeared almost simultaneously, the tendency was for one to displace the other very slowly. In fact, the number of mule spindles continued to increase throughout the century, though falling relatively far behind ring spindles.[95]

[94] Gibb, *op. cit.*, p. 10.
[95] U.S. Census Bureau, *op. cit.*, Bull. 74, p. 51; Copeland, *op. cit.*, p. 70.

When an innovation appeared decades after the last significant advance had been made in a process, it seemed to displace the old at a much faster rate. But in such cases the previous innovators and imitators had usually recouped their investments many times over. Typical examples are the introduction of the English slasher in the 1870's and the revolving flat card of the 1880's, both of which practically eliminated their obsolete competitors within a decade. On the other hand, after the introduction of fly frames and automatic bobbin-changing looms, the sales of speeders and plain looms, respectively, continued to flourish for a number of years. In these later decades the pressure of obsolescence was, of course, greatly tempered by the fact that most innovations were little more than attachments. The appearance of the wool mule was no doubt a development that was sufficiently unforseen to make certain expenditures on "operator" innovations excessive in retrospect. But in other cases, as in the appearance of successively faster spindles, only the attachment or some part, not the entire machine, became unexpectedly obsolete.

It should also be noted that few things of great importance happened that produced the reverse effect of obsolescence— unexpected aptness. There were few innovations like the cotton gin and the sewing machine that made textile-producing innovations vastly more apt to the changing level of production skills and resources of the economy than had been anticipated.[96]

With respect to customer risks, innovations in textile machinery involved the possible inertia and prejudices of two basic kinds of customers: the buyers of textile goods and, after machinery making became an independent industry, the buyers of textile machinery. In the earliest decades of factory production in America there was a preference for imported goods that went beyond actual differences in quality. It was to reduce the resulting uncertainties that Moses Brown first con-

[96] *Infra,* Chapter VI, pp. 205–214.

centrated on thread rather than cloth and that the Scholfields learned to supplement home industry rather than compete with imports. As long as differences in quality remained, however, and this was true throughout the century and longer, American attempts to bridge the gap were bound to meet a certain amount of unpredictable prejudice. Nevertheless, it does not appear that this uncertainty applied to any of the major original or imported innovations after 1840 in such a way that heavy losses were suffered by any innovating mill.

The inertia and prejudices of the millowners, the buyers of textile machinery after 1840, appear to have been a greater obstacle to innovation than the prejudices of cloth and yarn buyers. In the case of old mills, the desire for uniformity discouraged major changes even in replacements for worn-out machines. In the case of new Southern mills, promoters were apt to consider the lowest-priced machine the best buy, and quality competition was discouraged. In some cases the machine-shop owners were not eager to give Southern mills advantages in productivity. According to Gibb, every one of the directors of the Lowell Machine Shop stood to gain more from the failure than the success of Southern industry.[97] Furthermore, among the large number of English overseers in American mills there was a prejudice against American innovations.[98] Finally, the overseers and superintendents were apt to be relatively old men after 1850 since the textile industry was itself old and slow-growing. They were likely to be more aware of existing narrow profit margins and of the advantages in letting others work out "the bugs" than of the gains (if any) from being first in the field. The training given to younger men in textile mills stressed existing practice to an extent that inhibited critical examination of fundamentals.[99]

The conservatism and inertia of the millowners were so

[97] Gibb, *op. cit.*, p. 299.   [98] *Ibid.*, p. 294.
[99] Navin, "Innovation and Management," pp. 22–23.

formidable that the machine shops considered the resistance to innovation not uncertain but predictably insuperable and therefore allowed themselves to slide into equal, and perhaps greater, conservatism. When the automatic loom appeared, the machine shops refused to undertake the additional selling expenses of promoting a machine that would require textile mills to triple capital expenditures on looms, to readjust long-established methods of wage payments for weaving, and to alter spinning machines to make stronger thread. The machine shops believed that, given the inertia of millmen, it would be more profitable to press the sale of common looms.[100] Consequently the Drapers undertook production themselves.

Interference risks were low from the time the industry was founded until 1900 and later. There were few directions from which serious interference might conceivably have come. The British cloth dumped in the United States in the 1790's had "little or no effect on the industry which [Moses Brown] proposed to develop," according to Ware,[101] because cloth, not yarn, was dumped. The large ventures at Beverly and Hartford, of course, failed during the 1790's; but, as previously described, it appears that production risks had proved to be the critical threat. In later years, changes in the tariff continued to be of crucial importance to textile makers, but there is little to indicate that these changes were directed against innovations as such or that they had a greater effect on firms that had just adopted an innovation, imported or otherwise.

Nor was there any significant interference by earlier innovators with imitation by later ones. Slater had tried to keep others from understanding and copying his cotton machinery but had failed utterly. Judge Daniel Lyman sold the plans to Gilmour's crank loom to David Wilkinson for a mere ten dollars.[102] Innovators soon realized that it was more profitable to sell than to

[100] Lincoln, "The Cotton Textile Machine Industry," p. 102.
[101] Ware, *op. cit.*, p. 31.   [102] Bagnall, *op. cit.*, p. 549.

monopolize technical knowledge. From its earliest years the Boston Manufacturing Company established a policy of selling machinery or granting licenses on its patents. Later innovators adopted the attitude that, if someone improved on their own improvements, so much the better because sales and royalties might be larger. Even the spindle controversy with all its injunctions against improvements based on infringements seemed to be interference that spurred rather than discouraged innovation. Long before the end of the century, however, it was recognized that the Drapers had built up a formidable patent pool and that if a machine shop was interested in promoting innovations along certain lines the Drapers had to be cut in on the profits. But since few shops were interested in innovation until the turn of the century, this recognition had little operational meaning.

Interference risks from the side of labor were negligible in America. To begin with, there was no large group of putting-out handicraft workers that had to be displaced. Once the factory system was established, further decades had to elapse before workers came to consider themselves members of a distinct class with a special interest in technological innovation. The farm girls who worked in the large New England mills until the 1840's remained only a few years, and by the time they were displaced by immigrant workers, the enthusiasm for innovation had been lost anyway. Before 1850 there had been only six conspicuous strikes in Massachusetts, and all of these had failed. Puplic sentiment did not support "striking females," and the girls employed in the mills were unable to gain even a ten-hour working day.[103]

The immigrants who first entered the industry in large numbers around 1850 likewise provided a difficult group for trade union organization, the chief obstacle being the continual possibility of replacing older immigrants with more recent ar-

[103] Ware, *op. cit.*, pp. 198–235, 276–277.

rivals. Only the more skilled and somewhat more scarce male workers, such as loom-fixers and wool weavers,[104] achieved much success at organization. It appears that there was some grumbling among weavers about the introduction of the automatic looms—grumbling which has even been described as "serious" by those associated with management.[105] In one Connecticut mill such grumbling was overcome by means of a 20–25 per cent increase in pay that was reduced within a year. In South Carolina, workers preferred the automatic looms although they received practically no increase in pay.[106] Since 85,000 automatic looms were installed by 1904, the resistance of American workers could hardly be considered significant in comparison with the resistance of British workers, who kept the proportion of automatic looms down to 5 per cent until World War II.[107]

Finally, improper timing did not cause the failure of many innovations that might otherwise have succeeded. Among the many failures after various crises there were firms whose equipment was no doubt in some way novel; but there is no evidence that many failed because of innovations or that with luckier timing the innovations might have been more successful. For example, Crompton's loom experiments did not involve expenses of sufficient magnitude to jeopardize Crocker and Richmond in 1837, nor does it seem likely that it might have saved the company had the Crompton loom been developed several years earlier.[108] Moreover, most innovations did not involve a change in scale that would mean a significant change in vul-

[104] Cole, *American Wool Manufacture*, II, 124.

[105] Lincoln, "The Cotton Textile Machine Industry," p. 100.

[106] Frank M. Messenger, "The Northrop Loom," *Proceedings of the Association of New England Cotton Manufacturers*, LX (1896), 125–127.

[107] Sidney J. Chapman, *Work and Wages: Part I, Foreign Competition* (London: Longmans, Green and Co., 1904), pp. 176–177; Gibson, *op. cit.*, pp. 68–89.

[108] Lincoln, "The Cotton Textile Machine Industry," p. 97; Crompton, *op. cit.*, p. 32.

nerability to business fluctuations. The Waltham venture was, of course, an exception; but it flourished throughout the difficult years 1815–1821; and the dividends of the Boston Manufacturing Company never fell below 12.5 per cent.[109] At other times falling prices made depressions periods for catching up with cost-cutting innovations and therefore proved a boon to machine shops and to those in a position to collect royalties.

Summary

The manufacture of cotton and wool textiles was the first activity that was rapidly altered by the Industrial Revolution in America. Between 1790 and 1835 all the basic ideas for harnessing carding, spinning, and weaving to water and steam power were brought over from England and improved with striking originality. The most important American innovation during this period was probably the ring spinning machine. In the process of introducing this innovation and others in cotton and wool mills, a number of uncertainties could not be easily eliminated and miscalculations often led to financial loss. The outstanding uncertainties were (1) the production risk of not knowing how a machine would function in the daily course of operations and (2) the customer risk of not knowing how customers would adjust to a commodity that might be novel in price, quality, and geographical origin. But as long as the individual machine was small-scale, wooden, and inexpensive, these risks were frequently taken. After 1835, however, textile machinery became metallic, complicated, large-scale, and expensive; and production came to be concentrated in large machine shops. The result was an attitude of such caution toward innovation that original changes were almost entirely limited to attachments and gradual increases in speed and scale. Fundamental novelties were still imported from Europe but were faithfully copied rather than adapted by American machine

109 Gibb, *op. cit.*, pp. 26–27, 738.

builders. An exception was the firm of George Draper and Sons which had a long history of promoting novel loom attachments and improved spindles. In the 1890's this firm developed the automatic loom after large but carefully planned expenditures. It was a unique attempt at fundamental innovation that was so successful that all competitors were gradually driven out of the plain-goods loom field.

IV

Machine Tools

MACHINE tools are power-driven machines for cutting or shaping metal in the form of bars, rods, wire, plates, sheets, or castings, excluding such machinery as is used in the production of the metals in these various forms. Metal-cutting machines tools remove metal in the form of chips; metal-forming machine tools press, forge, emboss, hammer, blank, or shear metal. The term "machine tool" does not refer to equipment portable by hand or to die-casting machines, extruding machines, rolling mills, welding equipment, or powder metallurgy presses.

The development of machine tools was a strategic phase of the Industrial Revolution. The pace of transforming industry by mechanization depends on the number of machines produced; and this number depends first on the cost and quality of metal and second on the means for shaping standardized machine parts rapidly and with precision. Industrialization depends on metallurgy, power, and machine tools.

Between 1775 and 1850 British engineer-entrepreneurs—John Wilkinson, Joseph Brahma, Henry Maudslay, James Nasmith, Joseph Whitworth, and others—took the lead in developing metalworking machinery.[1] They developed most of the general machine tools: boring machines, engine lathes, planers, shapers, steam hammers, and standard taps and dies. Their efforts were primarily directed toward facilitating the construction of steam engines, mining equipment, railroads, and ships. It remained for American inventors and innovators to create tools for the mass production of firearms, clocks, sewing machines, automobiles, and electricl equipment.

Thus American inventors and innovators developed the first widely used milling machines and turret lathes for the rapid reproduction of identical machine parts, and by 1900 they had made some of these machine tools fully automatic for the production of screws, gears, nuts, bolts, and valves. As early as the London Exposition of 1851, the system of manufacturing objects with interchangeable parts was known in Europe as the "American System."[2] Britain was importing American machinery to equip its armories by 1855, and within the next twenty years Russia, Turkey, Egypt, Prussia, Spain, Sweden, and Denmark followed suit.[3]

Soon American machine tools were themselves manufactured with interchangeable parts, and their price fell to half that of equivalent British machine tools in the 1880's, although

[1] Joseph Wickham Roe, *English and American Tool Builders* (New Haven: Yale University Press, 1916), pp. 11–108.

[2] Charles H. Fitch, "Report on the Manufactures of Interchangeable Mechanism," in U.S. Census Office, *Tenth Census: Manufactures* (Washington, 1883), II, 3.

[3] *Ibid.*, p. 4; Roe, *English and American Tool Builders*, p. 140; Felicia J. Deyrup, *Arms Makers of the Connecticut Valley* (Smith College Studies in History, vol. XXXIII; Northampton, Mass., 1948), p. 149.

the wages of the semiskilled workers employed in manufacturing them were considerably higher in the United States.[4] By 1905 British and other European factories were making bicycles, watches, and automobiles with American machine tools.[5] The value of metalworking machinery exported from the United States in 1900 was $7,200,000, or more than twice the value of machinery of all classes imported that year. Total exports of American machinery of all classes in 1900 amounted to $55,500,000.[6] Total production of machine tools amounted to $44,400,000.[7] Although the United States was still relatively short of labor and capital in the nineteenth century, and therefore at a comparative disadvantage for the export of machinery, the pace of innovation was sufficiently rapid to offset these handicaps.

The course of innovation changed from capital-using and labor-saving improvements in the early years of the century to both capital- and labor-saving improvements by 1850. Eli Whitney and others increased output and capital per worker by reducing the number of operations per worker to one or two and providing a machine for almost every task. By 1855 there were separate machines for such processes as screw-slotting, screw-pointing, screw-threading, screw-thread finishing, and screw-clipping.[8] Then the trend of innovation changed toward increasing operations per machine, thus reducing the need for human supervision and handling. Output per worker now increased faster than capital per worker. Outstanding

---

[4] Bertold Buxbaum, "Der englische Werkzeugmaschinen- und Werkzeugbau im 18. und 19. Jahrhundert," *Beiträge zur Geschichte der Technik und Industrie*, XI (1921), 140.

[5] U.S., Bureau of the Census, *Census of Manufacturers, 1905* (Washington, 1907), Bull. 67, pp. 13–14.

[6] *Ibid.*, pp. 7–8.

[7] U.S. Census Office, *Twelfth Census: Manufactures* (Washington, 1902), X, 381–383.

[8] Fitch, *op. cit.*, p. 4.

among the new innovations were the "universal" miller, the "universal" grinder, and a series of "automatics" from gear cutters to lathes. By 1875 screw machines were substituting one tool for another automatically by means of a system of cams and turning out entire screws in a single operation. By 1900 these machines could work on five screws simultaneously, thus keeping all tools busy most of the time. The ratio of capital to value of output in the arms industry was reduced from almost 2:1 in 1822 to about 1:1 by 1900.[9] A ratio from .9:1 to 1.2:1 appeared to be typical of industries manufacturing mechanisms with interchangeable parts around 1900.

Table 1. Capital and value of output in selected industries, 1900 *

Industry	Capital	Value of output
Bicycles	$29,784,000	$31,916,000
Sewing machines	20,073,000	21,130,000
Typewriters	8,400,000	6,932,000
Metalworking machinery including custom work and repairs	54,294,000	44,385,000
Electrical apparatus and supplies, including custom work and repairs	83,131,000	91,349,000
Locomotives and other products of locomotive works	40,814,000	35,209,000
Totals	$236,496,000	$230,921,000

* U.S. Census Office, *Twelfth Census: Manufactures* (Washington, 1902), X, 157, 243, 325, 381, 404, 437.

Innovations by Arms Makers and Watchmakers, 1798–1855

The first establishment that contributed machine-tool innovations during the nineteenth century was the armory of Eli Whitney. Whitney received his earliest contract for muskets after writing to Oliver Wolcott, Secretary of the Treasury, on May 1, 1798:

[9] Deyrup, *op. cit.*, pp. 220–221.

I should like to undertake the manufacture of ten to fifteen thousand stand of arms. I am persuaded that machinery moved by water, adapted to this business would greatly diminish the labor and greatly facilitate the manufacture of this article. Machines for forging, rolling, floating, boring, grinding, polishing, etc. may all be made use of to advantage.[10]

English armories had simplified arms making so that each workman would specialize in one part of a musket lock. Whitney limited his workmen to one or two operations and therefore required several workmen for each part. By 1801 he had water-powered drilling and barrel-boring machines and had developed the system of filing and drilling to conform to patterns called jigs. Around 1815 he eliminated much hand filing by inventing a milling machine which applied a spinning irregular cutter to work moved across the cutter's path by means of a synchronized power feed. Around 1820 he developed the system of forging in hand dies.[11] The exact nature and date of most of his machines are unknown because after his discouraging experience with the cotton gin Whitney took out no further patents.[12] Interchangeability of parts, however, was still limited to sets of ten as late as the 1840's at the Whitney Armory, and even this much precision required a great deal of hand filing.[13]

[10] *New Haven Colony Historical Society Papers,* V (New Haven, 1894), 117.

[11] *American Machinist,* vol. XXVI, June 27, 1912; *New Haven Colony Historical Society Papers,* V, 117–122; William P. Blake, *History of the Town of Hamden, Connecticut* (New Haven: Price, Lee and Co., 1888), pp. 138, 296, 300; Denison Olmsted, *Memoir of Eli Whitney, Esq.* (New Haven: Durrie & Peck, 1846), pp. 53–54; Deyrup, *op. cit.,* p. 91; Constance McL. Green, *Eli Whitney and the Birth of American Technology* (Boston and Toronto: Little, Brown and Co., 1956), pp. 123–124, 169–170.

[12] Letter from Eli Whitney, Jr., to P. C. Watson, Assistant Secretary of War, Sept. 9, 1863, quoted by Felicia J. Deyrup, *op. cit.,* pp. 87–88.

[13] Deyrup, *op. cit.,* pp. 144–145.

Whitney needed two years to design and build the machinery for his New Haven armory and six more to deliver all the arms contracted for. He overcame numerous mechanical difficulties, as well as prejudice and ridicule, and he was the only one of the contractors of 1798 whom the Ordnance Department considered successful. His was one of two private armories to survive the War of 1812 and the only private armory founded before 1830 to survive to (and beyond) the Civil War. After Whitney's death in 1825 the armory was managed by his nephews, Eli Whitney Blake and Philos Blake. From 1835 until 1842 it was managed by ex-Governor Edwards, and from 1842 to 1888 by Eli Whitney, Jr. In 1888 the armory was sold to the Winchester Repeating Arms Company.[14]

Simeon North developed a system of arms manufacturing similar to Whitney's, more or less independently, at Middletown, Connecticut. He received his first contract in 1799, and it is sometimes claimed that he developed filing jigs and other devices before Whitney. His was the other private armory that survived the War of 1812. It did not, however, survive himself, largely because of faulty cost accounting and because of the absorption by profit of money that should have been reserved for depreciation.[15]

The United States armories at Springfield, Massachusetts, and Harper's Ferry, Virginia, adopted Whitney's system of manufacturing arms around 1815 [16] and soon became the coun-

[14] Stephen V. Benét, ed., *A Collection of Annual Reports and Other Important Papers Relating to the Ordnance Department, Taken from the Records of the Office of the Chief of Ordnance, from Public Documents, and from Other Sources* (Washington: Government Printing Office, 1878), I, 176–177; Roe, *English and American Tool Builders*, p. 160; Deyrup, *op. cit.*, p. 47–48, 54.

[15] S. N. D. North and R. H. North, *Simeon North, First Official Pistol Maker of the United States* (Concord, N.H.: Rumford Press, 1913), pp. 64, 84, 160–169; Benet, *op. cit.*, pp. 176–177; Deyrup, *op. cit.*, 53–54; Roe, *English and American Tool Builders*, p. 163.

[16] Deyrup, *op. cit.*, p. 49.

trys' primary machine-tool innovating establishments.[17] The first barrel-turning machine and the first power-driven rifling machines were introduced at Harper's Ferry around 1817.[18] The use of gauges for anything but the inspection of finished arms was almost unknown among the private arms makers of New England, but gauging during manufacture reached a high state of development at the Springfield Armory by 1819.[19] Blanchard's profile lathe of 1818 for making gunstocks was the predecessor for later metalworking profiling machines which by means of templates and formers could mill surfaces too intricate for milling machines. To improve this machine, the War Department took the unusual step of having Blanchard work with his profile lathe at the Springfield Armory and recieve 37 cents for each stock turned rather than royalties for the use of his machine. By 1827 Blanchard had invented 14 machines. Some of these appear to have been overspecialized and probably failed to repay their cost.[20]

The Springfield Armory took the lead in experimenting with steam-powered machinery in 1833 when steam engines cost $13,000 for a mere 20 horsepower and when New England mechanics were as yet so inexperienced with steam that an attempt at installation was once frustrated by such a minor matter as frozen valves. Nevertheless, the experiments proved that steam power was economical for certain operations.[21]

During the nineteenth century milling machines were the most numerous and characteristic machines used for interchangeable manufacturing. In firearms production they constituted 25 to 30 per cent of the total number of machines. But

---

[17] *Ibid.*, pp. 90–155.

[18] *American State Papers: Class V, Military Affairs,* II, 544, Document 246, "Armory at Springfield," March 3, 1823, cited by Deyrup, *op. cit.*, p. 90.

[19] Deyrup, *op. cit.*, pp. 96–98.   [20] *Ibid.*, pp. 97–98.

[21] *Ibid.*, pp. 99, 147.

in 1827 these machines were only 33 per cent more efficient than hand filing. In the course of the 1830's as a result of a series of inventions by Thomas Warner and others at the Springfield Armory, the efficiency of milling machines increased by more than 400 per cent.[22]

Not all the experiments at the armories led to success. For example, the Springfield Armory experimented unsuccessfully with rolling barrels and with stocking machinery using eccentric cutters.[23] It does not appear, however, that such experiments were ever carried to levels that would have jeopardized the armory's solvency had it been privately operated. On the contrary, Deyrup has concluded that "it is in fact remarkable that any musket contractors succeeded under the prices established at the Springfield Armory, for the latter from the end of the War of 1812 to the early 1830's was outstanding for its excellent management and high efficiency." [24] The techniques developed at the armories were not only made freely available to private arms makers, but were actually forced on them because all arms makers had to conform to public standards of quality and cost.[25]

Until about 1840 the government was the primary market, the primary source of capital, and, after the initial work of Whitney and North, the primary machine-tool innovator. Particularly the Springfield Armory, according to Deyrup, "served as an early yardstick for measuring the performance of private industry and as a laboratory in which was developed a body of knowledge of improved weapon designs and better manufacturing methods easily accessible to the other arms makers." [26] Furthermore, manufacturers depended on government contracts almost exclusively for sales and for capital in the form of

[22] Fitch, *op. cit.*, pp. 22–24; Deyrup, *op. cit.*, p. 153.
[23] Deyrup, *op. cit.*, pp. 152, 157.   [24] *Ibid.*, p. 149.
[25] *Ibid.*, pp. 3–5.   [26] *Ibid.*, p. 5.

advances.[27] On his first contract, advances to Eli Whitney from the government exceeded $130,000.[28]

After 1840 further refinements in metal-manufacturing methods were developed by newcomers in the arms industry, such as Robbins and Lawrence of Windsor, Vermont; the Ames Manufacturing Company of Chicopee, Massachusetts; E. Remington and Sons of Ilion, New York; and the Colt Patent Fire Arms Manufacturing Company of Hartford, Connecticut. Other industries did not adopt the principle of interchangeable parts until 1837 when Chauncey Jerome made the attempt in the brass clock industry. After 1850 small steam engines, watches, sewing machines, and machine tools themselves were made with interchangeable parts, and so were locomotives around 1860.[29] The development of interchangeable manufacturing was a prior condition to the commercial success of sewing machines, harvesters, typewriters, and a whole series of motors.

The firm of Robbins and Lawrence was perhaps the most prominent of the new arms makers that appeared around 1840. It was founded in 1844 at Windsor, Vermont, as Robbins, Kendall, and Lawrence, with a contract for making 10,000 rifles for the government. Although Richard S. Lawrence had previous experience as a gunsmith, 38 per cent of the rifles made were rejected by the government because of poor material and poor workmanship. Eventually, however, the firm employed two of the most ingenious American mechanics, Frederick W. Howe and R. D. Stone. Their inventions helped lay the founda-

[27] *Ibid.*, p. 46.

[28] As a matter of fact, the Ordnance Department lost track of just how much money Whitney had received. The contract had stipulated $134,000, but the final balance due to Whitney was only $2,400. See Benet, *op. cit.*, I, 26; Carl W. Mitman, "Eli Whitney," *Dictionary of American Biography* (New York: Scribner's, 1929), XX, 159–160.

[29] Victor S. Clark, *History of Manufactures in the United States* (Washington: Carnegie Institution, 1929), I, 509; Fitch, *op. cit.*, pp. 47–48.

tion for what is often considered the greatest era of American machine-tool progress, the years between 1850 and 1877. Together with Lawrence, Howe and Stone developed the metal-profiling machine, barrel-drilling machines, rifling machines, the universal and other milling machines, and, above all, the turret lathe.[30] There had been predecessors to the turret lathe, but previously no one had effectively used a vertical turret, and no one had attempted to sell turret lathes commercially.[31]

In fact, as late as the 1830's even slide-rest lathes were not in general use in American machine shops.[32] It is estimated that there were only four slide-rest planers, on which the construction of precise and powerful lathes depends.[33] During this decade, however, the first commercial machine-tool makers had branched off from textile machinery production. They included the Silver and Gay shop of Chelmsford, Massachusetts; Gage, Warner, and Whitney of Nashua, New Hampshire; Samuel Flagg of Worcester, Massachusetts; and the Putnam Machine Company of Fitchburg, Massachusetts. For the most

[30] Fitch, *op. cit.*, pp. 3 ff. A turret lathe called "capstan lathe" existed in embryonic form in England in the late 1830's. Some variations called "set screw machines" and "flyer nose machines" existed in the Silver and Gay shop of Chelmsford, Mass., around 1840. But until Frederick W. Howe (and perhaps Stephen Fitch of Middlefield, Conn.) adapted them to interchangeable manufacturing, these machines remained specialized curiosities with no general market. See Guy Hubbard, "The Development of Machine Tools in New England," *American Machinist*, LX (Feb. 21, 1924), 272–274.

[31] Richard S. Lawrence, account of his life for his son, Ned, Dec. 17, 1890, published as Appendix A in Roe, *English and American Tool Builders*, pp. 281–291; *ibid.*, pp. 186–201; Bertold Buxbaum, "Der amerikanische Werkzeugmaschinen- und Werkzeugbau im 18. und 19. Jahrhundert," hereafter cited as "Der amerikanische Werkzeugmaschinenbau," *Beiträge zur Geschichte der Technik und Industrie*, X (1920), 128; Deyrup, *op. cit.*, pp. 144–159.

[32] Fitch, *op. cit.*, p. 9.

[33] William Sellers, "Machinery Manufacturing Interests," in Chauncey M. Depew, ed., *One Hundred Years of American Commerce* (New York: D. O. Haynes and Co., 1895), II, 348.

part these companies closely followed British precedents in their construction of engine lathes, planers, and the like.[34]

The large-scale manufacture of American machine tools of original design thus began with Robbins and Lawrence. Commercial machine tools became one of the firm's leading products, and after winning a medal at the London Exposition of 1851, it became the primary supplier of the British Enfield Armory.[35] Nevertheless, the firm failed around 1855 after building railroad cars and rifle-making machinery in anticipation of contracts which did not materialize. R. D. Stone later worked for the pioneering Jones and Lamson Machine Company that bought the Robbins and Lawrence works in 1859.[36] Frederick W. Howe later redesigned Elias Howe's and the Wilcox and Gibbs sewing machines and planned the tools for their interchangeable production. He became superintendent in 1868 and then partner of the pioneering Brown and Sharpe Manufacturing Company. Finally he assisted Charles Goodyear, Jr., in the development of shoe machinery.[37]

In 1848 Samuel Colt ceased having his pistols manufactured at the Whitney Armory and established the Colt Patent Fire Arms Manufacturing Company at new quarters in Hartford, Connecticut. Five years later his market and his funds had increased sufficiently to warrant the construction of an entirely new armory. This new armory was operated by steam power from the beginning, and handwork was practically eliminated by over 1,400 machines. Colt's superintendent, Elisha K. Root, took a leading part in designing this machinery. He invented the crank drop hammer; machines for boring, rifling, making

[34] Bertold Buxbaum, "Der amerikanische Werkzeugmaschinenbau," p. 123; Roe, *English and American Tool Builders*, pp. 4, 5, 115–127, 216–237.

[35] Fitch, *op. cit.*, p. 4.

[36] Roe, *English and American Tool Builders*, pp. 198–201.

[37] Carl W. Mitman, "Frederick Webster Howe," *Dictionary of American Biography*, IX, 286.

cartridges, stock turning, and splining; a chucking lathe; and a double-turret lathe. He also worked out an entire system of jigs, fixtures, tools, and gauges. Eventually he received the highest salary in the State of Connecticut. But although the Colt Armory was probably the most advanced metalworking establishment in the world in 1856, it did not use the interchangeable system. For the Colt Armory with its high standards of precision, the parts for each revolver still had to be numbered, so that each weapon was unique. It was only with the Civil War that manufacturing methods reached such a level of precision that parts made in one factory fitted reasonably well with parts made in other factories. Many of the inventors and innovators responsible for these and later developments were former Colt employees, including Francis A. Pratt, Amos Whitney, Christopher Spencer, Charles E. Billings, Asa Cook, Charles B. Richards, and George A. Fairfield.[38]

A remarkable aspect of the early firearms and machine-tool industries was the way in which new innovating firms almost invariably grew out of old innovating firms. From the earliest experiments of Eli Whitney and the government armories, an intricate genealogy can be traced through Robbins and Lawrence and the Colt Armory down to Pratt and Whitney and the most active innovators of the end of the century. Such a genealogy has, in fact, been developed by Roe; and if elaborated fully, it would include many firms that made only minor contributions as well as firms whose innovations occurred in related fields. Thus the Ames Manufacturing Company of Chicopee, Massachusetts, was founded in 1834 under the partial direc-

[38] See William B. Edwards, *The Story of Colt's Revolver: The Biography of Col. Samuel Colt* (Harrisburg, Pa.: Stockpole Co., 1953); Roe, *English and American Tool Builders*, pp. 167–174; Deyrup, *op. cit.*, pp. 145–148; Fitch, *op. cit.*, p. 6; Buxbaum, "Der amerikanische Werkzeugmaschinenbau," pp. 129–130; Jack Rohan, *Yankee Arms Maker: The Incredible Career of Samuel Colt* (New York: Harper and Brothers, 1935).

tion of James H. Burton, who had been superintendent at the Harper's Ferry Armory. A number of innovations gave the firm a high reputation, and in the early 1850's it shared the British Enfield contract with Robbins and Lawrence.[39] An employee of the Ames Manufacturing Company, Albert K. Eames, became associated with the armory of E. Remington and Sons at Ilion, New York; and there he pioneered new methods of barrel rolling, strap drop forging, and drill presses. E. Remington and Sons then introduced interchangeable manufacturing methods to the production of agricultural implements in 1856 and pioneered the mass production of typewriters in 1873.[40] Given the lack of technical periodicals and professional organizations and the embryonic stage of engineering schools, the spread of knowledge across the country necessarily depended on such personal means of transmission.

[39] Deyrup, op. cit., pp. 125–126, 149; Roe, English and American Tool Builders, pp. 228–229; Vera Shlakman, Economic History of a Factory Town: A Study of Chicopee, Massachusetts (Smith College Studies in History, vol. XX, nos. 1–4, Oct. 1934—July 1935).

[40] Carl W. Mitman, "Eliphalet Remington," Dictionary of American Biography, XV, 495–496; Deyrup, op. cit., p. 157; Fitch, op. cit., pp. 6–9, 70–85.

The typewriter provides an illustration of the pioneering of items whose use involved taste as well as efficiency, that is, items which, in at least that one sense, could not be regarded as solely producers' goods. The experts at the Remington Armory easily solved the mechanical problems of the operation and production of the typewriter. Nevertheless, a legal sham battle had to be arranged among purported inventors, and over $250,000 had to be invested before the market was considered profitable. Even then typewriters were regarded as a luxury and an affectation. Mark Twain, for example, wanted it kept secret that he owned one. As with many other inventions, the official adoption of the typewriter by government agencies (the courts) appeared to be the break which led to its widespread acceptance. See Herkimer County Historical Society, The Story of the Typewriter (Herkimer, N.Y., 1923), pp. 30–108; Chauncey M. Depew, ed., One Hundred Years of American Commerce (New York: D. O. Haynes and Co., 1895), II, 544–545; Buxbaum, "Der amerikanische Werkzeugmaschinenbau," p. 144.

Throughout the middle decades of the nineteenth century, metalworking techniques that had been developed in the arms industry were applied with varying success to other industries. Chauncey Jerome's use of interchangeable parts in brass clock-making was highly successful in 1837.[41] In the manufacture of screws a number of firms around Providence overestimated their chance of success and sustained comparatively heavy losses.[42] In the watch industry, interchangeable manufacturing methods were first applied by Aaron Dennison in 1850. Because of the extreme precision required, $\frac{1}{5,000}$ of an inch, none of the standard machine-tool makers were able to supply Dennison's needs; and his company had to spend three years building its own machines. The company failed in the panic of 1857, but it had finished enough watches to establish the fact that the model in production was a good one and that the machine method of manufacture was successful and efficient.[43] Under new business management as the Waltham Watch Company,[44] but until 1861 with Dennison and the same machinery, the plant was again making 50 watches a day by 1859, 250 by 1864, and 1,200 by 1883. According to Moore, the market for American-made watches seemed unlimited; competition was negligible; prices and profits were high; and only delivery was im-

[41] Chauncey Jerome, *History of the Clock Business for the Past Sixty Years and a Life of Chauncey Jerome Written by Himself* (New Haven: F. C. Dayton, 1860), pp. 60–64; Fitch, *op. cit.*, pp. 68–69.

[42] "The Manufacture of Screws in Rhode Island," *Iron Age*, XXXVI (July 9, 1885), 15

[43] Fitch, *op. cit.*, pp. 60–67; Depew, *op. cit.*, p. 542; Charles W. Moore, *Timing a Century: History of the Waltham Watch Company* (Cambridge: Harvard University Press, 1945), p. 154; Harry C. Brearly, *Time Telling through the Ages* (New York: Doubleday, Page & Co., 1919), pp. 173–174.

[44] The name, Waltham Watch Company, was not actually adopted until 1906. Before 1885 the firm's name was the American Watch Company; from 1885 until 1906 it was known as the American Waltham Watch Company (Moore, *op. cit.*, pp. 12, 16, 56, 155).

portant. It should be noted that the watches first made were
of a standard English lever type to which the public had become accustomed.

Again, the special knowledge that had been developed was
transmitted by personal contact. Most other watch companies
in America were founded with the assistance of former employees of the Waltham company.[45] Throughout the century
watchmaking machinery was not available ready-made on the
open market but had to be specially designed and often built
by the manufacturers themselves.[46]

Innovations by Specialized Toolbuilders, 1855–1900

After 1855 machine tools were themselves manufactured
along interchangeable lines, and specialized machine-tool
builders, such as William Sellers and Company of Philadelphia,
Pratt and Whitney of Hartford, Connecticut, and Brown and
Sharpe of Providence, Rhode Island, took the lead at innovation. Pratt and Whitney and Brown and Sharpe also replaced
Robbins and Lawrence and the Ames Manufacturing Company
as the leading suppliers of European armories.[47] After the
Civil War, new companies tended to specialize in one general
type of machine tool, such as milling machines, gear shapers,
or chucking grinders. Under the influence of expanding Western markets for agricultural machinery, mining machinery, and
railway equipment, the center of the machine-tool industry
shifted to Ohio, particularly to Cincinnati, between 1880 and
1900.[48] Production in the East did not decline but rather failed
to expand at the same rate as production in Ohio. Nevertheless,
technological leadership remained in the East at the turn of the
century.[49]

[45] Brearly, *op. cit.*, pp. 177 ff.   [46] *Ibid.*, p. 174.
[47] Buxbaum, "Der amerikanische Werkzeugmaschinenbau," p. 135.
[48] *American Machinist*, XXV (Nov. 6, 1902), 1622, 1639.
[49] Roe, *English and American Tool Builders*, p. 278.

The Brown and Sharpe Manufacturing Company was founded as a machine shop for making clocks and instruments by David Brown and his son, J. R. Brown, in 1833. Lucian Sharpe joined the firm in 1853 and provided two essential ingredients for its later success, business ability and capital. It was the distinction of Brown and Sharpe to have brought precise measuring tools within reach of the ordinary machinist. J. R. Brown's vernier caliper of 1851 was accurate to $\frac{1}{1,000}$ of an inch, and his micrometer of 1867 was the first to be manufactured commercially. These economical and precise measuring instruments were a prerequisite for precise manufacturing methods. Among the machine-tool inventions credited to J. R. Brown and such employees as Frederick W. Howe and E. H. Parks are a turret screw machine with a self-revolving turret, automatic gear cutters, and, above all, the universal miller, the formed milling cutter, and the universal grinder. Like other pioneering firms, Brown and Sharpe expanded throughout the century and later.[50]

Among the firms equal to Brown and Sharpe was William Sellers and Company of Philadelphia.[51] In many ways Sellers' work complemented that of J. R. Brown. After Brown had made accurate measuring universally possible, Sellers proposed

[50] Roe, *English and American Tool Builders*, pp. 202–215; Buxbaum, "Der amerikanische Werkzeugmaschinenbau," pp. 135 ff.; Russell A. Bond, "Automatic Machine Tools," *A Popular History of American Invention*, Waldemar Kaempffert, ed. (New York: Charles Scribner's Sons, 1924), II, 337–338; Deyrup, *op. cit.*, pp. 144–145; Fitch, *op. cit.*, p. 24; *American Machinist*, XXV (Nov. 6, 1902), 1569–1638; Carl W. Mitman, "J. R. Brown," *Dictionary of American Biography*, III, 143–144.

[51] Buxbaum, "Der amerikanische Werkzeugmaschinenbau," pp. 130 ff.; Roe, *English and American Tool Builders*, pp. 247–252; Frank Barkley Copley, *Frederick W. Taylor, Father of Scientific Management* (New York: Harper and Brothers, 1923), I, 107 ff., II, 24 ff.; Fitch, *op. cit.*, pp. 51 ff.; Carl W. Mitman, "William Sellers," *Dictionary of American Biography*, XVI, 576–577; *Journal of the Franklin Institute*, LXXI (1861), 344; Sellers, *op. cit.*, pp. 346–352.

a standardized system of screw threads, boltheads, and nuts. The proposal was made in 1864; it was adopted by the United States Government in 1868 and by most European countries before 1900. Like Joseph Witworth in England, Sellers made his machines heavier, eliminated embellishments, and used only gray paint. Outstanding among the firm's ninety patents were a nut and bolt cutting machine, the spiral gear planer, automatic gear cutters, turntables, steam hammers, boring machines, and large multiple punches. Sellers and Company built the machinery that worked the metal structurals for the Philadelphia Centennial and the Brooklyn Bridge. In related fields it contributed innovations in riveters, boilers, hoisting cranes, and hydraulic machinery. From 1873 until 1887 Sellers was also president of the Midvale Steel Company, where he employed Frederick W. Taylor, "the father of scientific management" and the inventor of a revolutionary steam hammer, automatic grinders, false tables, chucks, forging and tool-feeding mechanisms, and boring and turning mills.[52]

Probably the only firm whose international prestige matched that of William Sellers and Company and Brown and Sharpe was Pratt and Whitney of Hartford, Connecticut.[53] When the firm was founded in 1860, Francis A. Pratt and Amos Whitney were still employed at the Colt Armory, for which Pratt had once designed the Lincoln miller. Their first machine, an automatic silk winder, was invented by Christopher Spencer, who had also worked for Colt. During the Civil War, Pratt and Whitney began making machine tools for guns and sewing machines, and the firm's net assets increased from $3,600 in

---

[52] Copley, *op. cit.*, I, 196, 201.

[53] Roe, *English and American Tool Builders*, pp. 175–185; Buxbaum, "Der amerikanische Werkzeugmaschinenbau," pp. 136 ff.; Fitch, *op. cit.*, pp. 4 ff.; *American Machinist*, XXV (Nov. 6, 1902), 1569–1638; Carl W. Mitman, "Francis A. Pratt," *Dictionary of American Biography*, XV, 172–173; *Accuracy for Seventy Years—Pratt and Whitney* (Hartford: Pratt and Whitney Company, 1930).

1862 to $350,000 in 1869.[54] The firm's patents included improvements on planers, millers, gear cutters, and turret screw machines and a method of feeding bar stock to lathes that eliminated manual chucking. Like J. R. Brown and William Sellers, Francis A. Pratt saw that the irregularity of measures hampered the interchangeable system, and it was largely through his efforts that a standard system of gauges was established in the United States and Europe. In 1879–1881 Pratt and Whitney supported the efforts of George M. Bond and William A. Rogers, a Harvard professor, to develop a comparator accurate to $\frac{1}{50,000}$ of an inch. After an expenditure of several thousand dollars, Bond and Rogers were successful, and the result was the famous Pratt and Whitney standard measuring machine. As with former Colt and Waltham employees, men trained at Pratt and Whitney played a large part in founding new firms. Among them were the inventors of the precision boring machine, the disk grinding machine, and the multiple-spindle lathe. At the turn of the century the firm merged with the Niles-Bement-Pond Company.

The firm of William B. Bement of Philadelphia, founded in 1851, pioneered heavy tools similar to those built by William Sellers and Company.[55] Bement's firm contributed improvements to the steam hammer and testing machines and tools for working sheet metal; but it "relied little on patent protection, trusting to quality and constant improvement." [56] Two years after Bement's death in 1897, the firm joined the Pond Machine Tool Company, the Niles Tool Works, and the Philadelphia Engineering Company to form the Niles-Bement-Pond Company.

The Jones and Lamson Machine Company originated in 1845

[54] Roe, *English and American Tool Builders*, pp. 175–179.

[55] Roe, *English and American Tool Builders*, pp. 255 ff.; Buxbaum, "Der amerikanische Werkzeugmaschinenbau," p. 130; *American Machinist*, XXV (Nov. 6, 1902), 1569–1638; Fitch, *op. cit.*, pp. 52 ff.

[56] Roe, *English and American Tool Builders*, p. 255.

when Nathan and E. G. Lamson began a cutlery factory at Shelburne Falls, Vermont.[57] In 1859 the firm was reorganized as Lamson, Goodknow, and Yale and purchased the works of the bankrupt Robbins and Lawrence Company. Jones and Lamson continued to manufacture Robbins and Lawrence turret lathes and continued to employ R. D. Stone, who subsequently developed a lathe with a power feed. After the Civil War, however, the management of Jones and Lamson became associated with unsuccessful ventures in quarrying machinery and cotton manufacturing; and in the depression of 1883 the entire plant came into the hands of Floyd Brothers, a group of Boston financiers. In 1888 the machine shop was sold as a going concern to several Springfield, Vermont, merchants. This group hired the inventor James Hartness as superintendent, giving him one-third ownership in exchange for his patents. Under Hartness and the businessman, William D. Woolson, who also owned one-third of the stock, Jones and Lamson regained a leading position in the machine-tool industry. It employed such outstanding engineers and mechanics as E. R. Fellows, G. O. Gridley, and William L. Bryant. Among the innovations contributed by Jones and Lamson were the flat-turret lathe, the Lo-swing lathe, the gear shaper, and the chucking grinder. It became the firm's policy to specialize in turret lathes of a single general design, and when other innovations occurred in the course of its work, it supported separate companies for their commercial development. Among the companies so formed were the Fellows Gear Shaper Company and the Bryant Chucking Grinder Company.

[57] Roe, *English and American Tool Builders*, pp. 255 ff.; Fitch, *op. cit.*, pp. 21 ff.; Buxbaum, "Der amerikanische Werkzeugmaschinenbau," p. 130; *American Machinist*, XXV (Nov. 6, 1902), 1569–1638; Joseph Wickham Roe, *James Hartness* (New York: American Society of Mechanical Engineers, 1937); Hubbard, "The Development of Machine Tools in New England," *American Machinist*, LX (June 26, 1924), 951 ff., LXI (June 10, 1924), 68 ff.

Two former Colt men, Charles E. Billings and Christopher Spencer, organized the firm Billings and Spencer in 1869.[58] Spencer had previously invented the automatic silk winder that was the first machine produced by Pratt and Whitney; then he had managed his own Spencer Repeating Rifle Company in Boston, Massachusetts, from 1861 to 1869. In 1865 Spencer had invented a sewing-machine spoolmaker, and the production of machine tools for sewing-machine factories became an important part of Billings and Spencer's business. The firm's outstanding innovation was the plank drop hammer which gradually replaced the earlier screw and crank drops in forging since the force of its blows could be adjusted more easily and precisely. After Spencer left the firm, Charles E. Billings made a number of improvements on drills and chucks and invented a way of drop-forging commutator bars for electric dynamos.

By 1874 Christopher Spencer had secretly invented an automatic turret lathe.[59] He withdrew from Billings and Spencer and organized the Hartford Machine Screw Company together with George A. Fairfield, an ex-Colt employee who had become president of the Weed Sewing Machine Company. The new firm was highly successful, but Spencer failed to gain as much from his invention as he had expected. His patent attorney had overlooked a key feature: the cylinder with adjustable cams that made the automatic substitution of one tool for another possible in any desired way. Spencer withdrew from his new firm after six years, in 1882, and organized the Spencer

[58] Roe, *English and American Tool Builders,* pp. 173 ff.; Fitch, *op. cit.,* pp. 22 ff.; Buxbaum, "Der amerikanische Werkzeugmaschinenbau," p. 137; Deyrup, *op. cit.,* p. 205; Carl W. Mitman, "Christopher Spencer," *Dictionary of American Biography,* XVII, 446–447, and Philip B. McDonald, "Charles E. Billings," *Dictionary of American Biography,* II, 264–265.

[59] Roe, *English and American Tool Builders,* pp. 176 ff.; Fitch, *op. cit.,* pp. 4, 22; Bond, *op. cit.,* pp. 332–333; Buxbaum, "Der amerikanische Werkzeugmaschinenbau," p. 137; Carl W. Mitman, "Christopher Spencer," *Dictionary of American Biography,* XVII, 446–447.

Arms Company to manufacture a repeating shotgun he had invented. This company failed after one year, and Spencer returned to experiments with machine tools, particularly screw machines.

Near the end of the Civil War, E. P. Bullard, who had worked for both Colt and Pratt and Whitney, began forming his own companies, among them, in 1877, the Bridgeport Machine Tool Works that was later, in 1894, incorporated as the Bullard Machine Tool Company.[60] In 1883 Bullard invented the first accurate boring machine. Previously boring had been feasible only for large rough work. When accuracy was required, the work had been performed on the faceplate of a lathe. Bullard, however, practically made the boring mill itself a vertical-turret lathe.

Still another former employee of Colt and Pratt and Whitney, William Gleason, organized his own works at Rochester, New York, in 1865 and developed the first bevel gear planer around 1874. Before this machine tool had been invented, the manufacture of bevel gears for most purposes had been limited to cast iron or wood.[61]

In the 1890's E. C. Henn and Reinholt Hakewessel, former Pratt and Whitney men, invented the first practical automatic multiple-spindle lathe.[62] In this lathe four bars of stock were fed through four hollow spindles to tools which automatically switch from one bar to another. In 1901 after numerous difficulties, which will be described later, Henn, Hakewessel, and Cleveland businessmen organized the National Acme Manu-

[60] Roe, *English and American Tool Builders,* pp. 184–185; Buxbaum, "Der amerikanische Werkzeugmaschinenbau," p. 141.

[61] Roe, *English and American Tool Builders,* p. 183; *Fourscore Years of Bevel Gearing: The Story of the Gleason Works* (Rochester, N.Y.: Gleason Works, 1945).

[62] Frederic H. Chapin, *National Acme: An Informal History* (New York: Newcomen Society, 1949); Roe, *English and American Tool Builders,* pp. 265–266; Bond, *op. cit.,* pp. 333–337; Hubbard, "The Development of Machine Tools in New England," *American Machinist,* LXI (Aug. 24, 1924), 334 ff.

facturing Company with a capitalization of $6,500,000 for the production of automatic screw machinery on the multiple-spindle principle.

Two other former Pratt and Whitney men, Worcester R. Warner and Ambrose Swasey, established an outstanding machine-tool works in Cleveland in 1881. Warner and Swasey were the first American toolbuilders outside of the East that built machine tools of the highest quality. The firm contributed important improvements in boring, drilling, and milling machines.[63] Another Pratt and Whitney man, Frederick M. Gardner, developed the disk grinding machine during the 1890's while employed by a firm he had helped to organize, Charles H. Besley and Company of Beloit, Wisconsin.[64] A former employee of Brown and Sharpe, Charles H. Norton, developed a cylindrical grinding machine that made grinding competitive with turning on a lathe. Although the grinding machine was more than twice as expensive as a lathe and required more power, its cutting action was sixteen times as efficient and its accuracy was unparalleled. Accuracy is at the heart of cheap interchangeable manufacturing, and grinding machines made accuracy greater and cheaper in two ways: first, directly, and second, by improving the quality and reducing the cost of measuring instruments. Norton developed this invention while employed by the Norton Emery Wheel Company of Worcester, Massachusetts.[65] In 1900 when the invention was ready for commercial production, a separate company, the Norton Grinding Company, was organized so that the assets of the Norton Emery Wheel Company would not be jeopardized.[66]

During the 1890's the pioneering companies developed

[63] Guy Hubbard, "100 Years of Progress in the Development of American Metalworking Equipment," *Automotive Industries*, CXIII (Sept. 1, 1955), 87, 298; Roe, *English and American Tool Builders*, pp. 262 ff.

[64] Roe, *English and American Tool Builders*, pp. 275–276.

[65] The identity of names is a coincidence.

[66] Mildred McClary Tymeson, *The Norton Story* (Worcester: Norton Co., 1953), pp. 83 ff.

pneumatic hammers, riveters, and drills; forming tools for bicycle wheel hubs; oil tube drills; and high-speed tools. Particularly significant, however, was the impact of improved
electric motors and generators on machine tools. Laminated
armatures required accurately made punchings of sheet metal
of a size and in numbers previously unknown. Electrical manufacturers placed orders for machinery capable of performing
this task with leading toolbuilders, such as William Sellers and
Company and Bement, Miles and Company. Large power
presses solved the problem, and once developed, these were
applied to other manufacturing processes. Some generator
rings and magnet frames were so heavy that the use of portable
machine tools appeared the obvious way of shaping and drilling such masses; and again, once they had been developed,
other uses for them appeared.[67]

Pioneering and Caution

Among both arms makers and tool builders innovating firms
were conspicuous for two reasons: they constituted a small
minority, and they were the most successful and long-lived
firms. In the decade of the Civil War, fifty-two arms makers
were active in New England.[68] Of these only one had been
among the private armories active before 1830, and this one
had belonged to the most active innovator—Eli Whitney.[69]
Most of the others had disappeared in the 1830's and 1840's.[70]
There were about forty-six machine-tool builders active during
the Civil War.[71] Some of these failed after the war, and some
after the crisis of 1873, but others were founded in their place,

[67] U.S. Census Office, *Twelfth Census*, X, 387–388; Victor S. Clark,
op. cit., III, 155.

[68] Deyrup, *op. cit.*, pp. 222–226.   [69] *Ibid.*, pp. 89–99, 120.
[70] *Ibid.*, p. 120.

[71] *Ibid.*, p. 194; Roe, *English and American Tool Builders*, pp. 123–163,
216–230; Buxbaum, "Der amerikanische Werkzeugmaschinenbau," pp.
126–140,

and by 1877 there were again forty-four establishments building machine tools.[72] By 1900 there were 150 establishments building machine tools as their primary product, worth $24,700,-000.[73] In addition 247 establishments built machine tools worth $19,700,000 more or less incidentally to their other operations.[74] Of all these firms, only a few had produced innovations, and still fewer were outstanding pioneers.[75]

The principal characteristic of the pioneering firms, according to a British observer of 1876, was "boldness of design and disregard of precedents," as well as recognition that "even failures teach useful lessons." This observer also noted that

in general, however, workmanship in America is a strange mixture of the most accurate and the most imperfect fitting which can be seen anywhere in the world . . . in two works, perhaps within a few minutes' walk of each other, there may be produced work so different as to serve as examples of practice separated by fifty years of progress.[76]

Among most firms innovation was negligible, and the result was

quite a stereotyped production. . . . The business is learned, and we may say conducted as a manufacturing rather than an engineering one; the result being, as is generally the case under such circumstances, that the cost of producing is often considered before quality and adaptation.[77]

Such firms often attempted to reduce costs by diminishing the amount of metal used in construction although the cost of metal amounted to only one-eighth of the sales price. In one

[72] Buxbaum, "Der amerikanische Werkzeugmaschinenbau," p. 145.
[73] U.S. Census Bureau, *op. cit.,* Bull. 67, p. 7; *American Machinist,* XXV (Nov. 6, 1902), 1638.
[74] U.S. Census Office, *Twelfth Census,* X, 381–383.
[75] Buxbaum, "Der amerikanische Werkzeugmaschinenbau," p. 139.
[76] *Engineering,* XXI (May 26, 1876), 3.
[77] *Ibid.,* XXI (July 7, 1876), 427.

case, a complicated and expensive machine tool was ruined by an attempt to save only 5 per cent of the metal.[78] In other cases metal of poor quality was used. The feet and spindles of lathes were generally too weak and thin, and planing was rough and inadequate. Systems of gears were especially inferior, and some planers used antiquated chain drives.[79] The typical firm also attempted to increase sales by "grotesque ornaments and gaudy color [which] as a rule rather than an exception distinguish American machines." [80] When practical electric motors became available for powering machines in factories, several machine-tool builders had to be compelled by their customers to design their machine tools so that they could be powered by such motors.[81] In 1902 Professor John E. Sweet of Cornell, an authority on machine tools for a generation, observed that only firms of national reputation seemed to make bold departures and that "the average maker forgets that the way the other man made his reputation was exactly by these bold departures, superior workmanship, and high prices." [82]

If engineers or mechanics lacked authority in a firm, innovation was apt to be discouraged. At the Waltham Watch Company, "anything approaching an automatic machine was frowned upon," and automatic machinery was adopted only after an employee had constructed a machine to run half automatically against the positive orders of the management.[83] Between 1857 and 1900, thirty-seven watch companies were organized; and twenty-two failed, eighteen within five years.[84] The general cause of failure, according to Brearly, was "lack of cooperation between technical watch-making skill and business

[78] *Ibid.*, XXII (Oct. 6, 1876), 294.

[79] Buxbaum, "Der amerikanische Werkzeugmaschinenbau," pp. 139–140.

[80] *Engineering*, XXI (May 26, 1876), 3.

[81] *Iron Age*, LV (Feb. 21, 1895), 390.

[82] *American Machinist*, XXV (Nov. 6, 1902), 1586.

[83] Moore, *op. cit.*, p. 59.   [84] *Ibid.*, pp. 301–308.

management." [85] Such firms as the Elgin National Watch Company succeeded because its promoters "organized the company at the suggestion of a few trained men from Waltham, to whose technical experience and knowledge they gave entire liberty of action from the first." [86]

In almost every one of the two dozen firms that successfully pioneered innovations after 1845, a trained machine-tool expert had either full control of business operations or at least an important voice as partner. Throughout the century, the majority of pioneers continued innovating for two decades or more, and there is considerable evidence that they developed their innovations with great caution. Eli Whitney, for example, never lost sight of the prosaic requirements that determined the profitability of the most ingenious machinery. In 1812 he wrote to the War Department:

The machinery should be so proportioned and the extent of each establishment such, as to keep *all* the machinery constantly employed. . . . The amount of the capital must be at least equal to double the value of the arms delivered in one year—and this amount will not be sufficient unless the finished work be turned in and payment for the same recd. every ninety days. The establishment of such a Manufactory is . . . a progressive operation—and can in no case be accomplished in less than two years—and should be continued at least twenty years to warrant such an investment of capital.[87]

In his third contract with the government, unlike almost every other arms maker, Whitney thought of insisting that "insurance against all risks, with the addition of such further percentage for wear and decay as shall be sufficient to preserve the said Capital unimpaired, shall be charged as making a part

[85] Brearly, *op. cit.*, p. 177.   [86] *Ibid.*
[87] Memorandum to War Department, June 29, 1812, quoted in Jeanette Mirsky and Allan Nevins, *The World of Eli Whitney* (New York: Macmillan, 1952), pp. 244–245.

of the Cost of Manufacturing arms." [88] On another occasion he offered the superintendent of the Springfield Armory a barrel-turning invention which he considered technically satisfactory but which he had decided not to build himself because "the probability is that some person would contract to make the barrels and not only take advantage of my invention but intice away the workmen whom I had instructed in the use of the Machine before I could be half compensated for the expence of making it." [89]

Evidence of great caution among later pioneering firms lies in their reluctance to sponsor inventions offered to them by outsiders. Thus, in the late 1880's Pratt and Whitney and Warner and Swasey refused to back James Hartness and his flat-turret lathe. [90] In the 1890's the Hartford Machine Screw Company and Warner and Swasey rejected Henn and Hakewessel's idea for multiple-spindle automatic lathes. [91] Often when a novel machine tool was developed within a firm, a separate company was organized to avoid risks for the original firm. In this way the Norton Emery Wheel Company established the Norton Grinding Machine Company, and Jones and Lamson founded the Fellows Gear Shaper Company.

The widespread reluctance to support innovation may be illustrated by the experience of Frederick W. Taylor, who is generally considered the outstanding inventor of machine tools in the last two decades of the century. [92] As previously mentioned, he developed a revolutionary steam hammer, automatic

[88] Quoted in Mirsky and Nevins, *op. cit.*, p. 273.

[89] Letter to Superintendent Roswell Lee, Jan. 3, 1818, quoted by Mirsky and Nevins, *op. cit.*, p. 269.

[90] Roe, *James Hartness*, p. 10.

[91] Hubbard, "The Development of Machine Tools in New England," *American Machinist*, LXI (Aug. 21, 1924), 315–316.

[92] Bond, *op. cit.*, pp. 340–342; Buxbaum, "Der amerikanische Werkzeugmaschinenbau," p. 145; Roe, *English and American Tool Builders*, pp. 250–251.

grinders, false tables, chucks, forging and tool-feeding mechanisms, and boring and turning mills, and, above all, he was the discoverer of high-speed tool steel.[93] Although Taylor was associated with the pioneering firm William Sellers and Company, whenever he appeared in the drafting room, "nearly everyone took on a smile" and "apart from Sellers, everyone . . . so far from having any sympathy with his experiments, was actively opposed to them." [94] Taylor's biographer writes, no doubt with exaggeration, that "it is extremely unlikely that there was then in industry another chief executive [besides Sellers] who would have given young Taylor any encouragement at all." [95] And yet, as quoted in the preceding chapter, Taylor himself was an exponent of extreme caution.[96]

One of Taylor's great interests was the room left for improvement on familiar processes. He experimented for six months on the correlation between cutting angles and maximum tool speed, using up 2,000 tons of metal in the process. He found no correlation; but testifying about this experience before a House Committee in 1912, he stated that the experiments were nevertheless a "gold mine" because any knowledge, however partial, "was vastly better than the utter lack of information or the very imperfect rule of thumb which existed before." [97] For example, he had discovered the superiority of water over oil lubrication and had realized fuel savings by noting the importance of heavier belts frequently tightened with precision.

But even at Midvale, Taylor was not allowed to experiment with tungsten steel because the company, now under Charles J. Harrah, Jr., was not manufacturing it.[98] Tungsten steel had been developed between 1860 and 1870 by Robert Mushet in

[93] Copley, *op. cit.*, I, 196, 201, II, 84–106.   [94] *Ibid.*, I, 124, 239.
[95] *Ibid.*, I, 238.   [96] *Supra*, Chapter II, p. 96.
[97] Copley, *op. cit.*, p. 240.
[98] Frederick W. Taylor, *On the Art of Cutting Metals* (New York: American Society of Mechanical Enginers, 1907), pp. 219–221.

England and was used to cut metals too hard for carbon steel tools. At Cramp's Shipyards in 1894–1895, Taylor discovered that with tungsten steel tools the cutting speed could be increased 41–47 per cent for hard forgings and 90 per cent for soft metal. Thus it was relatively more profitable to use tungsten steel on soft metal. Taylor left Cramp's after six months because the management, like manufacturers generally, according to Taylor, did not realize that "the small saving in grinder's wages, in the wages of the smith and in tool steel, which is made by having a tool last a long time, is much more than overbalanced by the diminished output of the machine which corresponds with the slow cutting speed." [99]

By 1898 Taylor was employed by the Bethlehem Steel Company, and there he discovered a type of steel that retained its hardness when red hot. Together with J. Maunsel White, he found that, although the quality of tungsten-chromium tool steel deteriorates after 1,500 degrees Fahrenheit, as was generally known, this process is reversed after 1,725 degrees. Above 1,850 degrees, improvement in quality was marked and became greatest just before the melting point. [100] With this knowledge he designed a novel set of high-speed machine tools. At the Paris World's Fair of 1900, Taylor's high-speed tools were considered the outstanding development in metalworking machinery. [101]

The principle involved was so simple, however, that the discovery was rapidly and widely infringed. For five years the Bethlehem Steel Company waged an unsuccessful suit against the Niles-Bement-Pond Company, which was assisted by other manufacturers. [102] In spite of this perennial danger of infringement, Taylor concluded that

[99] *Ibid.*, p. 189.   [100] Copley, *op. cit.*, II, 84–86, 91–106.
[101] Buxbaum, "Der amerikanische Werkzeugmaschinenbau," p. 145.
[102] Copley, *op. cit.*, II, 86–87.

the greatest difficulty in commercial life is to get the opportunity to successfully carry out the experiment; frequently more ingenuity is required in providing the opportunity than in making the experiment itself. Special ingenuity is required to see how [the] experiment can be made profitable to [an] employer in [a] comparatively short time. Necessity in many cases [calls] for beginning at the wrong end of the experiment to furnish a convincing object lesson to your employer.[103]

Risks and Failures

In appraising the riskiness of machine-tool innovation it must be remembered that machine tools were not expensive and that innovations were generally attempted by those who already possessed toolmaking facilities. In the 1830's a fourteen-foot double-engine lathe cost $350 and was the most expensive machine tool coming into common use in large machine shops.[104] By the 1850's a plain milling machine was the typical machine tool used in interchangeable manufacturing, and it sold for about $300. What was then perhaps the most complicated machine tool known, the universal milling machine, cost about $850.[105] Around 1880 the value of machinery, excluding belts and shafting, per worker in a plant manufacturing interchangeable mechanisms was betwen $300 and $350.[106] The most accurate machine tool known at this time, the automatic pinion cutter of the Hampden Watch Company, cost $4,000.[107] In the 1890's, flat-turret lathes sold for about $1,100; [108] the first high-precision Norton grinding machine was designed to sell for $2,500; [109] and the cost of building the

[103] Notes quoted by Copley, *op. cit.*, I, 247.

[104] George Sweet Gibb, *The Saco-Lowell Shops: Textile Machinery Building in New England, 1813–1949* (Cambridge: Harvard University Press, 1950), p. 635.

[105] Fitch, *op. cit.*, p. 4.

[106] *Ibid.*, p. 5.

[107] *Ibid.*, pp. 60–67.

[108] Roe, *James Hartness*, p. 36.

[109] Tymeson, *op. cit.*, p. 85.

first multiple-spindle automatic lathes was about $500 each.[110] The price of the average metal-cutting machine tool did not reach $2,000 until 1923 and $5,000 until 1947.[111]

By contrast, the price of textile machinery rose much faster. Around 1820 the Boston Manufacturing Company was already selling dressers for $1,000 and double speeders for $2,000.[112] Moreover, the scale of operations in a textile mill was much greater. Northrop automatic looms sold for only $150 each around 1900, but a mill was likely to install hundreds or thousands of such looms or none.[113] Machine tools, on the other hand, could always be sold one at a time.

The fact that the innovators after 1850 already possessed or had free access to toolmaking facilities is important in several respects. It meant that special expenses for equipment to make a novel tool would be small. Those who were interested in invention and innovation were therefore in a position to keep these activities a minor part of their total operations if they chose to do so.

In the period when machine-tool innovation was incidental to making arms for the government, what risks there were generally fell on the taxpayers. Later risks fell on the arms makers or toolbuilders themselves. When machine tools were manufactured for sale, a guarantee of successful performance was always understood as a condition in furnishing machines.[114] If a machine proved imperfect, it had to be taken back and the money refunded. In some cases periods of free trial were al-

[110] Hubbard, "The Development of Machine Tools in New England," *American Machinist*, LXI (Sept. 18, 1924), 454.

[111] Figures supplied by Mr. Tell Berna, General Manager of the National Machine Tool Builders' Association, Cleveland, Ohio, from reports to the Association by manufacturers.

[112] Gibb, *op. cit.*, p. 47.

[113] Thomas R. Navin, Jr., *The Whitin Machine Works since 1831: A Textile Machinery Company in an Industrial Village* (Cambridge: Harvard University Press, 1950), p. 535.

[114] *Enginering*, XXII (June 2, 1876), 454.

lowed.[115] In others, as in the case of the first flat-turret lathes, sales were made on agreement to take the pay out of savings in operating costs.[116]

Among the production risks in machine-tool innovation, technical failure of experimental equipment was no doubt a common occurrence beginning with the days of Eli Whitney and Roswell Lee of the Springfield Armory. But to repeat, the fact that interest in machine-tool innovation was usually limited to those who had access to the experience and equipment of a going concern made it possible to keep expenditures specifically devoted to innovation within safe limits. Henn and Hakewessel, as an exception, did invest too many of the resources of their Standard Manufacturing Company in developing the multiple-spindle lathe. Their small shop, which had specialized in bevel protractors and sensitive drills, failed; and by the time a working model of the multiple-spindle automatic lathe had been developed, the country was in the midst of the depression of the 1890's.[117]

There were a number of other production risks, however, which had little to do with a firm's innovating activities as such. For example, the armory of Simeon North shared the lead with Eli Whitney in promoting musket interchangeability; but, unlike Whitney, North did not understand the economics of manufacturing with machinery. His difficulties around 1828 were partly the result of his failure to allow for depreciation.[118]

The earliest machine-tool innovations were designed to overcome the shortage of skilled labor, but so long as they did not eliminate skill altogether, this shortage could prove troublesome. The shortage was a bottleneck not only in arms production, but also in the production of the very machinery that was supposed to eliminate this bottleneck. The lack of skills has

[115] *Ibid.* [116] Roe, *James Hartness,* p. 37.

[117] Hubbard, "The Development of Machine Tools in New England," *American Machinist,* LXI (Aug. 21, 1924), 315–316.

[118] Deyrup, *op. cit.,* pp. 53–54.

probably been exaggerated; [119] but nevertheless it helped delay the completion of Whitney's first contract by six years. As Whitney himself wrote; "my workmen without an exception, were . . . and have always been almost wholly of my own instructing. I am indebted to no man for planning or executing any part of my Machinery." [120] If the government had not been his customer, the delays involved in these efforts might well have been fatal to his enterprise. Other production difficulties confronted Robbins and Lawrence when their British customers failed to send reliable gauges and models for a rifle contract and when a drought forced Pennsylvania sawmills to shut down in the summer of 1856, delaying the delivery of rifle stocks.[121]

A production risk that definitely affected innovation as such was unexpected obsolescence. In an industry which was technologically as active as the manufacture of machine tools, obsolescence was a well-known phenomenon by 1870. Even in the watch industry, which had to design its own more precise machine tools, obsolescence came to be recognized as unpredictable in detail but still inevitable and therefore subject to planning.[122] In the machine-tool industry, obsolescence was anticipated to the extent that it was "thought folly to waste material and labor in securing a little extra advantage in the operation of a machine which it is expected must soon make way for another." [123] Nevertheless, the rate of obsolescence for a particular machine could not be predicted, and an enterprise built exclusively on a single novel machine was necessarily in danger.

[119] Gibb, *op. cit.*, p. 10.

[120] Letter to Callender Irvine, Nov. 25, 1813, quoted by Mirsky and Nevins, *op. cit.*, pp. 253–254.

[121] Hubbard, "The Development of Machine Tools in New England," *American Machinist*, LX (Jan. 24, 1924), 131, 171.

[122] Moore, *op. cit.*, p. 62.

[123] *Engineering*, XXI (June 2, 1876), 454.

This danger was enhanced by the ease of circumventing patents and the ease of entry. The basic elements of metalworking machines had almost all been developed before the end of the eighteenth century.[124] When a new type of metalworking machine became commercially feasible, it could often be constructed with several different combinations of these basic elements. The number of patents a man held were therefore more a mark of prestige than a charter to prosperity. No doubt, patents delayed competition somewhat, but a British observer found that "a shameful copying of everything which reaches a successful sale" was the rule in the United States.[125] Thus, Christopher Spencer and Frederick W. Taylor found their patents for the automatic turret lathe and high-speed tools, respectively, unenforcible; and Henn and Hakewessel encountered little difficulty in circumventing the patents of Allen Johnston in the multiple-spindle automatic.[126] Some innovators, among them Eli Whitney and William Bement, did not even find patents worth the effort and expense of their acquisition.

After the turn of the century, the importance of patents increased considerably because of the reinterpretation of patent laws by the courts which made possible the hoarding of patents without use. By 1912 the various patents of Henn and Hakewessel were declared worth $12,000,000.[127]

A factor that increased the danger of unexpected obsolescence was the ease of entry due to low capital requirements. Warner and Swasey in the 1880's and Henn and Hakewessel's National Acme Machine Screw Company in the 1890's began

[124] Abbott Payson Usher, *A History of Mechanical Inventions* (rev. ed.; Cambridge: Harvard University Press, 1954), pp. 222–237, 360–367, 376–378.

[125] *Engineering*, XXI (June 2, 1876), 454.

[126] Hubbard, "The Development of Machine Tools in New England," *American Machinist*, LXI (Aug. 14, 1924), 315–316.

[127] Chapin, *op. cit.*, p. 17.

with only $10,000.[128] Even a nineteen-year-old boy, Edward A. Muller of Cincinnati, could organize his own company on the basis of a slight improvement of lathes in 1886, merge it with the Bradford Mill Company, and thus found the important Bradford Machine Tool Company.[129] With such ease of entry it would be unreasonable to suppose that some records of small firms which failed and which might have promoted an innovation have not been lost. If one therefore claims that machine-tool innovation was not particularly risky, one can mean no more than that innovation did not on balance result in losses for any one of the well-known firms. This claim is significant because the majority of known innovating firms continued introducing important technological changes for several decades after their initial success. They could and almost did by themselves sustain the pace of technological change.

There can be no question, however, that less-well-known firms also contributed some less-well-known innovations. Almost anywhere small manufacturers of metal goods were likely to think of improvements for their machinery. For example, during the 1870's Allen Johnston of Ottumwa, Iowa, invented a series of sewing-machine attachments and organized the Johnston Ruffler Company for their manufacture. The attachments required metal screws; and, as production increased, Johnston found it economical to manufacture his own screws. Eventually he began making improvements on the screw machines he had purchased.[130] His first patent, issued January 28, 1879, covered a "thread cutting tool for metal screw machine." [131] His second, issued a few days later on February 4, 1879, was called simply "improvement in metal screw machines." [132] Within the next

---

[128] *Ibid.*, p. 14; Roe, *English and American Tool Builders*, p. 262.

[129] John G. Glover and William Bouck Cornell, *The Development of American Industries* (New York: Prentice-Hall, 1930), p. 527.

[130] The Allen Johnston Papers, now in the possession of Mr. Allen Sharp, 1540 North Van Buren, Ottumwa, Iowa.

[131] U.S. Patent no. 211,742.   [132] U.S. Patent no. 211,911.

decade, Johnston obtained fourteen other patents on screw machines and their tools. Some of the ideas represented by these patents he applied in his own works; some he licensed to others such as the Chicago Screw Company; and some had no direct commercial consequences. Outstanding among his ideas was the conception of an automatic lathe with several spindles which could be switched from one cutting tool to another.[133] This idea anticipated the work of Henn and Hakewessel, as previously mentioned. The significance of all such isolated developments to the improvement of machine tools as a whole, however, cannot be easily appraised. In any case, the work of the pioneering firms did not depend on them. In addition to these unknown successful firms, there were the unknown, or almost unknown, failures. Again, not all of their records have been lost.

A case of unexpected obsolescence, for example, led to the failure of Francis Curtis, who patented an automatic screw machine in 1871 and placed it on the market with the financial backing of Henry Devens of Brattleboro, Vermont. Curtis' machine was not a variety of turret lathe but a machine with a hollow spindle and a cam shaft with disks operating draw bars to feed the stock, turn the body of the screw, cut it off, slot it, finish the head, and eject the finished product into a pan. It was used at the Springfield Armory and at the Wheeler and Wilson sewing-machine plant at Bridgeport, Connecticut. One worker could operate eight of these machines, and the productivity of labor in screw making doubled. In 1874, however, the machine was entirely superseded by Spencer's automatic turret lathe; and Curtis eventually died in poverty.[134]

Such cases occurred now and then, but unexpected obsolescence was nevertheless not as likely as its reverse, unexpected

133 U.S. Patent no. 337,499 and others.

134 Hubbard, "The Development of Machine Tools in New England," *American Machinist,* LXI (July 21, 1924), 197–198.

technological aptness. For example, the turret lathe was a specialized machine with no general market before 1850, when a variety of complementary developments in the economy led to a rapid spread of the interchangeable system. On the side of supply, these developments consisted of cheaper metals to be shaped by machine tools, harder metals for the cutting edges of tools, cheaper and better lubricants, and cheaper power to drive the spindles. On the demand side, these developments were the broad economic trends in the United States that created mass markets for food, clothing, machines, and power, to such an extent that farm machinery, sewing machines, machine tools, and steam engines could themselves be mass-produced. During the 1890's the reduction in electricity costs, particularly at Niagara Falls, and the consequent development of artificial abrasives like carborundum made possible the application of grinding machines to roughing out as well as light finishing.[135] The cutting action of the new grinding machines was sixteen times as rapid as that of any machine tool that had previously been built,[136] but through a coincidence it appeared on the market almost simultaneously with Taylor's high-speed tools. One innovation did not, however, make the other superfluous. There were important differences in quality, cost of operation, and other factors. For example, grinding wheels could not be used in that large class of work which involved profiling because a profiled wheel cannot traverse and thus neutralize wear and maintain accuracy. The development of a great variety of machines using electrical and internal-combustion motors created ample needs for each type of machine tool.

Customer and interference risks were of little significance in

[135] Joseph Horner, "Modern Grinding: Methods and Machines," *Cassier's Magazine*, XXX (1906), 113–124, 261–273; Hubbard, "100 Years of Progress in the Development of American Metalworking Equipment," p. 315.

[136] Tymeson, *op. cit.*, p. 85.

machine-tool innovation. The buyer of a novel machine tool could generally rest assured that the innovation had been developed by a firm experienced and concerned with problems almost exactly like his own. Before investing in mass-production equipment, a machine-tool producer had ample opportunity to observe the behavior of a new tool in the course of his own operations. Firms which produced new types of milling machines and lathes had frequently perfected these by using them to produce old types.

With respect to interference risks, the ineffectiveness of the patent system has been described. This inffectiveness meant that many innovators were not much concerned about interference by someone whose patent might be infringed. By the same token, as already mentioned, the risk of unexpected obsolescence increased. It is hard to say whether innovation was on balance encouraged or discouraged by the weakness of the patent law, but the rapid pace of change suggests that any discouragement could not have been significant.

A rare case of serious interference involved Eli Whitney during the War of 1812. Callender Irvine, Commissary General of Purchases for the army, apparently wanted complete control of musket manufacture in 1813 and decided, therefore, to eliminate the private armories. His ultimate aim was to increase the size and number of public armories and to enforce uniform adoption of the Wickham musket in which he had a stake.[137] In letters to General John Armstrong, Secretary of War, Irvine accused Whitney of unnecessary delays and of using funds advanced to him for purposes unrelated to arms making. He claimed that only someone unacquainted with arms making would spend such large sums for buildings and machinery.[138] Although Irvine caused Whitney considerable uncertainty and annoyance, no other unfavorable consequences followed.

[137] Mirsky and Nevins, *op. cit.*, p. 248.   [138] *Ibid.*, pp. 250–254.

The low cost of building an experimental machine tool kept the risk of poor timing with respect to business fluctuations a relatively minor threat. If a toolbuilder's financial position was sound in his regular business operations, the fact that a few thousand pounds of iron and some workers had been used in unfinished experiments was an unlikely cause of serious losses. Indeed, one of the compensations of slack business for the engineer-entrepreneurs in charge of the leading firms was the chance of devoting more time to innovations. It is not surprising, therefore, that the automatics, the universals, the gear shapers, and the grinding machines were developed most rapidly during the depressions of the 1870's and the 1890's. The relatively prosperous 1880's were years of quantitative rather than qualitative progress.[139] Depressions tended to shift the attention of businessmen to ways of cutting costs and therefore favored those toolbuilders that had labor-saving automatics ready for the market. For example, in 1895 one observer noted:

Again, the wonderfully brisk competition that has sprung up within the last very few years in the bicycle industry has made acceptable any device that will increase the output and thereby lessen the cost of manufacturing, and at the same time preserve the needed accuracy. The market has been open to the inventor with the certain assurance of ample reward if successful.[140]

In a few cases, however, a small company gambled most of its resources and credit on an innovation and failed primarily because of a sudden depression. This was the fate of Aaron Dennison's pioneering venture to manufacture watches with interchangeable parts. His American Horloge Company failed in the panic of 1857, but two years later the Waltham Watch Company succeeded with exactly the same machinery and with Dennison as superintendent.[141] It should be remembered

[139] Buxbaum, "Der amerikanische Werkzeugmaschinenbau," p. 142.
[140] *Iron Age*, LV (March 7, 1895), 496.
[141] Brearly, *op. cit.*, pp. 173–174.

that depressions occurred about every ten years and that if Dennison had organized his watch company much earlier than 1850 he would have encountered the previous depression. For innovations that required ten years of development or more, the risk of failure in a depression could not easily be eliminated.

It also appears that the difficulties of Henn and Hakewessel in securing financial backing were primarily due to their failure to attain a working model (that infringed no one's patents) until after the depression of 1893 had begun. The significant point in their experience, however, is that they succeeded in spite of the depression.[142]

The general riskiness of machine-tool innovation should be appraised by the fact that almost every firm which contributed major innovations after 1840 continued operating successfully after 1900 and that, with the exception of the American Horloge Company, the few which dissappeared did not fail on account of unsuccessful innovation. The firms which disappeared were Robbins and Lawrence of Windsor, Vermont, and the Ames Manufacturing Company of Chicopee, Massachusetts. The Jones and Lamson Machine Company of Windsor, Vermont, also failed but was reorganized under different management at Springfield, Vermont. The Niles Tool Works, Bement, Miles and Company, Pratt and Whitney, and several other firms merged around 1900 to form the Niles-Bement-Pond Company.[143]

Robbins and Lawrence failed (1) because they had agreed to build cars for a Vermont railroad that refused to buy these cars when its president quarreled with one of the partners and (2)

---

[142] Chapin, *op. cit.*, p. 14; Hubbard, "The Development of Machine Tools in New England," *American Machinist*, LXI (Aug. 14, Sept. 18, 1924), 315–316, 453

[143] *American Machinist*, XXV (Nov. 6, 1902), 1569–1638; *Thomas Register of American Manufacturers* (New York: Thomas Publishing Co., 1909), pp. 424, 1156–1162, 1459; Roe, *English and American Tool Builders*, pp. 172–291.

because they had tooled up for rifle production on the promise of a contract for 300,000 rifles for the British Government. This contract failed to materialize when the Crimean War ended unexpectedly.[144] After one generation of outstanding work, the Ames Manufacturing Company failed, according to Shlakman, because of too great reliance on the past reputation of the firm and lack of initiative in investigating new fields of endeavor. Moreover, between 1861 and 1867 dividends were paid "without any thought of either protecting the working capital or building up a capital reserve." [145] The difficulties of Jones and Lamson involved (1) an attempt to manufacture quarrying machinery which infringed a basic patent of one of their own former employees and (2) an unsuccessful attempt to manufacture cotton textiles.[146]

The other leading innovators continued to expand. The net assets of Pratt and Whitney, for example, increased from $2,600 in 1862 to $75,000 in 1866. By 1869 assets were $350,000; and by 1893, $3,000,000.[147] Ten of the most prominent firms increased the number of their employees from 1,560 in 1877 to 9,845 in 1902, an increase of more than 600 per cent, which must be multiplied by the rise in productivity per employee for an estimate of total expansion.[148]

Summary

Until 1855 machine-tool innovations in the United States were promoted mostly by arms makers. After 1855 the pro-

[144] Richard S. Lawrence, account of his life for his son, Ned, Dec. 17, 1890, published as Appendix A in Roe, *English and American Tool Builders,* pp. 281–291; Hubbard, "The Development of Machine Tools in New England," *American Machinist,* LX (Jan. 24, 1924), 131, 171.

[145] Shlakman, *op. cit.,* p. 164.

[146] Hubbard, "The Development of Machine Tools in New England," *American Machinist,* LX (June 26, 1924), 953–954.

[147] Roe, *English and American Tool Builders,* pp. 175–179.

[148] *American Machinist,* XXV (Nov. 6, 1902), 1638.

moters were specialized machine-tool builders. In both industries innovating firms were a small minority, copying firms a majority. Although individual attempts at innovation often failed at the level of invention, these failures never led to insolvency once a firm had established itself. On the contrary, the firms that had attempted a series of innovations not only continued operating successfully after 1900, but they were also the most successful firms. There were exceptions, but the causes of failure of well-established firms never included later unsuccessful attempts at machine-tool innovation.

Among established firms, risks were low for two reasons. First, their innovations were planned by mechanics and businessmen who thoroughly understood the economics and technology of metalworking. Second, it was easy to keep resources devoted to single experiments within safe limits because the cost of a new machine tool was low, generally between $300 and $3,000. For new firms with few assets the development of an innovation could mean a serious commitment, and a single failure could mean the end of an enterprise. There can be no doubt that such failures occurred, but their significance appears to have been largely peripheral. The failures of some rarely contributed to the success of others, and the pace of technological progress was easily sustained by firms that had been innovating for decades.

V

Electric Power

NO doubt the most conspicuous change in production methods during the nineteenth century was the greater substitution of energy derived from coal and falling water in place of energy derived from muscles in the operation of tools and machines. At first this energy was transmitted from steam engines or water wheels by chains, belts, gears, and shafts. But such transmission worked without great loss only for short distances, and it made the consumption of power uneconomical on a small scale and inflexible on a large scale. The development of electric generators, transmission lines, and motors during the last third of the nineteenth century made possible the elimination of each of these difficulties. By 1907 the United States Bureau of the Census could state that "the use of electric motors has become almost universal, so that relatively few mills or factories of any size are established in which the power is not distributed largely by means of electric motors attached directly to the tools or machines, or by short lines of shafting." [1] Forty years later 93 per cent of the mechanical power used in American industrial plants was applied by electric motors.[2]

Although the electrification of industrial plants did not become widespread until after 1900, all the basic technological changes were introduced commercially before that year: dynamos, turbogenerators, high-voltage transmission lines, central power stations, transformers, and electric motors for anything from sewing machines to steel mill equipment. This chapter is confined to these technological innovations, that is, all those involved in the generation and transmission of electric power and its reconversion into mechanical energy for manufacturing. Specialized innovations in telegraphy, telephony, transportation, lighting, batteries, electrolytic processes, electric furnaces, electromagnets, and measuring instruments will not be considered, except in cases in which the effect on the introduction of electric power machinery was direct and immediate.

Eighty Years of Discovery—Thirty Years of Innovation

In 1819 the Danish professor Hans Christian Oersted discovered that an electric current will deflect a compass and that a magnet exerts a force on wire carrying a current. In the following years a number of scientists, among them Michael Faraday of England, André Marie Ampère of France, and Joseph Henry of the United States, developed theories of electromagnetism and constructed devices later called electric motors and generators. Thomas Davenport of Rutland, Vermont, is often credited with being the first to produce a commercially successful electric motor. In 1837 he received a patent on "improvements in pro-

[1] U.S. Bureau of the Census, *Census of Manufactures, 1905* (Washington, 1907), Bull. 73, p. 19.

[2] Editorial Staff of *Electrical World, The Electric Power Industry, Past, Present, and Future* (New York: McGraw-Hill, 1949), p. 8.

pelling machinery by magnetism and electro-magnetism." He
used a fifty-pound motor for drilling holes up to one quarter of
an inch in all the ironwork and steelwork of his blacksmith shop.[3]
In 1838 Charles Page of Boston claimed a saving of fifteen dollars
a day by drilling steel plates with a battery-driven motor. He
received a Congressional appropriation of $20,000 and developed
motors capable of sawing heavy timber and of propelling a
twelve-ton locomotive at nineteen miles an hour.[4] But since the
energy used by such motors was originally generated by expensive chemical batteries, these motors could not compete with
steam engines. According to various estimates around 1850, the
cost of lifting an equal weight with electric power instead of
steam was twenty-five times greater.[5] Zinc and acid in batteries
could not compete with coal and water in steam engines.

The introduction of electric motors on a large commercial
scale had to follow the introduction of improved generators.
Electric power was to be derived from the primary sources of
energy already in use, coal and falling water, but it was to provide greater flexibility and lower cost. It was to make possible
the cheap transmission of power over great distances, the use of
power in small shops and homes, the saving of power in factories
with machines operated intermittently, and the construction of
prime movers of unprecedented efficiency.

Between 1860 and 1863 in Italy, Antonio Pacinotti improved
the design of generators and constructed a machine that could
be operated in reverse as a motor. The principle of reversibility
had been stated by Francis Watkins of London in 1835, but Watkins had been forgotten and Pacinotti came to be regarded as
the initiator of an important new development.[6] Soon a number

[3] Malcolm MacLaren, *The Rise of the Electrical Industry during the
Nineteenth Century* (Princeton: Princeton University Press, 1943), p. 83;
A Chronological History of Electrical Development (New York: National
Electrical Manufacturers Association, 1946), p. 25.

[4] MacLaren, *op. cit.*, pp. 87–88.   [5] *Ibid.*, p. 89.

[6] *Electrical World*, II (Dec. 8, 1883), 243.

of men almost simultaneously discovered and announced the principle of the self-exciting generator. In 1870 Z. T. Gramme patented a generator which he claimed reduced the cost of electroplating. At the Vienna Exhibition of 1873 one of Gramme's generators was hooked up in reverse to operate a pump. Another was installed commercially to operate a hoisting conveyor to unload beetroots outside a sugar factory at Sermaize, France. Still other Gramme motors were used to operate sewing machines, lathes, planers, drills, hammers, and a printing press at the Paris Exhibition of 1881.[7]

In the United States the commercial introduction and technological development of generators were inspired by opportunities in electroplating and lighting. In 1872 Edward Weston, a New York chemist, began constructing dynamos for electroplating and found it comparatively easy to prove to manfacturers that steam engines and generators would be less costly than batteries. He was the first to use laminated armatures and pole pieces in America and thus raised the efficiency of generators from about 45 to 85 per cent. In 1877 he organized the Weston Dynamo Electric Machine Company with an authorized capitalization of $200,000.[8]

At the same time the possibility of generating electric current more cheaply turned the attention of inventors toward lighting. Brighter street lights and the elimination of soot, fumes, and indoor fire danger promised great rewards. In contrast with lighting, the existing methods of powering factories seemed relatively adequate and not easily improved by converting energy from one form to another and back. During the late 1870's the

[7] MacLaren, *op. cit.,* pp. 89–91, 116; *Electrical World,* II (Dec. 8, 1883), 243.

[8] David O. Woodbury, *A Measure of Greatness: A Short Biography of Edward Weston* (New York: McGraw-Hill, 1949), p. 72; *A Chronological History of Electrical Development,* pp. 38–40; Harold C. Passer, *The Electrical Manufacturers, 1875–1900* (Cambridge: Harvard University Press, 1953), p. 31.

first arc-lighting systems were exhibited on American streets, and a number of inventors appeared close to solving the problems of incandescent lights. The opportunities in lighting soon overshadowed those of electroplating, and even Weston's firm changed its name to the Weston Electric Light Company in 1879.

Lighting systems involved longer and more complicated circuits than electroplating and therefore inspired many technological changes. Thus Charles Brush had to design improved dynamos with constant current and high-voltage characteristics before he could introduce his pioneering arc lights on a commercial scale.[9] Likewise, the introduction of high-resistance, low-voltage incandescent lamps by Edison required improved dynamos and a novel transmission system. His work in improving armature design and introducing feeder-main-type circuits (which reduced copper costs by about 94 per cent) was as important as his search for a better filament.[10] All these improvements together made possible the first commercial central power station in 1882. Edison, of course, realized that he was also creating outlets for industrial electric motors, particularly small ones. In 1878 he wrote in his notebook, "Generally poorest district for light, best for power, thus evening up whole city—note effect of this on investment." [11] What is relevant for this study is that Edison's attempt to establish a central power station was the first such attempt and that it was commercially successful.

As early as 1880 Edison had used only electricity for transmitting power from a steam engine in his lamp factory. Although he recognized its future possibilities, he was not himself interested in promoting electric power for industry.[12] He left this field to some fifteen small manufacturers, among them the Electro-

---

[9] Passer, *op. cit.*, pp. 13–17, 64.

[10] MacLaren, *op. cit.*, pp. 123–125, 162; Passer, *op. cit.*, pp. 80–82, 177–178.

[11] T. C. Martin, *Forty Years of Edison Service* (New York: New York Edison Co., 1922), p. 11.

[12] Passer, *op. cit.*, p. 218.

Dynamic Company of Philadelphia and the Fuller Electrical Company of New York. By 1887 these fifteen had manufactured some 10,000 motors of one horsepower or less.[13] Such motors powered fans, sewing machines, watchmaker's lathes, and dental equipment.[14]

Larger motors were not produced for industrial purposes in America until 1884 when Frank Julian Sprague resigned from Edison's staff and organized the Sprague Electric Railway and Motor Company with the financial assistance of E. H. Johnson, vice-president of the Edison Electric Light Company. The authorized capital of this firm began at $100,000 and was increased to $1,000,000 after two years. It produced motors of fifteen and more horsepower, explicitly designed for industrial use on Edison lighting circuits. The motors were manufactured at the Edison Machine Works and were installed in elevators, clothing factories, printing presses, and a variety of other places, including a Springfield, Massachusetts, steam-power station which had been distributing power to various customers by means of shafting and wire rope.[15] In 1887 at Richmond, Virginia, the Sprague company established the first large streetcar system. Its capitalization was increased by $800,000, of which $600,000 was preferred stock purchased by the Edison Electric Light Company. In 1889 the Sprague company merged with the newly formed

[13] *Ibid.*, p. 276; MacLaren, *op. cit.*, p. 92. Most of these were unsatisfactory in many respects. At least one observer realized that improvement in quality, to be commercially feasible, depended on increased demand, which would make possible economies of scale in the methods of production, thus keeping the price per motor sufficiently low (S. S. Wheeler, "The Practical Requirements of Small Motors," *Electrical World*, IX [Feb. 19, 1887], 93–95).

There were about forty enterprises, mostly very small, supplying dynamos, lamps, and related electrical apparatus (T. C. Martin, "The Electrical Industry in America in 1887," *Electrical World*, IX [Jan. 29, 1887], 50).

[14] *A Chronological History of Electrical Development*, pp. 50–56.

[15] Passer, *op. cit.*, pp. 238–240.

Edison General Electric Company.[16] It had been the first to attempt the production of large motors for sale, and it was successful. Sprague became a consulting engineer to Edison General Electric, but he resigned when the company decided to promote low-voltage traction against his advice.[17] He then organized the Sprague Electric Elevator Company.

The Westinghouse Electric Company of Pittsburgh pioneered the use of alternating current for lighting, alternating-current motors, and turbogenerators. After the basic components of each of these had been invented by others, primarily Europeans, George Westinghouse bought the patent rights and, together with his engineers, developed experimental devices into marketable producers' goods.

In promoting alternating current in 1885 he first obtained Gaulard and Gibbs transformers from England, a Siemens alternating-current generator from Germany, and technical advice from Ganz and Company of Budapest and Werner Siemens of Berlin. Ganz and Company suggested a parallel circuit as workable, but Siemens saw no practical future for alternating current.[18] By 1886 William Stanley, a Westinghouse engineer, had improved both transformers and alternators to the point that a commercial a.c. lighting system could be successfully installed at Buffalo.[19] The chief advantage of alternating current was the possibility of stepping up voltage by means of transformers for cheap transmission and then reducing it again for safe consumption. Lower transmission costs increased the market area for electric current and made possible the location of steam-generator stations closer to fuel and water supplies or in low-rent areas.

Alternating current required a new type of motor, and in 1888

[16] *Ibid.*, p. 248.
[17] Frank Julian Sprague, "Digging in the Mines of the Motors," *Journal of the American Institute of Electrical Engineers*, LIII (May, 1934), 702.
[18] Passer, *op. cit.*, p. 132.
[19] William Stanley, "Alternating Current Development in America," *Journal of the Franklin Institute*, CLXIII (June 1912), 561–580.

inventions in this direction were announced by Galileo Ferraris in Italy and by Nikola Tesla in the United States. The Westinghouse company purchased the patent rights of both inventors [20] only to find that complex frequency, phasing, and voltage problems remained to be solved. A commercially successful a.c. power system for operating mining equipment was installed at Telluride, Colorado, as early as 1891, but Westinghouse was not fully prepared to supply a.c. power motors until about 1893.[21] The following account by B. G. Lamme, one of the leading associates of Westinghouse, may illustrate the caution and imagination with which such equipment was introduced:

In 1890 the Westinghouse company, which had been developing the Tesla polyphase motor laid aside the work, largely on account of there being no suitable general supply systems for this type of motor. The problem was again revived in 1892, in an experimental way, with a view to bringing out an induction motor which might be applied on standard frequencies such as could be used in commercial supply circuits for lighting and other purposes. It should be understood that at this time such circuits were not in existence but were being contemplated. In 1892, after the polyphase motor had been further developed up to the point where it showed great commercial possibilities, the best means for getting it on the market were carefully considered. It was decided that the best way to promote the induction motor business was to create a demand for it on commercial alternating current systems. This meant that, in the first place, such systems must be created. Therefore, it was decided to undertake to fill the country with polyphase generating systems, which were primarily to be used for the usual lighting service. It was thought that, with such sys-

---

[20] Tesla received $1,000,000 for about forty patents in addition to royalty rights which he voluntarily renounced in 1892 (John T. O'Neil, *Prodigal Genius: The Life of Nikola Tesla* [New York: Ives Washburn, 1944], pp. 74–82).

[21] Henry G. Prout, *A Life of George Westinghouse* (New York: Charles Scribner's Sons, 1922), pp. 124, 144–145; MacLaren, *op. cit.*, pp. 97–99; Passer, *op. cit.*, pp. 277–282.

tems available, the time would soon come when there would be a call for induction motors. In this way experience would be obtained in the construction and operation of polyphase generators and the operating public would not be unduly handicapped in the use of such generators, compared with the older single-phase types.[22]

In the meantime, the company pioneered the electrification of steel-mill equipment at the nearby Edgar Thomson Works of Andrew Carnegie.[23]

Steam turbines were brought to a fairly practical stage by Gustaf de Laval of Sweden in 1882 and, along different principles, by Charles A. Parsons of England in 1884. From the beginning steam turbines were designed to power electric generators. By 1895 hundreds of small-capacity turbines were coupled to generators and used commercially in Europe. Westinghouse bought the Parsons patents in the fall of 1895 and improved the design before undertaking the first commercial installation in 1898 in the power plant of the Westinghouse Air Brake Company. Three years later the Westinghouse turbogenerator installed at Hartford, Connecticut, was the first employed in an American central power station.[24] Steam turbines drastically reduced the manufacturing, operating, and maintenance costs of large prime movers and led to a phenomenal growth in electric central power stations within ten years. Like a.c. lighting systems and a.c. motors, their introduction was first attempted by the Westinghouse company and resulted in success.

Of all the firms attempting to introduce new types of heavy electrical equipment, there was one that failed to succeed in the process—the Bradley Electric Power Company of Yonkers, New

[22] B. G. Lamme, "The Technical Story of the Frequencies," *Transactions of the American Institute of Electrical Engineers*, XXXVII (1918), 68.

[23] MacLaren, *op. cit.*, p. 96.

[24] Prout, *op. cit.*, pp. 201–211; MacLaren, *op. cit.*, pp. 197–198; Passer, *op. cit.*, pp. 310–311.

York. In 1888 Charles S. Bradley, a former Edison employee, had received a patent on a machine with a revolving field and a stationary armature that would change alternating into direct current more economically than hooking an a.c. motor to a d.c. generator. This device, the rotary converter, made possible the use of cheap a.c. current for such d.c. purposes as electroplating and electric traction. Its future may have seemed assured, but the innovating company, organized in 1893, did not survive the depression beginning that same year and sold out to General Electric. The sales of General Electric itself had fallen, and about 5,000 of its 8,000 employees had been dismissed. But General Electric did not wish to pass up this opportunity for acquiring a basic patent.[25] The Westinghouse company, however, introduced most of the major improvements on the rotary converter, adapting it to a variety of frequencies, phases, and special uses.[26]

The first attempt to generate and transmit electric power on a very large scale was made at Niagara Falls. A group of New York financiers, including J. Pierpont Morgan and William K. Vanderbilt, organized the Cataract Construction Company in 1889 and paid $482,500 for necessary property rights. At the time there was no precedent and no way of knowing whether technical problems of this magnitude could be solved.[27] A variety of mechanical, electrical, and pneumatic transmission systems were considered. Then a commission of scientists from four countries was organized to conduct a contest among twenty-

[25] *Electrical World*, XXI (March 11, 1893), 178–179; John W. Hammond, *Men and Volts: The Story of General Electric* (New York: J. B. Lippincott, 1941), pp. 230–238; John T. Broderick, *Forty Years with General Electric* (Albany, N.Y.: Fort Orange Press, 1929), p. 31; Passer, *op. cit.*, p. 300.

[26] Passer, *op. cit.*, p. 301.

[27] Edward Dean Adams, *Niagara Power: History of the Niagara Falls Power Company, 1886–1918* (Niagara Falls, N.Y.: Niagara Falls Power Co., 1927), I, 134.

eight European and American firms. Twenty entries were received but none was considered adequate. Further estimates and plans were requested from three American and three Swiss firms, and again all were rejected.[28] The Cataract Construction Company then developed its own plans and requested criticism from Westinghouse and General Electric. The Westinghouse engineers proposed many changes, and finally after four years, in October 1893, a contract for three 5,000 horsepower generators and other equipment was awarded to the Westinghouse company. By 1900 $7,000,000 had been invested, and generating capacity amounted to 50,000 horsepower.

The Cataract company had expected most of this power to be sold in Buffalo. The first customer, however, was the aluminum-producing Pittsburgh Reduction Company; [29] and within two years firms making carborundum, calcium carbide, sodium peroxide, soda ash, sodium, chlorine, and other chemicals were consuming 68 per cent of the power generated. This electrochemical demand had not been anticipated,[30] and an additional $3,000,000 was invested to raise generating capacity to 110,000 horsepower by 1904.

In 1892 the Thomson-Houston Electric Company and the Edison General Electric Company merged to form the General Electric Company, capitalized at $50,000,000. Thomson-Houston had been the leading imitative firm in the electrical industry. It had generally waited until someone like Brush, Edison, Sprague, or Westinghouse had shown the profitability of an innovation, and it had then entered the field quickly and often with superior equipment. By 1891 its annual sales were $10,-300,000, which compared with $10,900,000 for Edison General

[28] *Ibid.*, I, 172, 186, II, 223.

[29] James W. Rickey, "Hydro Power for the Production of Aluminum," *Transactions of the Electrochemical Society*, vol. LXX (1936); Charles C. Carr, *Alcoa: An American Enterprise* (New York: Rinehart & Co., 1952), pp. 85–92.

[30] Passer, *op. cit.*, pp. 293–294.

Electric and $5,000,000 for Westinghouse. After Edison himself had turned his attention to other fields, the Thomson-Houston management had been more imaginative than that of Edison General Electric; and probably for that reason most of the top executives of the new firm, General Electric, were Thomson-Houston men.[31] During the 1890's the new firm rivaled, and perhaps surpassed, Westinghouse in seeking technological improvements. In its a.c. motors General Electric tended to emphasize operating economy and good speed regulation rather than simplicity. It promoted the use of a.c. power in isolated plants and was the first American company to make revolving-field-type generators. Shortly after 1900 it introduced the first large (5,000 kw.) turbogenerators in America.

More than 300 patent suits were pending between General Electric and Westinghouse by 1896, and after months of negotiation a patent agreement was reached. Henceforth General Electric could produce 62.5 per cent and Westinghouse 37.5 per cent of any equipment line covered by the agreement without paying royalties. Needless to say, the agreement impaired the competitive position of other manufacturers, and a considerable number sold out either to General Electric or to Westinghouse within ten years.[32]

One of these other manufacturers, the Stanley Electric Manufacturing Company, had pioneered high-voltage transmission lines. This company was organized in 1891 by William Stanley, who had previously developed practical transformers and alternators for Westinghouse. The new firm began with transformers, but because Westinghouse would not sell his generators to buyers of Stanley transformers, it was soon forced to expand.[33] To avoid patent infringement, Stanley had to change the design of his motors and generators, and these changes created selling

[31] *Ibid.*, pp. 150, 192, 320–329.   [32] *Ibid.*, pp. 329–334.
[33] Letter from William Stanley to B. G. Lamme, Dec. 29, 1913, cited by Passer, *op. cit.*, p. 396.

points that helped the firm capture about 15 per cent of the polyphase generator market during its first four years of production. By 1900 its sales exceeded $1,000,000 annually, which compares with $10,000,000 for a.c. equipment by General Electric and Westinghouse combined. Stanley's principal contribution, however, was the introduction of transmission lines with voltages up to 60,000. Neither Westinghouse nor General Electric considered such voltages feasible. But Stanley and his engineers developed the necessary insulators and could therefore lengthen transmission distances to more than two hundred miles. As a result, a great number of once unprofitable and remote water-power sites could be exploited. Although patent infringement suits forced Stanley to sell out in 1903, his novel attempt to raise transmission voltages, as well as his other activities, had been commercially successful.[34]

Progress and Entry

In 1900 the electrical manufacturing industry was a young, highly progressive industry that was not characterized by ease of entry in some branches. Since 1880 its annual output had expanded almost forty times, from $2,700,000 to $105,800,000.[35] In 1890 its output had been less than one-fourth that of the agricultural implement and machinery industry; but now, in 1900, it was slightly larger. In 1900 the heavy-equipment branch, which is considered here, produced generators worth $10,500,000 and motors worth about $18,000,000.[36] Approximately 4.4 per cent of the mechanical power used in manfacturing was already applied by electric motors—495,000 of 11,300,000 horsepower.[37]

[34] Passer, *op. cit.*, pp. 306–310.
[35] U.S. Census Bureau, *op. cit.*, Bull. 73, p. 9. This figure includes $13,-400,000 of electrical goods produced by firms primarily making other products.
[36] *Ibid.*, pp. 13, 19.
[37] U.S. Census Office, *Twelfth Census: Manufactures* (Washington, 1902), VII, cccxvi.

The great expansion of electrical manufacturing was in large part due to rapid advances in underlying sciences. New theories by Maxwell, Helmholz, and Lord Kelvin often led directly to superior armatures and transmission circuits. One of Edison's closest advisers, Francis R. Upton, was a mathematician and physicist, who had worked with Helmholz in Germany. It was Upton's job to keep Edison informed on advances in theoretical physics and to work out problems involving advanced mathematics, which Edison could pose but not solve. Westinghouse also followed scientific developments closely and often got in touch with scientists shortly after they had published their findings. The Cataract Construction Company began its plans for Niagara power by organizing an international commission of famous scientists and engineers. By 1900 a number of top scientists were employed by the leading companies: Charles Steinmetz, for example, worked out his new system of mathematics for solving alternating-current problems while an employee of General Electric. The pure scientists, however, were not always in the lead. A number of them advised Edison that a practical incandescent lighting system was theoretically impossible, and Lord Kelvin considered the use of alternating current at Niagara Falls a "gigantic mistake." [38]

The progressiveness of an industry is influenced by the extent to which old and established firms are willing to innovate. If innovations must be introduced by newcomers, the difficulties of organizing a business are added to those of innovation. No firm in the electrical industry was old, but rapid expansion soon created an approximation of age through size and reputation. In the manufacture of heavy electrical equipment, the two leading firms, Westinghouse and General Electric, continued innovating long after they had achieved undisputed leadership. Neverthe-

[38] R. H. Parsons, *The Early Days of the Power Station Industry* (Cambridge: Cambridge University Press, 1940), p. 8; Adams, *op. cit.*, II, 256; Passer, *op. cit.*, pp. 82–83.

less, it appears that the most radical departures from existing trends were innovations by newcomers. Thus Westinghouse himself was a newcomer to the electrical industry when he introduced alternating current; and Frank Julian Sprague, William Stanley, and the Cataract Construction Company were new as entrepreneurs when they sponsored their most novel contributions.

Ease of entry into an industry affects the number of newcomers who can initiate radical departures. Entry may be restricted by the difficulty of acquiring complex experience, by patents, by control of market outlets or essential supplies, or by the amount of capital required. Each of these was significant in the manufacture of heavy electrical equipment, almost from the beginning, and as a result entry was difficult.

Perhaps the greatest barrier to newcomers was the difficulty of acquiring complex experience. Edison had worked with telegraph circuits for years and was closely associated with Western Union before he innovated in lighting circuits and power stations. Westinghouse could draw on the electrical engineering experience of his Union Switch and Signal Company. Of the three innovators who organized independent manufacturing companies, Sprague and Bradley had worked with Edison, and Stanley with Westinghouse. Thomson-Houston, the leading imitators, were the largest arc-lighting producers when they branched out into other fields.

The difficulty of overcoming a five-year handicap in alternating current was one of the reasons impelling the Edison General Electric Company to merge with Thomson-Houston.[39] Ten years earlier, however, the Edison Electric Light Company had decided not to sue infringers of its direct-current patents because "the business ascendancy which we have acquired is of itself sufficient to give us a practical monopoly."[40] The buyers of heavy

[39] Passer, *op. cit.*, p. 325.

[40] Edison Electric Light Company, *Annual Report, October 23, 1883*, quoted by Passer, *op. cit.*, p. 100.

electrical equipment were generally less interested in price than reliability, and only years of experience could assure reliability.

Patents were important in restricting entry. Since most electrical inventions were as new as the industry itself, the number of unexpired basic patents was bound to be high. Nevertheless there were rival patents, both domestic and foreign, and a newcomer could acquire these and involve established firms in lengthy suits, if necessary. At times, when the purpose of a device was known, it was possible to achieve the same effect in a different way. Thus Stanley hoped to avoid the Tesla patents in his first motors by substituting an alternating for a rotating magnetic field. But in the end, patent conflicts forced the largest firms (Edison General Electric, Westinghouse, Sprague, and Thomson-Houston) into mergers or cross-licensing agreements, and such newcomers as the Lorain Steel Company, the Walker Manufacturing Company, the American branch of Siemens and Halske, and Stanley were forced out of business.[41] Furthermore, patents made it hard for new companies to gain a toe hold in the heavy-equipment business by starting with single items. The large full-line producers insisted, often on the grounds of efficient performance, that they must supply all the components of a power system or none. This policy could be enforced because patents made the withholding of strategic devices possible. The policy compelled Stanley to branch out into motors and generators from transformers and probably helped account for the failure of Bradley and his rotary converters.[42]

Control of market outlets restricted entry primarily through the system basis of sales just mentioned; or, alternatively, it might be said that high capital requirements restricted entry because only full-line producers who were capable of acquiring a strong patent position could survive as heavy-equipment producers in the 1890's. Moreover, in a rapidly developing industry much depended on who could pay the highest salaries to the

[41] Passer, *op. cit.*, pp. 145, 274, 306, 324–334.
[42] *Ibid.*, pp. 300, 306–307, 352; Hammond, *op. cit.*, pp. 230–231.

best engineers. Westinghouse, for example, could induce important Sprague engineers to resign and join his organization in 1889 when he decided to bring out a direct-current streetcar system.[43] General Electric hired Charles Steinmetz by buying the small Eickemeyer firm of Yonkers, New York.[44] Having a superior technical staff, the large firms quickly duplicated and improved on any innovation that might be introduced by a newcomer. Such was the case with the single-reduction-gear motors for streetcars, introduced by the small Wenstrom company in 1890, and with the multiple-unit control systems for electric railways, introduced by Sprague in 1897.[45] The incidents mentioned occurred in transportation equipment, but they also occurred in the power field when the need arose—for example, when Stanley introduced a generator not requiring brushes or slip rings. The intense product competition between Westinghouse and General Electric in motors and generators during the 1890's repeatedly indicated the ability of each to copy and temporarily to surpass something newly introduced by the other.[46] Finally, since the pricing policies of General Electric and Westinghouse were based on a large sales volume, a newcomer attempting to begin on a small scale with a little capital would have been under an additional disadvantage.[47]

Almost every innovating firm had access to a large volume of capital from the very beginning. Edison had the backing of a group of New York financiers, including Egisto P. Fabbri, a J. P. Morgan partner, and Norvin Green, the president of Western Union.[48] From 1878 until 1884, when the Edison Electric Illuminating Company of New York finally showed a profit, these financiers provided Edison with $490,000 for experimental and

[43] Passer, *op. cit.*, p. 257.   [44] MacLaren, *op. cit.*, p. 127.

[45] Passer, *op. cit.*, pp. 259, 274.   [46] *Ibid.*, pp. 296–305.

[47] *Ibid.*, p. 264.

[48] Payson Jones, *A Power History of the Consolidated Edison System, 1878–1900* (New York: Consolidated Edison Co. of New York, 1940), pp. 28–29.

administrative expenses.[49] Westinghouse, meanwhile, could draw on the assets of his Union Switch and Signal Company, the Westinghouse Air Brake Company, and the Philadelphia Company, a gas distributing firm. Sprague's first company was financed by E. H. Johnson, partner of the Edison Lamp Company and vice-president of the Edison Electric Light Company. Sprague's motors were manufactured at the Edison Machine Works and promoted by Edison interests as "the only practical and economic motor existing today." [50] Most extensive of all were the financial resources of the Cataract Construction Company backed by such New York investment banking houses as Brown Brothers and Company; Winslow, Lanier and Company; and Drexel, Morgan and Company. It began with a cash outlay of $100,000 and spent $7,000,000 on construction alone before 1900. The least successful innovators, Stanley and Bradley, were also those with access to the least amount of capital.

The Cautious Engineer-Entrepreneurs

Most of the innovators in the electrical industry were alike in at least two respects. They had a background of technical experience; and, in the process of making an innovation, they were as cautious as possible.

[49] Edison himself, however, had to finance his lampworks, machine works, and tubeworks by selling most of the stock that he had received for assigning patents to the Edison Electric Light Company (Passer, *op. cit.*, pp. 87–88, 98, 201).

[50] Circular quoted by Passer, *op. cit.*, p. 239. See also *Electrical World*, IX (Jan. 15, 1887), iv, for a typical Sprague advertisement: "These Patents are fundamental, and cover the only possible methods of operating constant speed motors on constant potential currents. . . . Suits for damages will be promptly brought against infringers.

"The Sprague Motors have been formally adopted for use on the Edison Currents. . . .

"This is the only company in the United States devoting its entire energies to the different questions involved in the transmission of power, and it is putting into practical use more motors of over one-half horsepower than all other companies combined."

It was in his study of the electrical manufacturers that Passer evolved his concept of the "engineer-entrepreneur" or the man who combines technical skill and commercial insight to develop a new product.[51] Except for the Niagara project, the place in the economy which new types of electric power equipment might occupy was first seen by men with a technical background. Edison and Westinghouse had little formal education, but each had turned to problems of lighting and power only after years of technical and business experience in other fields. Each had contributed significant inventions to these other fields. The remaining innovators, Sprague, Bradley, and Stanley, worked only in the electrical manufacturing industry; but they had years of experience as technicians before they took the initiative in placing a new product on the market.

To say that the electric power innovators were as cautious as possible does not mean that they were so regarded by all their contemporaries or that they never lost money investigating unpromising inventions. It does mean that they chose to introduce an invention on a commercial scale only after doubts about its technical feasibility had been carefully eliminated and that even then investment proceeded as experimentally and painstakingly as possible. Edison considered his financial backers excessively timid, and "the opposition of ALL the electric part of the Westinghouse organization [to alternating current] was such that it was only Mr. George Westinghouse's personal will that put it through." [52] These attitudes are relevant, but they indicate nothing about the caution with which innovations were actually carried out. Edison and Westinghouse took certain risks and sometimes lost in trying to perfect inventions. Edison believed he could generate electricity directly from coal, without interven-

[51] Passer, *op. cit.*, pp. 1, 66–67, 180–181, 356–360. Cf. *supra*, Chapter I, pp. 9–10.
[52] Reminiscences of G. Pantaleoni, Westinghouse files, quoted by Passer, *op. cit.*, p. 132.

ing steam engines or turbines.[53] Westinghouse thought he could use the heat of the atmosphere to generate power.[54] But both men knew very well that such schemes did not yet warrant a large-scale program of development.

Before designing the Pearl Street central power station, Edison built a small central power system for his lighting demonstrations at Menlo Park. This system was carefully observed and analyzed, and the result was incorporated in a better system the following year. A third experimental station was built in London in 1882 to develop larger dynamos and to test the entire system on a commercial scale. After the Pearl Street station had operated profitably for about two years, the London experimental station was dismantled. Edison also took a survey and found that users of all but 850 of the 16,000 gas jets in the Pearl Street district were willing to switch to electric light if its price were the same as gas. He had the district canvassed thoroughly to determine the number of gas jets burning each hour, and with this information he studied voltage conditions on a model network of the entire district. After the station and the power network were built, months were spent testing for leakages and other difficulties before the system was placed in operation.[55]

In a similar way, the Westinghouse alternating-current system was tested near the laboratory at Great Barrington, Massachusetts, and later in three- and four-mile transmission systems near Pittsburgh before the first large installation was attempted at Buffalo.[56] Sprague did not invest in plant or sales organization

[53] *Electrical World*, IV (Oct. 18, 1884), 151. This belief was shared by others, including Professor Elihu Thomson of the Thomson-Houston Company (*ibid.*, IX [Feb. 26, 1887], 109).

[54] Prout, *op. cit.*, pp. 314–318.

[55] Frank J. Sprague, "Digging in the Mines of the Motors," *Electrical Engineering*, 50th Anniversary Number, LIII (May 1934), 697; Passer, *op. cit.*, pp. 90–91, 186–187; Francis Jehl, *Menlo Park Reminiscences* (Dearborn, Mich.: Edison Institute, 1937–1941), II, 880.

[56] Passer, *op. cit.*, pp. 137–138.

until after his motors, manufactured by the Edison Machine Works, had commercial success.[57] Stanley constructed an experimental high-voltage line and operated it successfully for long periods of time before he undertook his first commercial installation in California.[58]

Perhaps no innovation was ever carried out with greater caution than the Niagara Falls power project. According to Edward Dean Adams, president of the Cataract Construction Company:

It was recognized by all persons in interest that there were no precedents to follow and that the special problems at Niagara were only to be worked out practically and commercially by the aid of the most advanced developments of several branches of engineering, operating in close accord. Because of their novelty, every detail should have deliberate consideration from all possible points of view, and much time should be provided for this study.[59]

After a preliminary contract had been signed, but before the purchase of the Niagara rights and properties had been finally negotiated, Edison was asked by cable in September 1889, "Has power transmission reached such development that in your judgment scheme practicable?"

Edison answered from Le Havre, "No difficulty transferring unlimited power. Will assist. Sailing today." [60]

Edison's estimate involved a power loss of about 26 per cent from turbine to Buffalo consumers and an annual rate of return of about 16 per cent on a $5,000,000 investment. Edison's plan was not considered sufficiently economical or profitable in view of the room it obviously left for technological improvement. Moreover, a decision on power transmission could easily be postponed until the mile-long discharge tunnel had been completed.[61] The company did not feel that it was risking loss of the initial investment of $2,630,000 for the tunnel because the pros-

[57] *Ibid.*, pp. 238–239.   [58] *Ibid.*, p. 309.
[59] Adams, *op. cit.*, I, 159.   [60] *Ibid.*, I, 144.
[61] *Ibid.*, I, 145–157, 159.

pects of selling 20,000 horsepower at Niagara Falls for $180,000 annually were considered good, and this amount was sufficient to cover the capital charges.[62]

Four years of considering numerous proposals from every conceivable point of view and with the costly assistance of the world's most eminent scientists and engineers elapsed before a contract for electrical equipment was finally awarded to Westinghouse in October 1893. In its contract the Westinghouse company had to guarantee, in detail, the efficiency, temperature, tensile strength, and interchangeability of each component and to accept responsibility for all patent suits that might involve the Niagara Falls Power Company.

These cautious procedures were significant because they led to technological and commercial information that allowed innovators to adjust their plans to actual technological and economic possibilities and needs, thus reducing uncertainty and the chance of loss.

Risks

The preceding sections have indicated that technological innovation in the generation and transmission of electric power, as well as its application to industrial motors, was, with one minor exception, successfully achieved by the firms making the first attempts at each innovation. According to criteria used in this study, therefore, one would not consider the series of innovations to have been very risky. Among the factors which reduced risks, the difficult entry into the industry, the ample technical and financial resources of the innovators, and the effectiveness of cautious procedures were outstanding.

The production risks of technical failure, excessive labor or

[62] *Ibid.*, I, 158. S. Dana Greene, general manager of General Electric, predicted in 1895 that as long as business conditions were "moderately prosperous" 25,000 horsepower would be used near the Falls (*Cassier's Magazine*, VIII [July 1895], 340).

material costs, or obsolescence were not significant. Some highly productive innovations, such as the substitution of carbon for copper brushes, were so simple that, if patents were not involved, they could be quickly and easily adopted.[63] Other innovations, such as a.c. motors, could be and were tested and demonstrated in the electrical manufacturers' own plant in uses typical of almost any customer's plant.[64] Nevertheless, at times technical success required more time and money than had been anticipated. The Pearl Street central power station opened nine months later than expected and cost nearly $600,000 instead of the estimated $250,000. One of the difficulties was the oscillation which occurred when both dynamos operated simultaneously, and the solution of this problem required a complicated synchronization of steam-engine governors.[65] At times there were shortages of supplies and trained personnel; but given the financial resources of the actual innovators in the last third of the nineteenth century, these problems could generally be overcome without much delay. They were not usually problems of the magnitude of Edison's search for a filament.

More serious, perhaps, was the problem of obsolescence. At various times there was uncertainty whether direct or alternating current, high- or low-voltage transmission, commutation or induction motors, and any of a number of possible phase and frequency systems would ultimately be adopted. But the limited number of firms in the industry and their great technical resources made catching up fairly easy, provided they did not wait as long as Edison, in the case of alternating versus direct current, to concede error.

Customer risks—those involving refusal to adopt new types of producers' goods for noneconomic reasons—were not important handicaps to innovators in heavy electrical equipment. In a community that had recently adjusted itself to steam-powered

[63] Passer, *op. cit.*, p. 251.   [64] *Ibid.*, p. 340.
[65] *Ibid.*, pp. 119–120.

factories, horse-drawn streetcars, and gaslight, a further change
to electric motors, trolleys, and lamps was not much of a challenge. It was a change that could be evaluated on the basis of
demonstrable differences in safety, cleanliness, and cost. For this
reason, perhaps, the change occurred with great rapidity. The
innovating manufacturers, moreover, usually created their own
immediate customers by helping to organize lighting and power
companies, accepting securities in payment for equipment, and
providing technical and business assistance. In many cases, the
innovators themselves vastly underestimated the possibilities
and demand for their innovations. In spite of all the scientific
advice marshaled by the Cataract Construction Company, the
rapid growth of electrochemical demand for current was not
foreseen. Except for the depression of 1893, inelasticity or in-
sufficiency of demand was not a serious problem.[66]

In the electrical industry the principal threats to innovators
were interference risks. For example, when the rise of Westinghouse and alternating current hurt the competitive position of
Edison General Electric, Edison wrote that his "personal desire
would be to prohibit entirely the use of alternating currents"; [67]
and, on the grounds of safety, he promoted bills in several legis-
latures that would reduce voltages to levels sharply increasing
a.c. costs. None of these was adopted, but the New York state
legislature was persuaded by Edison interests to make electrocu-
tion the means of capital punishment and to adopt Westinghouse
alternators for the purpose. It was apparently part of a scheme to
identify alternating current with danger and death.[68] Westinghouse eventually countered with legislative recommendations
against direct connections of lighting circuits with underground
mains, a feature essential to Edison's system. Later Westing-

[66] *Ibid.*, pp. 293, 356, 362–363.
[67] T. A. Edison, "Dangers of Electric Lighting," *North American Review*, CXLIX, Nov. 1889, 632.
[68] Passer, *op. cit.*, p. 169.

house tried to thwart Stanley's innovations not only by refusing to sell accessories to Stanley's customers but also by advising bankers not to deal with Stanley.[69] These attempts to repress innovation failed, however.

More serious interference risks came from the patent system, as already described. By discouraging entry, patents made the innovations of pioneering firms safer, but they increased the difficulties of latecomers attempting improvements. Westinghouse instituted a patent suit against Thomson-Houston in 1887 and obtained an agreement that severely limited Thomson-Houston's activities in the a.c. field.[70] Other latecomers, whether innovating or not, were forced out of business altogether, particularly after the Westinghouse-General Electric patent agreement of 1896.[71] But the role of patents should not be exaggerated. Both the Edison distribution patents and the basic alternating-current patents of Westinghouse were interpreted too narrowly by the courts to permit much interference with competitors.[72] Moreover, as already mentioned, there was often the possibility of acquiring a competing patent. The same year that Westinghouse bought the Gaulard and Gibbs patents for his a.c. system, Edison agents bought the rights to the Zipernowsky-Deri-Blathy alternating-current system of Ganz and Company of Budapest.[73]

The only unsuccessful innovating firm, the Bradley Electric Power Company of Yonkers, failed primarily because of the panic of 1893. It is impossible to say whether it would have succeeded under different circumstances. As it was, a producers' goods maker organized in 1893 required more than the patent on rotary converters to stay in business. It was probably the riski-

[69] Letter from William Stanley to B. G. Lamme, Dec. 29, 1913, cited by Passer, *op. cit.*, pp. 306–308.

[70] Passer, *op. cit.*, pp. 145–146.   [71] *Ibid.*, pp. 39–40, 333–334.

[72] *Ibid.*, p. 163.   [73] *Ibid.*, p. 172.

ness of business in general, not innovation in particular, that led to failure.

Summary

In the last three decades of the nineteenth century, electrical manufacturing grew into a $105,000,000 industry. By 1900 factory steam engines driving machines by means of belts and shafts were being replaced by electric motors that sharply reduced operating and maintenance costs. More important, electricity made mechanization feasible for entirely new types of operation. The innovations that resulted in this transition were introduced by a few firms which, with one exception, succeeded in the initial attempt. This record of success may be attributed to the technical experience and caution of the innovators and to the difficulty of entering the heavy-equipment part of the electric industry. Entry was limited because of patents, heavy capital requirements, and the difficulty of acquiring complex experience and market outlets. Of all the factors threatening innovation as such, patent decisions against newcomers appear to have been most serious. The alternative, however, would probably have been a greater risk of obsolescence to the original pioneering firms. But since attempts to innovate were generally successful, that is, profitable, the innovations actually attempted cannot be described as risky. The only innovating firm that failed was a new firm that could not survive the depression beginning in the year of its organization.

VI

Conclusion

ANY broad study of American economic history must necessarily cover much familiar ground, and many apparent revelations will actually be restatements of well-known characteristics and trends.[1] It is widely accepted that, as Professor John E. Sawyer has put it:

The relatively open and uncluttered scene, the abundance of natural resources, the availability of labor and capital from abroad, the timing of 19th century American expansion in relation to the long evolution of technology and of the institutions of market capitalism in the Western world—these constituted a set of conditions and objective possibilities without historical parallel, nor likely to be duplicated again.[2]

[1] In this chapter only information not previously cited will be documented in footnotes.

[2] John E. Sawyer, "Entrepreneurship in Periods of Rapid Growth: The United States in the 19th Century," *Entrepreneurship and Economic Growth* (papers presented at a conference sponsored jointly by the Com-

The present study has simply taken these conditions and possibilities and reformulated them as an explanation of the high incidence of success and, therefore, the low riskiness of technological innovation in manufacturing methods, given the degree of caution of American innovators. The fluid social structure with its materialistic orientation, the nonexistent or weak labor unions, the distinterested governments, and the competitive framework of industry are together the epitomy of low customer and low interference risks. American society in the nineteenth century was basically predictable for innovators in producers' goods because it was not a society hostile to cheaper and better methods of production. The coming of the next business depression and the exact way in which an innovation would mesh with developments in other industries were less predictable; but this uncertainty did not increase the chance of loss. On the contrary, in depressions during the nineteenth century many financially strong firms eagerly sought cost-cutting innovations, and technological developments in other industries were apt to be complementary rather than competitive, reinforcing, not undermining, the market prospects of an innovation. In this process of expansion and proliferation even obsolete methods of production faced markets that were growing, although at a slower rate, for years after a new method had been introduced. And when the decline finally came, it was apt to be slow.

Interference Risks

In the early decades, interference risks were low because novel manufacturing methods simply were not interfering with the welfare of American groups other than importers. For example, the labor that some innovations "saved" was often nonexistent, was British, or was willingly abandoned by women in house-

mittee on Economic Growth of the Social Science Research Council and the Harvard University Research Center in Entrepreneurial History, Cambridge, Mass., Nov. 12 and 13, 1954), sec. C, p. 2.

holds. When Congress appropriated money for 50,000 muskets in 1798, arms makers other than Eli Whitney could barely undertake production of 30,000 and were therefore not much upset by Whitney's offer to make 15,000 or by his contract for 10,000.[3] Moreover, as late as the 1840's American factories outside of the largest cities were not operated by members of a self-conscious class of laborers. Even in New England, the overwhelming majority of factory hands were still drawn from local farms and worked in the mills for only four or five years.[4] These workers were not afraid of losing their jobs to machines. They actually abetted the process of technological change. According to one observer of 1829:

From the habits of early life and the diffusion of knowledge by means of free schools there exists generally among the mechanics of New England a vivacity in inquiring into the first principles of the Science to which they are practically devoted. They thus frequently acquire a theoretical knowledge of the processes of the useful arts, which the English laborers may commonly be found to possess after a long apprenticeship and life of patient toil. For this reason the American mechanic appears generally more prone to invent new plans and machines than to operate upon old ones in the most perfect manner. The English mechanic, on the contrary, confining his attention simply to the immediate performance of the process of art to which he is habituated from early youth, acquires wonderful dexterity and skill.[5]

Twenty-five years later, in 1854, British industrial experts noted that, in contrast with their own country, both masters and men in America were convinced that labor-saving inventions were for their mutual benefit and that "every workman seems

[3] Jeannette Mirsky and Allan Nevins, *The World of Eli Whitney* (New York: Macmillan, 1952), pp. 137–143, 187.

[4] Victor S. Clark, *History of Manufactures in the United States* (Washington: Carnegie Institution, 1929), I, 398–399.

[5] Zachariah Allen, *The Science of Mechanics as Applied to the Present Improvements in the Useful Arts* (Providence, 1829), p. 349.

to be continually devising some new thing to assist him in his work." [6] They attributed this behavior to the scarcity of labor, flexible customs, sound practical education, and restless optimism. Again in 1904 a British observer wrote:

The apparent ease with which experiments can be conducted and changes made in factory organization in the United States at once suggests that the employer there is less hampered than his rival by interference on the part of his hands, and of this there seems little doubt. The American workman is readier to face new situations, and expects less permanence in the nature of his economic surroundings. . . . Therefore, the thought of resisting or impeding advance is seldom so seriously entertained in America as in England. . . . An English workman finds it almost impossible to imagine that the adoption of labour saving methods could result in higher wages and more employment; but the American knows that an increased demand for labour has followed the recent improvements.[7]

After the Civil War more laborers worried about technological threats to their particular jobs. As early as 1866 cobblers demonstrated against shoe machinery in New England, particularly at Lynn, Massachusetts, and teamsters cut the first oil pipelines. But such opposition was almost totally ineffective and rare. The resistance to technological change could more aptly be described as occasional "nonco-operation." Whenever such attitudes became too outspoken, as in the case of hand molders

[6] Great Britain, House of Commons, *Report of the Committee on the Machinery of the United States* (Parliamentary Papers, L, 1854–1855), pp. 578, 584. See also *New York Industrial Exhibition: Special Reports of Mr. George Wallis and Mr. Joseph Whitworth* (Parliamentary Papers, XXVI, 1854). Both are summarized by D. L. Burn, "The Genesis of American Engineering Competition, 1850–1870," *Economic History,* II (Jan. 1931), 292–311. See also John E. Sawyer, "The Social Basis of the American System of Manufacturing," *Journal of Economic History,* XIV, *The Tasks of Economic History* (1954), 361–379.

[7] Sydney J. Chapman, *Work and Wages: Part I, Foreign Competition* (London: Longmans, Green and Co., 1904), pp. 176–177.

versus molding machines in the textile machinery industry around 1900,[8] employers encountered little difficulty in bringing in new men to learn a process. In the late nineteenth century labor relations in the United States were often turbulent; but other issues took precedence over those involving technological change. Innovators did not have to be afraid of interference with innovations as such.

Unlike British employers, therefore, Americans were almost never compelled to pay unskilled machine operators skilled craftsmen's wages, or to limit the number of machines per op-

[8] George Sweet Gibb, *The Saco-Lowell Shops: Textile Machinery Building in New England, 1813–1949* (Cambridge: Harvard University Press, 1950), pp. 440–441. In the glass industry, flint glass workers and glass bottle blowers tried to oppose semiautomatic jar-making machinery in the early 1890's. They insisted that wages paid should be proportional to the output of any machine. As a result, the D. C. Ripley Glass Company of Pittsburgh, the patent owners, decided to abandon the process. Ripley, however, profited by licensing a number of nonunion shops, particularly in Huntington, W.Va. By 1898 the Glass Bottle Blowers Convention decided that the introduction of machinery was inevitable and that the only thing for local unions to do was "to make the best settlement and upon the most advantageous terms that they can get" (*Proceedings*, Glass Bottle Blowers Convention, 1898, p. 75, as quoted by George E. Barnett, *Chapters on Machinery and Labor* [Cambridge: Harvard University Press, 1926], pp. 68–75).

The International Typographical Union, the oldest national organization of labor in the United States, made no attempt to stop the substitution of lintoype for hand composition, but on the contrary favored "the recognition of such [typesetting] machines" and recommended "that subordinate unions . . . take speedy action looking to their recognition and regulation, endeavoring everywhere to secure their operation by union men upon a scale of wages which shall secure compensation equal to that paid hand compositors" (*Reports of Proceedings of the Thirty-sixth Annual Session of the International Typographical Union*, p. 181, as quoted by Barnett, *op. cit.*, pp. 8–10). On the other hand, the rapid introduction of stone-planing machinery after 1895 led to union action which forced the exclusion of such machinery from many localities between 1899 and 1910. Nevertheless, during these years one-half of the stonecutting workers were displaced by machinery (Barnett, *op. cit.*, pp. 36–64).

erator, or to hire superfluous operators for automatic machines. They did not even have to face many uncertainties about government action to protect the workers' health, such as the British Cotton Cloth Factories Act that limited the practice of "steaming" to maximum temperatures and humidities and minimum amounts of air per head.[9] Moreover, there were no workingmen's compensation laws for industrial accidents throughout the nineteenth century, the first being adopted by Maryland in 1902 and the second by Montana in 1909. Even these two acts were later declared unconstitutional. In nineteenth-century America, interference risks from the side of labor were low.

From the side of government, interference risks were equally low and partly for the same reasons. State, local, and national governments were unsympathetic with labor and were likely to comply with manufacturers' wishes in labor disputes. In some agricultural states there had, of course, been considerable prejudice against manufacturing in the early decades. Jeffersonian Republicans were cool toward industrialization because they feared that factory workers would not uphold political liberties. They felt life near a factory was bound to be irregular, unhealthy, servile, and generally demoralizing and unconducive to good citizenship. It was therefore typical that a biographer of Samuel Slater in the 1830's would write a chapter called "The Moral Influence of Manufactories in the United States" and include "documentary testimony" in the form of answers to a questionnaire on morals sent to a number of factory owners.[10] But even Jeffersonians were not opposed to technological change as such. Jefferson himself loved tinkering with machines and gadgets as much as any New England mechanic, and by 1816 he regretted that

[9] Melvin Thomas Copeland, *The Cotton Manufacturing Industry of the United States* (Cambridge: Harvard University Press, 1912), p. 93.

[10] George S. White, *Memoir of Samuel Slater: The Father of American Manufactures* (2d ed.; Philadelphia, 1836), pp. 117 ff.

I am quoted by those who wish to continue our dependence on England for manufactures. There was a time when I might have been so quoted with more candor, but within thirty years which have since elapsed, how are circumstances changed! . . . Experience has taught me that manufactures are now as necessary to our independence as to our comfort. . . . In so complicated a science as political economy, no one axiom can be laid down as wise and expedient for all times and circumstances, and for their contraries.[11]

The Constitution, moreover, provided for exclusive patents "to promote the progress of science and useful arts." Some local governments encouraged industrialization by providing for tax exemption and subsidies. Beginning with George Washington and Alexander Hamilton, officials of the Federal Government promoted mechanization by patronizing textile factories, issuing testimonials, and even arranging for imports of superior sheep as a patriotic necessity.[12] The Federal Government also took the lead in developing or supporting interchangeable manufacturing, battery-driven electric motors, the Bessemer process, hydraulic steel-mill equipment, the large-scale use of alloys and aluminum,[13] and many other innovations. It freely lent its military technicians when no others were available [14] and promoted technical education in providing for the land-grant colleges. Finally, the tariff increased the profits of manufacturing in general and therefore encouraged the rapid adoption of novel manufacturing methods. On most kinds of machinery the tariff varied

[11] Letter to Benjamin Austin, Jan. 9, 1816, *The Writings of Thomas Jefferson* (Washington: Jefferson Memorial Association, 1903), XIV, 389–392.

[12] Arthur H. Cole, *The American Wool Manufacture* (Cambridge: Harvard University Press, 1926), I, 61–64, 72–85.

[13] Charles C. Carr, *Alcoa: An American Enterprise* (New York: Rinehart & Co., 1952), pp. 111, 129.

[14] See Forest G. Hill, "The Role of the Army Engineers in the Planning and Encouragement of Internal Improvements" (unpublished doctoral dissertation, Columbia University, 1950).

from 25 to 35 per cent from 1818 until the Civil War. After the war the rate was 45 per cent, except for a reduction to 35 per cent from 1894 to 1897.[15]

Nor did the patent system as yet facilitate interference with innovation by one firm with another. Indeed, a British observer in 1876 found the American patent system incapable of preventing "a shameful copying of everything which reaches a successful sale to an extent for which there is no parallel in Europe."[16] In order to recover damages for infringements, a victim had the difficult task of proving the amount of profits made by the illegal use of his invention and also that he could and would have made the same sales but for the infringement.[17] Even when suing, patent holders mainly wanted their royalties, not restriction of use and further development by others. By and large, patent holders were thus not afraid that modification by anyone else would render their own patents less profitable. Nor were they generally in a position to use patents for collecting monopoly revenues on the output of a new type of machine as well as on the machine itself. Until the 1890's the size of a firm was generally small compared with the size of an industry, and widespread licensing or selling of machines was more profitable and feasible than attempting to monopolize the output of machines. For one thing, new machines and processes rarely produced something radically new or cheap in such industries as textile making, metalworking, and iron and steel making. Among the exceptions was the introduction of the Bessemer process and Bessemer steel; and, as a matter of fact, a number of firms did combine to use the patents at low royalty for monopolizing Bessemer steel output. In the young electrical industry, the size

[15] *Tariff Acts Passed by the Congress of the United States from 1789 to 1909* (Washington: Government Printing Office, 1909), pp. 100, 124, 328, 383, 478.

[16] *Engineering,* XXI (June 2, 1876), 454.

[17] *Tilgham* v. *Proctor,* 43 O.G. 628, C.D. 1888, and *Tatum* v. *Gregory,* 60 O.G. 1753, C.D. 1892.

of the firm was large relative to the industry; a larger proportion of patents covered basic inventions; and Westinghouse and General Electric considered it profitable to discourage Stanley and others from experimenting.

Until the 1890's the attitude of the courts toward patent suppression made it difficult to keep later innovators with a different approach from encroaching on the first innovator's terrain. In the 1890's one court still maintained that, according to the Constitution, patent rights were consideration for promoting useful arts and that patents held without use were "entitled to scant recognition at law, though necessarily to some, but to none whatever in equity." [18] At the same time another court had already declared that patents were "clearly within the constitutional provisions in respect to private property" and that the patent holder "is neither bound to use the discovery himself nor permit others to use it." [19] This latter position was not reinforced by a Supreme Court decision until 1908,[20] thus leaving matters somewhat confused during the last decade of the nineteenth century. By this decade, however, technological progress in some industries had reached such a pace and complexity that newcomers with hopes of innovating could be thwarted merely by withholding access to patents actually developed. Thus even an established firm such as Edison General Electric in 1892 considered itself unable to overcome a five-year handicap in alternating-current equipment without using patents developed by Westinghouse or Thomson-Houston.

Other interference risks from the side of business involved the

[18] *Evart Manufacturing Co.* v. *Baldwin Cycle Chain Co.*, 9 Fed. 262 (1898). See also Walton Hamilton, *Patents and Free Enterprise* (U.S. Temporary National Economic Committee, Monograph 31; Washington, 1941), pp. 51–61.

[19] *Heaton-Peninsular Button Fastener Co.* v. *Eureka Specialty Co.*, 77 Fed. 288 (1896).

[20] *Continental Paper Bag Co.* v. *Eastern Paper Bag Co.*, 210 U.S. 405 (1908).

sort of threats, rumor spreading, and conspiracies that might have confronted any enterprising competitor. But from Callender Irvine's promotion of the Wickham musket at the expense of Eli Whitney's to Edison's activities against Westinghouse and alternating current, such methods appeared to be irritants rather than genuine threats. In the climate of the nineteenth century, there was little hesitation about breaking exclusive agreements and testing the sensational claims of newcomers. Interference risks from the side of business, although often dramatic, were not significant in the aggregate.

In short, from all the major directions—labor, government, and business—interference risks remained low throughout most of the nineteenth century. To the extent that these risks changed at all, however, they increased rather than decreased and became significant after the turn of the century. A self-conscious laboring class gained more and more power in bargaining with employers. Business firms combined to form pools, trusts, and oligopolies, patent laws were reinterpreted, and production methods grew more complex. After 1900 the responses of employees and competitors to an innovation were no longer as predictable as they had been in 1850.

Customer Risks

Generalizations about the inertia and prejudice that led to customer risks are not easily formulated because two types of customers must be considered: those who bought the novel machines and those who bought the products of novel machines. The difference between these two types of customers is not the same as that between producers and consumers, respectively, because the products of new machines might themselves be producers' goods in the form of semiprocessed materials or, as in the case of machine tools, further new machines. Even in the case of textiles, the inertia of clothing manufacturers, wholesalers, and retailers must be added to that of consumers.

In spite of these limitations, an over-all statement that customer risks were not serious for the innovations actually attempted in the industries studied is safe. Americans were able to experiment with new manufacturing methods because of lack of inertia and prejudice on the part of three groups: labor, consumers, and small capitalists.

British observers found that "traditional methods had little hold upon the American as compared with the English artisan, and processes holding the least promise of improvement were quickly tested."[21] Moreover,

the willingness on the part of the American Public to buy what is offered them, if it in any way answers the purpose, has given a great advantage to the North American manufacturer over his European competitor, who has to contend with habits and prejudices of centuries standing, and even now almost in full vigor. . . . In the United States they overlook defects more than in Europe, and are satisfied if a machine intended to supersede domestic labour will work even imperfectly, while we insist on its being thoroughly well made and efficient.[22]

The small capitalist could afford to finance an experimental machine because he could find a market for this machine or its products even before all defects had been eliminated. There was, however, a greater reluctance to experiment with expensive equipment even when the proposed owners of such equipment were themselves wealthier to a corresponding degree. Thus, one of the important factors that kept innovation more active in machine tools than in textile machinery after 1850 seems to have been the lower cost of a novel machine tool. Moreover, the least expensive machine tools were developed most rapidly in the United States and surpassed similar British tools at a time when

[21] Great Britain, House of Commons, *Special Reports of Mr. George Wallis and Mr. Joseph Whitworth*, p. 15.

[22] *Reports of Juries*, London Exhibition of 1862, class XXXI, pp. 2–3, quoted by Burn, *op. cit.*, p. 306.

expensive heavy tools remained inferior.[23] The same reluctance to introduce expensive changes also helps to account for the relative backwardness of the American iron and steel industry compared with other industries and compared with the major European iron and steel industries throughout most of the century. It can even be observed at the very beginning of American industrialization. Samuel Slater found a backer for his spinning frame immediately upon arriving in New York, but a generation later Thomas C. Lewis had to travel for a year before he found someone willing to finance a puddling and rolling mill. Even after the Civil War, ironmasters failed to install Player hot-blast stoves, Siemens furnaces, and Porter-Allen engines long after older equipment should have been scrapped. When Andrew Carnegie finally appeared on the scene, his "scrap-heap" policy evoked little admiration from his colleagues.

Reluctance to adopt expensive novel machines, however, even if due to inertia or prejudice, does not necessarily constitute a customer risk. It constitutes a risk only if there is a highly specialized producers' goods maker who has tooled up especially for producing the new equipment. Such producers practically did not exist for trains of rolls and furnaces in the iron and steel industry.

Customer risks were probably serious in retarding sales of the first American textile mills and cast steel makers; but insofar as losses occurred, they can hardly be attributed solely to irrational inertia and prejudice. The quality of the earliest American cloth and steel was not only inferior but irregular; and when superior qualities appeared, it was natural for potential users of these materials to wait to see if the new standards could be maintained. The production risks of one decade became the customer risks of the next.

[23] Great Britain, House of Commons, *Special Reports of Mr. George Wallis and Mr. Joseph Whitworth*, p. 112 *et passim*.

Timing Risks

The relation between technological change and fluctuations in the level of business activity has many aspects, but most of these fall outside the scope of this study. Not even the possibility that technological change made production more roundabout, capital commitments heavier, depressions deeper, and business, therefore, riskier has been a part of this investigation. This has been a study of the riskiness of producers' goods innovation only, not of business in general, and for a variety of reasons innovations were introduced with fairly uniform success in periods preceding crises and during the following depressions.

The threat to an innovation by an unexpected business depression has been called the risk of unlucky timing. It has been suggested that timing risks should be considered risks of innovation only insofar as poor timing might have caused greater losses among innovating organizations than among other new or expanding firms. Such losses might have been greater because an innovation used a higher proportion of fixed capital or incurred a greater expense in trying to "iron out bugs." All this is theoretically plausible, but no evidence indicates that it was practically important.

The impact of a depression on a producers' goods innovation was essentially its impact on the markets of industries in which that innovation might have been used. If the markets of these industries dwindled fast, manufacturers naturally were less attracted to further illiquid investment than if the contraction was mild, involving the value rather than the number of sales. Under the latter circumstance, buying cost-reducing equipment was often a successful and even mandatory policy. Those who had just installed such equipment or were ready to put it on the market were therefore frequently able to strengthen their position in an industry. An early example was the prosperity of the Boston Manufacturing Company, which expanded both plant and profits while other cotton mills failed and prices fell from 1815 to 1820. Later examples occurred during all the other depressions, particularly that of 1873. It will be recalled that although prices fell sharply in that depression, steel production continued to rise and pig iron production fell only to the level of 1871.[24] Those who had just introduced the new blast furnaces and steel mills crushed others who had not and paid dividends to their own stockholders.[25] The early 1870's were also the beginning of a new period of textile machinery innovation, including many imported innovations. The market for textiles shrank after 1873, but it was not so bad that some firms did not buy innovations and force others to follow suit. The machine shops therefore prospered, paying dividends averaging as high as 22 per cent from 1874 to 1879 and accumulating a cash surplus as well.[26] The machine-tool builders were hit rather hard, but none of the major innovating firms failed, and some even prospered with orders from foreign armories. Others used the slack times to perfect such tools as the automatic turret lathe, automatic gear cutters, and the universal grinder; and these were placed on the market during the depth of the depression.

The pattern was repeated with variations during all later depressions of the century, including that of 1893. By introducing cost-cutting innovations, Carnegie could expand production 70 per cent and profits 67 per cent from 1893 to 1895. Among the innovations at his plants was the fuel-saving substitution of electric motors for steam engines. These motors were designed in co-operation with Westinghouse engineers and were roughly similar to others being installed throughout industry. Westinghouse and General Electric had each developed their industrial alternating-current motors during the early 1890's and brought

[24] James M. Swank, *History of the Manufacture of Iron in All Ages and Particularly in the United States from Colonial Times to 1891* (Philadelphia: American Iron and Steel Association, 1892), pp. 36–37, 511.

[25] *Supra,* Chapter II, pp. 34, 41, 58–59.

[26] Gibb, *op. cit.,* pp. 200–202.

them on the market just after the business collapse.[27] Sales were nevertheless so encouraging that new models were brought out in 1894, 1895, and 1896. The chief bottleneck was not the customers' lack of cash but their lack of access to alternating-current power circuits.[28] The sales of alloy steel makers likewise continued to expand because the substitution of alloy steel cut the production costs of other manufacturers. Machine-tool builders were again hard hit, but none of the major innovating firms went out of business and many once more used the slack times for developing new ideas. In both the textile and the textile machinery industry, meanwhile, price competition had become so severe that margins for innovation and installation faded. The Drapers could not find loom builders who would make their automatic looms; and after they reluctantly brought their own model on the market in 1895, they found that saving half the labor cost of weaving was not always a sufficient reason for scrapping old looms. On the basis of this innovation, however, the Draper corporation soon eliminated practically all competition in plain-goods looms.

In general, timing risks were minimized in the nineteenth century for two reasons. One involved the organization of industries and the other the cautions approach of innovators. Most industries were organized into a large number of firms of unequal size and resources. The large number constituted a competitive market which tended to maintain the level of output in the face of price declines. The inequality among firms in size and credit rating made depressions a particularly auspicious time for adopting cost-cutting innovations and driving weak competitors out of business. For specialized producers' goods makers, the maintenance of output meant a continued market for replacements; and

[27] Edison's first commercial direct-current central power station was also introduced just before a depression, in Sept. 1882.

[28] Harold C. Passer, *The Electrical Manufacturers* (Cambridge: Harvard University Press, 1953), pp. 296–301.

the aggressive competition meant a market for innovations. That these innovations were developed cautiously has been pointed out for each industry studied and will be summarized later.

Years such as 1873, 1883, and 1893 were not, therefore, black years for men who had backed producers' goods innovations in manufacturing. This is not to say that depressions never contributed to the failure of unsuccessful innovators. No doubt Henry W. Oliver might have operated his Clapp-Griffiths steel converters a few years longer if the depression of 1883 had not intervened. A generation earlier William Kelly might likewise have continued his experiments after the depression of 1857. But largely because of ignorance of both chemistry and the requirements of mass production, these attempts had none of the ingredients of success anyway. Unlucky timing was not their only misfortune. By contrast, a genuine case in which unlucky timing played a part was Aaron Dennison's adaptation of interchangeable manufacturing to watchmaking. The watches made were standard types, but the machine tools that made some of the parts were novel. The company failed in 1857, but in 1859 production was resumed with the same equipment under different owners, and the venture became the successful Waltham Watch Company. Among all the innovations studied, failures due solely to poor timing appeared to be exceedingly rare.

Production Risks

For producers' goods innovators during the nineteenth century the greatest risks were production risks. These risks involved inability to predict whether an innovation would function at all and, if so, whether it would suit the changing level of skills and resources well enough to be profitable. Sufficient amounts of the right kind of labor, materials, and auxiliary equipment had to be available at suitable prices for use in conjunction with the producers' good. The new machine or process had to function with a degree of efficiency that was comparable or superior to alternatives. The commodity produced likewise had to be comparable or in some way superior to its substitutes. If superior alternatives were likely to be developed later, the delay had to be sufficient to allow the innovation the usual profits and capital amortization.

In the introduction of new methods of making iron and steel, fabricating textiles, working metals, and handling electric power, some of these risks had to be faced and losses resulted. Only uncertainty about the availability of labor can easily be discounted as having been a serious production risk. The lack of skilled workers may at times have delayed the installation of a new process, but there seems to be no record of heavy losses or failure for this reason. The skills that were lacking around 1800 were those of the machine-building trades, the machines themselves being designed to overcome the scarcity of other skills. Machine building, however, required skills much like those of carpenters, blacksmiths, and millwrights; and of these America had a considerable and talented supply. Employing such men, Slater and Whitney found that progress was slow, but not fatally slow. Later, Whitney-trained and Slater-trained men helped found other shops and the skill of machine building was handed down in several intertwined genealogies.

Nor was the lack of complementary trades in earlier and later stages of production much of a threat to mechanization. After the Newburyport Woolen Manufactory failed, the Scholfields could profitably adjust their carding machines to the requirements of household spinners. At other times it was realized from the beginning that all stages of manufacture had to be organized simultaneously, and this need inspired integration of processes and further innovation. As American industry expanded, there were times when a producers' goods maker moved West ahead of his labor supply and had to retreat. This happened to the machine-tool builders, Warner and Swasey, who moved to Chicago in 1881 and back to Cleveland in 1882. But these moves were not at the same time attempts at technological innovation.

A production risk that was serious, however, was the inability to predict the outcome of new chemical processes, particularly those which affected certain innovations in iron and steel making. In the design of mechanical and electrical equipment the relevant scientific principles were known or could be worked out as needed. But in smelting and refining iron, a critical area of uncertainty could not be removed. Chances had to be taken, and several times great losses and failures resulted. These losses were not caused by lack of proper raw materials in the same sense that early woolen factories suffered from the lack of merino sheep. Suitable ores, clays, and coal seams existed in America. But until the development and spread of chemical knowledge, technicians did not know how to test for suitability accurately and cheaply.

There were other novel manufacturing methods that failed to perform efficiently compared with established practice. For example, Thorp's ring spindles and the Springfield Armory's attempts at rifle-barrel rolling were failures. But these and similar failures involved only small-scale machines and resulted in only small-scale losses. Necessarily, such failures individually became less perilous to an enterprise as the average size of firms grew larger. As a matter of fact, in the last decades of the century, such failures resulted from only a small proportion of any established firm's total attempts at innovation. The explanation lies partly in the rise of engineers who knew how to avoid expensive errors and partly in the abundant opportunities for innovation, the limited number of persons acquainted with these opportunities, and hence a concentration on the most obvious possibilities.

The rise of engineers and the growth of science in the course of the nineteenth century cannot be overestimated as a factor that kept production risks low for innovations in manufacturing methods. A mechanic speaking in the 1890's recalled that in the 1840's, "when I was an apprentice, we simply had parts and plans on a poplar board, roughly pencilled and chalked in . . . nothing like the details and dimensions, with elaborate blue prints, as today." [29] An engineer referred to this early period as "the chalk age of mechanical engineering" and emphasized the advantages of having an engineering society to which papers could be presented and in whose transactions difficulties and discoveries might be published. He remembered that the leading technicians of his youth had "had no means beyond the little circle which each one had about him, of communicating to others the different problems of their day and of their generation." [30]

Offhand it might appear that ignorance and lack of precision made technological innovation rather hazardous. As a matter of fact, whenever the initial expense amounted to several thousand dollars, technological illiteracy discouraged original innovations almost entirely. Before 1860 even equipment of standard design was so liable to break down that innovations were viewed with extreme skepticism. One man remembered that

we had no opportunity of learning to give the proper proportion to shafts, wheels, and things of that kind, and the mill was put up rather haphazard. The consequence was, that just as soon as the mill was started the trouble commenced. I remember, in one week, working fifteen days—working nights and Sundays, etc.—and it was that way all the time I was there. I left there about a year after the mill was started, and they had not gotten over their troubles then—break-downs and other troubles which they met with. But the business has gone on.[31]

Under these circumstances expensive changes in equipment design were rarely endorsed and then only after the most pains-

[29] Comment by Ezra Fawcett in "The Old and the New," *Transactions of the American Society of Mechanical Engineers*, XVI (1895), 752.

[30] J. F. Holloway in *Transactions*, XVI, 756.

[31] Robert Allison in *Transactions*, XVI, 760.

taking and fumbling preparations. Scientific engineering vastly simplified these procedures and enhanced the predictability of results. Andrew Carnegie thus believed that chemical engineering removed nine-tenths of the risks from the iron industry. Similarly, it was found that the arithmetic estimates which had taken Boyden months of calculation in the designing his novel water turbines could have been solved in minutes by the use of calculus.[32] Before constructing his early central power stations, Edison had invariably built elaborate models of the circuits to be supplied, and then he had spent weeks measuring voltages. One day Edison asked Frank J. Sprague, a man with a technical college education, if he could not "figure it out." As a result, the work of weeks was reduced to hours and minutes.[33] The remarks of one expert made in 1907 with respect to the electrical industry can be extended to many other industries with equal validity:

A few weeks ago a gentleman asked me what I considered to be the most important event in the history of electrical development. In reply . . . I should answer the advent of the young man with a college training. . .

The technically trained man has shown the possibility of predicting results theoretically which previously had to be determined experimentally, at very great expense, and I am convinced that the entrance of the college man into electrical engineering has been the most important event in the history of the industry.[34]

The picture was, of course, somewhat different for the less expensive innovatoins, those in which the final mechanism would cost only a few hundred or perhaps one or two thousand dollars. Before equipment assumed large-scale, expensive

[32] William E. Worthen in *Transactions*, XVI, 749.

[33] *Electrical Engineering*, LIII (May 1934), 697; Harriet Sprague, *Frank J. Sprague and the Edison Myth* (New York: William Frederick Press, 1947), p. 12.

[34] Philip A. Lange in an address delivered at the Engineers' Club of Manchester, England, quoted by Harriet Sprague, *op. cit.*, p. 12.

proportions, many such innovations came from independent inventors who did not themselves contemplate the commercial use or sale of the new producers' good. These independent inventors were then, in "the chalk age of mechanical engineering," the men who took the risks of trying to acquire superior information—how to design a more efficient machine. Usually an inventor had to demonstrate the superiority of his machine to a person with the financial recources for establishing a going commercial concern, thus sharing his superior information before he could hope for installation and gains from royalties or profits. After perhaps many failures and much poverty in garrets, the last inventor and the first successful innovator could divide the spoils. No doubt innovators at times backed unsuccessful inventions of producers' goods. But invariably the caution of innovators increased disproportionately with the scale of investment. And, as the century wore on, innovations did require a larger and larger scale of investment, and amateur inventors encountered increasing difficulty in acquiring information and proving theories about producers' goods. As the Industrial Revolution advanced, larger and larger amounts of capital and more and more highly specialized training became prerequisites for developing new manufacturing methods. The amateurs therefore left these problems to engineers and turned their attention toward new fields: chemistry, internal combustion, and electronics.

As a matter of fact, the imaginations of amateurs had never been as much attracted by problems of machining gears and valves rapidly, cheaply, and with high precision as by the possibility of creating revolutions in transportation and communication or mechanizing familiar activities around home and farm. The inventors of novel manufacturing methods were almost always mechanics or engineers professionally familiar with the problems of an industry. Even during the "chalk age" these men were naturally less likely to overlook vital details than complete amateurs; and their suggestions were therefore more likely to be safe, that is, freer of hidden flaws.

For all these professionals the proliferating American economy created abundant opportunities for innovation as a result of interacting technological and economic factors. But only a few men even among the experts were in a favorable position for seeing these opportunities, and they had a tendency to underestimate the possibilities. Consequently they concentrated on the most obvious and safe innovations.

To understand this tendency to underestimate opportunities, one must remember that certain kinds of producers' goods are vertically related to others in preceding and succeeding stages of production. An innovation at any stage Q is therefore likely to change, either qualitatively or quantitatively, the demand for goods at the preceding stage P or the supply to a following stage R. If the change is quantitative, that is, if the innovation makes mass production possible at stage Q, it is likely to make similar innovations economical at the preceding stage P by increasing the demand for Q's inputs and at the following stage R by increasing the supply and reducing the price of Q's output.

The effect is then likely to be compounded because the secondary innovation at the preceding stage P may increase the supply to stage Q and reduce costs to such an extent that a tertiary scale-increasing innovation may new become feasible at Q. Likewise the scale-increasing innovation at succeeding stage R may increase the demand for Q's products in such a way that tertiary innovations are made feasible from this direction as well. Finally, if the output of stage R is also the input of stage P, then each innovation will have still further repercussions.

A similar but possibly somewhat less rapidly cumulative

effect may occur if the innovation makes mass production of consumers' goods possible.[35] If the consumers' goods industry X requires inputs A and B, an innovation may economize on the amount of A per unit of output. If it is assumed that demand is elastic, output will be increased, and therefore the demand for input B will increase. As a result, scale-increasing innovations may become economical in industry B, which, in turn, can make a further expansion of consumers' goods industry X possible. Moreover, if input B is also used in consumers' goods industry Z, innovations become possible there which may increase the demand for its other inputs C and D. The increase in the production of B can make possible further innovations in the industries that supply industry B, perhaps leading to repercussions along the lines of P, Q, and R, discussed above.

Such relations as these are not mere speculation but have actually characterized the Industrial Revolution since its beginning. In terms of *quantity,* lower-priced iron made the wider use of machinery possible, which allowed the development of large-scale machine tools, and this reduced the price of machinery still more. The resulting lower price of blast-furnace and rolling-mill machinery once more lowered the price of iron. In terms of *quality,* superior grades of iron or steel made possible degrees of machine-tool precision that allowed the construction of entirely new types of machines which could themselves be improved by novel alloys. The first reciprocating steam engine built by Watt, and sold to John Wilkinson to power the bellows of Wilkinson's ironworks at Broseley, could not have been constructed if Wilkinson himself had not invented a new method of precision boring.

Since the eighteenth century, the iron and engineering industries of Britain have influenced one another in this manner,

[35] See Marcus Fleming, "External Economies and the Doctrine of Balanced Growth," *Economic Journal,* LXV (June 1955), 249–250.

but in the United States the interrelatedness of innovations did not become conspicuous until the 1840's. In the earlier period the principal market for iron was among country blacksmiths; most machinery was built of wood and powered by pitch-back water wheels; and American machine-tool innovations were concentrated in the firearms industry. The demand for iron was so small that when the Baltimore and Ohio Railroad was begun in 1830 the capacity of all refining forges accessible to the coast was too small to furnish the 15,000 tons of strap iron required to face its wooden rails.[36]

By the 1850's, however, the expansion of the railroads, the coming of iron turbines, the Corliss steam engine, the application of interchangeable manufacturing to new products, and the like had made opportunities for innovation in various industries closely interrelated. The railroads inspired blast furnaces and rolling mills that were oriented from their beginning toward a larger volume of production than were any previous establishments. In the largest rail mill, the Trenton Works, costs were reduced so far that iron became competitive with wood and brick as a building material. In large blast furnaces, steam engines were replacing water power. Water power itself was harnessed more and more by standardized and mass-produced iron turbines. These were mostly Boyden turbines, developed in 1844, and since they required an unprecedented accuracy of workmanship, they depended on further improvements in metalworking.[37] They also depended on innovations in iron casting, which was required for pipes and casings; but these innovations were developed independently of this need.[38]

In the first half of the century, the steam engine had little effect on factory development;[39] but the Corliss valve gear,

[36] Senate Document 192, 20th Congress, 1st Session, quoted in Clark, *op. cit.*, I, 511.

[37] James B. Francis, *Lowell Hydraulic Experiments* (Boston, 1855), pp. 2–4, quoted in Clark, *op. cit.*, I, 407.

[38] Clark, *op. cit.*, I, 416.   [39] *Ibid.*, I, 403.

patented in 1849, rapidly accelerated its introduction by allowing great savings in steam when only a fraction of the machines in a factory were in use.[40] Around 1850 the first steam engines with interchangeable parts were placed on the market, and interchangeable manufacturing methods were also applied to farm machinery and sewing machines. The wider use of machine tools essential for interchangeable manufacturing now justified interchangeability in machine tools themselves.

The interrelatedness of innovation in key industries by 1850 set the basis for an accelerated pace of mutually reinforcing changes. This pace continued through wars and depressions into the twentieth century. It was not, however, as rapid as might have been feasible on the basis of technology alone. If the principles of technological development had been more thoroughly understood, the pace of innovation might have been accelerated by interindustry co-operation. As Professor Scitovsky has pointed out, planners do not have better foresight than isolated entrepreneurs; but they have the advantage of acting simultaneously on interrelated projects.[41] Independent

[40] H. W. Dickinson, *A Short History of the Steam Engine* (New York: Macmillan, 1939), p. 147

[41] Tibor Scitovsky, "Two Concepts of External Economies," *Journal of Political Economy*, LXII (April 1954), 143–151, LXIII (Oct. 1955), 450–451.

Professor John E. Sawyer has reversed this hypothesis, suggesting that economic development would have proceeded far more slowly if it had been left to centralized initiative. In his view American entrepreneurs tended to overestimate the returns and underestimate the difficulties of their projects. But these errors were frequently matched by similar errors in complementary projects, and all the errors collectively generated the conditions for realizing the original visions. This position obviously involves the assumption that centralized planning would have meant increased caution but not increased co-ordination among complementary projects—an assumption that may or may not have been justified for the nineteenth century. It should be noted that the projects which Sawyer had in mind were primarily "the building of basic facilities, canals, railroads, ports, cities." See John E. Sawyer, "Entrepreneurship in Periods of Rapid Growth: The United States in the 19th Century," pp. 1–7.

entrepreneurs, on the other hand, must depend largely on market prices to formulate their decisions; and these prices reveal mostly what is, not what can be. Innovations are therefore likely to proceed on a piecemeal, even hesitant basis.

Is a slower pace of innovation less risky than a fast pace? The answer could be negative if innovations became possible only because of complementary developments in other industries. But many producers' goods innovations do not depend on wider markets or cheaper or higher-quality supplies. The direct application of scientific discoveries to overhaul an old process and other revisions, some brilliant, some routine, are all likely to occur at a pace not necessarily affected by the rate of adjustment to complementary industries. In the nineteenth century one might say that such *intra-industry* innovations occurred at a faster pace, relative to objective possibilities, than *inter-industry* innovations that depended on changes in demand and supply among a variety of industries. When such independent streams of innovation were finally brought together, they were likely to result in more profitable and productive combinations than might have been the case if they had been combined in less perfected form. With a larger proportion of inherently safe opportunities available, innovation was likely to be less risky, even without considering other factors that worked in the same direction at the time.

The pace of inter-industry innovation was, however, not only retarded because entrepreneurs were not *organized* to act simultaneously on interrelated projects. It was also held back because innovating entrepreneurs and their technical assistants were largely *uninformed* about matters outside of their own industries.[42] The lack of personnel trained in more than one specialty, the lack of publications catering to businessmen of

[42] For some implications of this type of nineteenth-century isolation, see Arthur H. Cole, "A New Set of Stages," *Explorations in Entrepreneurial History*, VIII (Dec. 1955), 99–107.

more than one industry, and the entrepreneurs' limited resources due to the small scale of enterprise made it uneconomic
and even impossible to keep up with other industries. Detached
from the broad stream of technological and economic development and viewed only in terms of each entrepreneur's own
limited knowledge, any single innovation was bound to seem
less promising, that is, riskier, than it actually was. With their
limited horizons entrepreneurs could not foresee the many
complementary repercussions of changes they might authorize
in their own plants. They tended to view their own innovations
as the only change in a world that was static for their immediate purposes and analyzed an innovation's possible effects in a
manner somewhat like that of economists holding all other
things equal. When the future was viewed as uncertain, the
feeling of uncertainty therefore had overtones of pessimism
rather than optimism.

The fact that in certain producers' goods industries innovations time and again dovetailed with developments in complementary industries and resulted in windfall profits did not seem
to penetrate into entrepreneurial consciousness: no widespread
entrepreneurial learning process took place. If it had, a more
dynamic image of economic development, with elements other
than the alternation of prosperity and depression, the threat of
lower tariffs, and greater silver coinage, might have prevailed.
It might have been more obvious that continual innovation was
a matter of keeping industries in balance with one another
along the same road and not of pushing in different directions
toward rapidly diminishing, and then negligible, returns.[43] As a
matter of fact, such men as William Sellers, George Westinghouse, and Andrew Carnegie did view the economy in these
terms. They were among the few who could understand the

[43] Since the most distinguished economists of the century also thought
in terms of diminishing returns for capital, the businessmen's failure to
think otherwise can hardly be condemned.

real meaning of the engineer H. L. Gantt's contemporary observation that "the usual way of doing things is always the wrong way." [44]

If this attitude had been widely prevalent, innovators might have allowed a smaller margin for error, the pace of innovation might have been faster, and the number of unsuccessful innovations might have been considerably higher. As it was, however, the lack of co-ordination that made it inherently impossible for certain producers' goods innovations to proceed at a highly risky pace created at the same time a subjective outlook that made innovations seem riskier than they actually were.

Before going on, it might be well to recall a few specific illustrations of delayed innovation, windfall gains, and the dovetailing of innovations in separate industries in the nineteenth century. Some cases of undue delay could be found in changing blast-furnace construction, particularly in the types of blowing engines used. By 1875 furnace managers were convinced that "almost any expense to increase the economy of blowing engines is warranted." [45] They wanted an engine that was both economical of steam and free of breakdowns. Years passed, nevertheless, before furnace managers made any attempts to adopt the economical and tough compound engines that had proved themselves on the Atlantic Ocean. They believed that, being more complicated, such engines must also be more delicate.[46] In the same decade nickel and chromium alloys were applied to such engines. These alloys had been developed for entirely different, primarily military, purposes; but now they allowed the construction of lighter and more powerful blowing engines, which in turn allowed a number of highly

[44] Frank Barkley Copley, *Frederick W. Taylor, Father of Scientific Management* (New York: Harper and Brothers, 1923), I, 112.

[45] A. L. Holley, "Some Pressing Needs of Our Iron and Steel Manufacturers," *Transactions of the American Institute of Mining Engineers,* IV (Oct. 1875), 78.

[46] *Ibid.,* p. 80.

productive changes in blast-furnace design and blasting technique.[47] As a result, pig iron prices declined relatively and absolutely. A similar interaction had previously occurred in factory engines, metals, and forge equipment. The introduction of more powerful steam hammers made forging more economical and reliable, and consequently factory steam engines were no longer confined to the slow-running, beam types.[48]

Examples need not be confined to cases involving steam engines and ironmaking. A typical windfall gain was the unexpected demand for electric power by metallurgical and chemical firms at Niagara Falls. The electrolytic manufacture of aluminum at Niagara in turn facilitated the manufacture of alundum, a cheap new abrasive; and this development dovetailed with the invention of a grinding machine whose cutting action was sixteen times as efficient as that of any other machine tool and of such unparalleled accuracy that its feed mechanism could serve as a micrometer.[49]

The large hydroelectric power stations had themselves provided windfall profits to steel mills that were installing hydraulic forging presses for armaments. In this case there was a need for generator rings of a more uniform density than could be achieved with steam hammers.[50] These rings as well as the magnet frames of large generators were also too large to be machined by any but heavy portable tools. Once such portable tools had been constructed, a variety of other uses for them appeared.[51] The lower price of electricity that resulted from the hydroelectric stations in turn reduced the operating cost of these portable tools. Electric motors improved the accuracy,

[47] Charles M. White, *Blast Furnace Blowing Engines, Past, Present—and Future* (New York: Newcomen Society, 1947), pp. 18–20.

[48] Clark, *op. cit.*, I, 416–417.

[49] Mildred McClary Tymeson, *The Norton Story* (Worcester: Norton Co., 1953), pp. 85–87, 92–94.

[50] Clark, *op. cit.*, III, 86.   [51] *Ibid.*, III, 185.

speed, and quality of other machine tools and made them more automatic. Hydraulic forging presses, electrolytic chemical manufacturing, novel machine tools, electric motors, and the Niagara power installation each had more limited possibilities without the others; and when introduced independently, each must have seemed riskier than it actually was.

Any number of similar cases could be cited. Punch-type forming tools were first adapted to hard metals in bicycle manufacturing around 1890 but quickly found a windfall market in laminated armatures. The capacity and accuracy of such machines consequently had to be increased, and these improvements made them suitable for still other purposes. Cheap electricity made electric steel furnaces economical and increased the supplies of high-grade alloys; and one of these, silicon steel, reduced the cost of electricity by improving motor and generator cores. Like the coming of steam power, electric power facilitated the mining of coal and ores, specifically by allowing the mechanization of underground machinery and underground transportation on an unprecedented scale. There were many other cases of interaction—for example, the interdependence of superior alloys, more accurate machine tools, and ball bearings.

Obviously, not all producers' goods participated in this spiral. The mery-go-round admitted only producers' goods that were themselves producing certain types of producers' goods. Excluded, for example, was textile machinery. A superior carding machine might induce innovations in spinning either by way of price and scale or by way of quality. If the change in spinning were a great increase in scale, further innovations in the scale of carding are possible, but the reciprocal effect would definitely be limited. Thread is not used in the construction of carding machines; nor are the tools that shape carding machines, or the engines that power them, made out of cloth. Textile machines benefit as much as machine tools and motors from advances in metallurgy and power engineering. Their cost of construction and operation is likely to be reduced an equal amount by equal causes. That is their supply side. On the demand side, however, the fact that they borrow innovations from other industries without selling commodities to these industries means that they cannot expand and innovate with the increased scale of operations of these industries per se. During the nineteenth century the demand for metals, power equipment, and engineering tools grew at a much faster rate than the demand for textiles because of the strategic importance of these industries in the Industrial Revolution. The complementarity of innovations here was, in fact, the essence of that revolution. As a mechanic reminiscing in the 1890's pointed out:

In the olden time, shops made all the bolts, nuts, set-screws, oil-cups, in fact, everything required in the construction of machinery, and also all the small tools required, such as taps and dies, reamers, etc., while now all these things are specialties, and can be bought from the makers and dealers at prices which preclude the possibility of machine-shops making them, and we get a much better article than we could make.[52]

The interrelatedness and consequent expansion of demand in metallurgical and engineering industries were sufficiently conducive to innovation to offset the inhibiting effect of increasing lump-sum costs per innovation through larger and more complicated machines. Textile machinery also became larger and more complicated, but no interrelatedness led to an accelerated expansion of demand. The same change from wooden to metal construction that stimulated innovation in one set of industries was discouraging in others.[53]

[52] Comment by Robert Allison in *Transactions*, XVI, 761.

[53] Interrelatedness in terms of scale also existed among the tools, mechanisms, and degrees of specialization of lumberjacks, millwrights, and carpenters. This interrelatedness was developed to unprecedented

The comparative development of these two sectors of the economy before and after 1850 is best illustrated by statistics. From 1830 to 1850 the American population almost doubled; the number of cotton spindles tripled; and the annual production of pig iron also tripled. From 1850 to 1900 the population tripled. The number of cotton spindles multiplied 5 times, and the annual consumption of raw cotton fibers 6 times. Pig iron production, however, increased 26 times.[54] In 1869 the amount of mechanical power used in manufacturing was estimated at 2.3 million horsepower, and 48 per cent of this was still applied directly from water wheels and turbines. From 1869 to 1889 the amount of power derived from steam engines increased at an average annual rate 14 times greater than the rate of increase from water wheels and turbines.[55] Meanwhile from 1869 to 1899 the average number of horsepower per wage earner increased from 1.1 to 2.7 in cotton manufacturing and from 2.2 to 7.4 in the iron and steel industry.[56] During these three decades the consumption of raw cotton increased 4.4 times, the production of pig iron 7.5 times, and steel production 138 times.[57]

The low degree of reciprocal complementarity with other industries and the relatively slow expansion of demand after 1850 a priori made an equal expenditure on innovation riskier in the textile industry than in the other industries studied. This

---

levels in early America with its abundant forests and water-power sites. But the limitations of wood as a harnesser and transmitter of energy set low limits to the size and expense of particular pieces of equipment.

[54] U.S. Bureau of the Census, *Census of Manufacturers, 1905* (Washington, 1907), Bull. 74, p. 17, Bull. 78, p. 37; Swank, *op. cit.*, pp. 366–367; Copeland, *op. cit.*, pp. 5, 6, 34, 70.

[55] U.S. Census Office, *Twelfth Census: Manufactures* (Washington, 1902), VII, cccxvi.

[56] *Ibid.*, VII, cccxxx.

[57] U.S. Census Bureau, *op. cit.*, Bull. 74, p. 17, Bull. 78, pp. 37, 69; Swank, *op. cit.*, p. 511.

difference accounts in large part for the fact that few innovations were attempted and that it therefore appeared to be an "old" industry with most opportunities exploited. The metalworking and iron industries were equally old, but here entrepreneurs were confronted with an expanding series of opportunities, and they responded with innovations. They were by no means less cautious. On the contrary, case after case revealed the most painstaking procedure leading to the smallest possible commitment of capital. Unavoidable risks came primarily from ignorance of metallurgical chemistry, and indeed most of the innovators taking these risks were merely trying to introduce processes that had already achieved success abroad. Large-scale handling rather than metallurgy was the area of outstanding American originality. On the rare occasions when considerable sums were expended on textile machinery innovation, considerable results followed, particularly in the case of the Northrop loom. Thus it appears that the innovations actually attempted in textile machinery were not riskier than those attempted in more promising fields.

In none of the industries studied was the pace of innovation and imitation sufficiently rapid and unpredictable to make obsolescence or "the perennial gale of creative destruction" a great threat to innovators or even to routine manufacturers. The expanding, tariff-protected American economy easily allowed something old (with its slightly different quality) to keep growing for decades, although more slowly, after the new had been introduced. Ring spindles were a commercial success by 1845, but the number of mule spindles continued to increase until around 1900. The sales of speeders for roving cotton kept rising from the Civil War until the 1880's although superior fly frames had already appeared on the market. More than ten years elapsed before the Northrop automatic loom appreciably reduced the sales of other looms. Forges and bloomeries kept expanding after the introduction of puddling and rolling; charcoal smelting expanded until around 1890; the number of puddling furnaces reached a maximum twenty-five years after Bessemer steel was successfully made in 1867; and crucible steel production increased for some thirty-nine years after the first successful open hearth of 1870. Moreover, after expansion ceased, the rate of decline was usually slower than the immediately preceding rate of growth. In the post-Civil War period the exceptions were such cases as that of Francis Curtis' automatic screw machine of 1871, which was superseded by Spencer's automatic turret lathe of 1874. It was a typically small-scale device still in the experimental stage when superseded.

Schumpeter always emphasized what he considered the extreme riskiness of technological innovation:

The history of the productive apparatus of the iron and steel industry from the charcoal furnace to our own type of furnace, or the history of power production from the overshot water wheel to the modern power plant . . . illustrate the same process of industrial mutation—if I may use that biological term—that incessantly revolutionizes the economic structure *from within,* incessantly destroying the old one, incessantly creating a new one. This process of Creative Destruction is the essential fact about capitalism. . . .

Every piece of business strategy . . . must be seen in its role in the perennial gale of creative destruction . . . as an attempt by those firms to keep on their feet, on ground that is slipping away from them. . . .

Long-range investing under rapidly changing conditions, especially under conditions that change or may change at any moment under the impact of new commodities and technologies, is like shooting at a target that is not only indistinct but moving—and moving jerkily at that.[58]

[58] He recognized negatively, however, that "largest-scale plans could in many cases not materialize at all if it were not known from the outset that competition will be discouraged by heavy capital requirements or

The criticism of Schumpeter implied by the present study is, of course, more sweeping than the mere claim that old methods of production managed to survive for decades after they became partially obsolete. The primary objection to Schumpeter's theories is that they do not adequately explore the process of technological change as a series of complementary, mutually reinforcing developments.

Conspicuous Caution

Throughout this study there has been an emphasis on the cautiousness of innovators. Caution affects the procedures of innovators and is therefore crucial in determining the riskiness of innovation. The chance of loss can be reduced whenever more cautious procedures can lead to knowledge that increases the predictability of strategic factors.

In nineteenth-century America some factors were sufficiently predictable for innovators so that there was no need to make

---

lack of experience," as was indeed the case for many innovations examined in this study. See Joseph A. Schumpeter, *Capitalism, Socialism, and Democracy* (2d ed.; New York: Harper and Brothers, 1947), pp. 83–84, 88–89. (The italics are Schumpeter's.) It would appear that, like many other writers, Schumpeter based his conclusions exclusively on the statements of businessmen, while ignoring those of engineers. As pointed out in Chapter II, pp 35–36, businessmen's statements were often colored by a desire to justify high tariffs, monopolistic prices, and failure to adopt new methods as soon as proposed. They can be found in the contemporary nontechnical literature of almost any industry. For example, an editorial writer of the *Glass Budget* wrote on June 25, 1898: "Inventors, infringers and imitators are tumbling over each other in their hot haste to get there first. . . . Branch after branch of the glass industry is being invaded by machinery, production is being immensely increased, prices are being reduced below the living point. . . . The future is uncertain and full of dark problems upon which few can shed light." But according to Dr. Warren Scoville, "At the time this exaggerated statement was published, manufacturers were making only widemouth jars on machines" (Warren C. Scoville, *Revolution in Glassmaking* [Cambridge: Harvard University Press, 1948], pp. 178–179).

them special objects of worry and manipulation. The principles of *laissez faire* were so deeply entrenched that the reactions of government and labor were not likely to be astonishing. The government would be indifferent; and labor would be cheerfully compliant, or powerless, or interested in other problems. Conspiracies by competitors and attempts to withhold key patents were likely to be harmless or legally untenable until the very end of the century. A cautious procedure, therefore, was not essential for reducing interference risks.

Caution was of some importance in reducing customer risks. A cautious entrepreneur would develop his novel process or product on the smallest possible scale, among other reasons to see if inertia and prejudice were surmountable. Insofar as a large scale was not itself integral to the innovation, this procedure was followed by almost all innovators studied. Hence the first machines, furnaces, and power transmission lines were deliberately of less than optimum scale; and new motors and machine tools were not produced on an efficient mass-production basis until well after sales justified such methods. Some inertia and prejudice did exist and therefore warranted such procedures; but in comparison with Europe the reactions of consumers and machine users in America were fairly predictable. As previously cited, visitors from abroad were amazed at the American willingness to accept machines and the products of machines that were imperfect in quality provided they lowered costs. Europeans tended to insist on thorough workmanship and a great reduction in price before tolerating machine methods of production. This faultfinding attitude increased uncertainty and the length of the transition period for European innovators. The difficulty was further compounded by and partly the result of the fact that in Europe demand generally increased slowly enough to be supplied by old methods of production without great difficulty.[59]

[59] Burn, *op. cit.*, p. 306.

Caution could not do much to anticipate and overcome the risk of unlucky timing. It did, however, reinforce the tendency to adopt the tentative, small-scale approaches mentioned above. In any case, however, nineteenth-century depressions were not apt to discourage the introduction of novel manufacturing methods, if indeed they did not encourage such innovations.

If caution played a significant role in reducing production risks, it must have been possible and relatively inexpensive to learn how economically a new producers' good would function before staking large sums on an innovation. If such inquiries were possible and consistently attempted by innovators, then it could be that innovators were not necessarily the boldest gamblers in sight but rather those who first bothered to acquire superior information. Was Eli Whitney "bold" in working out the implications of interchangeable manufacturing and proposing them to the government? Given the competition, standards of production, and available labor supply of his time, Whitney's customer risks, timing risks, and production risks were rather low. His interference risk from Callender Irvine, inside the government, was temporarily considerable. But Whitney continued innovating not because he was the most intrepid arms maker in America but because a large head start made it easier for him than for other arms makers to see what further devices could safely be added. Moreover, as repeatedly emphasized, with the progress of engineering in the second half of the century, inventions could be more thoroughly and cheaply tested in laboratories; and more and more experts could be consulted. The roster of experts heard and the number of plans submitted before a design for the Niagara Falls hydroelectric project was approved provided almost a "Who's Who" of science and engineering. M. Lourdelot, a commissioner sent to America in 1885 by the French Minister of Commerce to report on trade and manufacturing methods in the United

States, believed that "the great element of competitive danger in America with Europe arises from . . . the close watching of details too often neglected in Europe." [60]

For some innovators the access to superior information might more properly be described as access to superior opportunities. For example, the manager of a works that included several stages of production would be in a favorable position for integrating these stages technologically. In his field he would be able to do what could not be done for the economy as a whole: he could develop interrelated changes simultaneously. Among others, Carnegie's engineers had this advantage. Outstanding business leaders such as William Sellers and George Westinghouse were able to develop their innovations because they had both technical ability and business experience in two or three interrelated industries. None of these men endorsed changes in production techniques because they liked to gamble on ventures too risky for others. They initiated and endorsed changes because they happened to be in a strategic position for seeing the changing requirements of a growing economy. Insofar as their plans involved less predictable aspects than the plans of routine businessmen, they also took greater pains with their predicting: they made the most elaborate experiments and used ingenious but inexpensive pilot plants.

Why was there, moreover, a disproportionately great reluctance to finance the more expensive innovations? Could this reluctance be attributed to the general shortage of capital in America or to the fact that holders of large amounts of capital, being less expert in technological matters, were also less enthusiastic about technological innovations as investments? In a country with vast undeveloped natural resources, technological innovations in manufacturing naturally seemed less promising than building transportation facilities, exploiting forests, developing mines, and speculating in real estate. But appearances

[60] *Iron Age*, XXXVI (Aug. 20, 1885), 35.

were deceptive. The relative shortage of labor and the ready availability of vast agricultural plains, forests, coal seams, and ore beds created unique opportunities for innovation in the machinery for processing cotton, wheat, lumber, and ore. Under these circumstances the new machinery itself required a novel American method of manufacturing—mass production with interchangeable parts. Moreover, the comparative disadvantage of manufacturing was in large part offset by the tariff, especially after the Civil War, and by geographical isolation.

It was apparently the scarcity of capital among those willing to innovate, rather than the general shortage of capital, that led to a greater rate of development of innovations involving devices which would ultimately cost three thousand dollars or less. The fact that attempts at very expensive innovations hardly ever failed suggests that more attempts at such innovations and less tinkering might have reduced losses still further and might have led to a faster rate of technological change. As Frederick W. Taylor once concluded, "The greatest difficulty in commercial life is to get the opportunity to successfully carry out the experiment." [61]

Nevertheless, there is little evidence to support Veblen in his opinion that the trend toward larger business units and toward control by men without technological training had led to a greater reluctance to innovate.[62] On the contrary, larger

[61] See also *supra*, p. 145; quoted by Copley, *op. cit.*, I, 247. Professor J. D. Bernal has observed the same disparity on a broader scale and has offered an explanation: "Where discoveries opened new fields . . . there were long delays in following them up and this only occurred when there was an overwhelming case for profitable exploitation. . . . Ever-increasing markets opened up by rail and steamship, put a premium on the multiplication of existing production rather than on technical advance" (J. D. Bernal, *Science and Industry in the Nineteenth Century* [London: Routledge and Kegan Paul, 1953], pp. 148–151).

[62] Thorstein Veblen, *Absentee Ownership and Business Enterprise in Recent Times: The Case of America* (New York: B. W. Huebsch, 1923), pp. 80–103.

business units in textile manufacturing and iron and steel making allowed specialization in the performance of various managerial functions, and specialization in turn meant greater proficiency in each function. Whenever specialization led to the introduction of expert accounting techniques, it provided a means for substituting scientific procedures for rule-of-thumb methods in production and was, therefore, conducive to innovation. Thus the Boston Manufacturing Company under the leadership of merchants and financiers became the most progressive cotton manufacturing enterprise around 1815; and thus the iron and steel industry was more progressive with businessmen such as E. B. Ward, Abram S. Hewitt, and Andrew Carnegie in charge than with old-fashioned practical ironmasters. Most business leaders did not allow their technical experts as much scope for innovation as Ward, Hewitt, and Carnegie; but men like these three nevertheless set the pace. After 1870 engineers did, of course, favor many projects that were not tried or that were tried only tardily and with reluctance. Perhaps it was Veblen's observation of this state of affairs that led him to the assumption of a greater readiness to innovate before 1860 when business managers were their own technical experts. The more authority engineers had in an enterprise after 1870, the more progressive it was likely to be, for by and large business managers without technological training were the most averse to innovations. But confronted with a massive display of technical evidence and expert testimony, businessmen could in time be moved to action.

The American innovations that looked so bold to foreign visitors were mostly in those fields in which interference and customer risks were much lower in America than in Europe. The typical "bold" American innovation was the initial substitution of an ingenious mechanism for manual labor. But there were also European innovations which looked bold to Americans. These innovations occurred in those fields in which interference risks were less important than production risks or in which a high initial expenditure was required. Innovations in metallurgy an in textile machinery between 1850 and 1890 were more "daring" in Europe than in America.

The Image of the Nineteenth Century

One cannot pretend that widespread caution made innovation in manufacturing methods as safe as operating a routine business. But the infrequency of losses suggests that the difference was not great: technological innovation in manufacturing methods had been reduced to a fairly predictable and safe routine long before the advent of giant corporations and their laboratories.

A close look at history should therefore correct anyone's impression that technological innovations actually attempted in manufacturing methods were generally risky. Such an impression may easily be transferred from observations of other economic activities in which many risks were, in fact, taken and in which losses did, in fact, occur. There were inventors of novel consumers' goods who lost their own and their friends' money on a variety of quixotic ideas. There were speculators in real estate, canals, and railroads who were carried away by optimism. These inventors and speculators were investing under circumstances in which information about important factors affecting the outcome could not be acquired in advance. As Professor Carter Goodrich has put it:

In spite of warnings and examples, States and municipalities continued to invest hopefully in improvements without having at their command either the engineering and economic skill needed to appraise the prospect of the undertaking, the fiscal strength to sustain it, or a system of public administration effective enough to protect their interest.[63]

[63] Carter Goodrich, "The Revulsion against Internal Improvements," *Journal of Economic History*, X (Nov. 1950), 165.

But in the four producers' goods industries examined here, essential information could generally be acquired; and financial and administrative problems, once a project was under way, were not formidable. Information about interference, customer, and timing risks was not vital because these risks were unlikely causes of frequent or heavy losses. Information about factors determining production risks was of paramount importance, but with painstaking effort it could generally be acquired, and the prevailing cautiousness of innovators almost invariably led to such effort.

It appears, furthermore, that innovators in manufacturing methods rarely overestimated their chance of success. On the contrary, they tended to underestimate their chances because they were unaware of innovations in other industries complementary with their own. Even when competitive rather than complementary innovations appeared, the rapidly expanding economy almost always had room for them all. At the level of innovation, however, technological complementarity was far more important than technological duplication or competition. Hence it was not necessary to destroy in order to create, or to be afraid of destruction while creating. On the contrary, creative actions mutually supported one another.

These generalizations are qualified by the significance of the most important exceptions. In the textile industry before 1830 there were not enough experts to appraise the claims of every mechanic who proposed a novel machine. In the iron and steel industry, throughout most of the country, the relative backwardness of chemistry made attempts to use a novel process or novel materials highly unpredictable. Yet even these two series of innovations were attempted in a cautious and painstaking manner. Without techniques for acquiring knowledge of crucial factors, however, such procedures could not reduce risks, and losses necessarily occurred.

The picture of nineteenth-century America reflected by these industries is that of an economy remarkably flexible and un-fettered by tradition, but, by the same token, poorly co-or-dinated and without much liaison among groups with com-mon interests. It was a society that experienced an unprece-dented technological revolution in manufacturing methods, a change that was brought about, not by heroic gambling, but by the cautious exploitation of vast and multiplying opportuni-ties.

Bibliography

General

Allen, Zachariah. *The Science of Mechanics as Applied to the Present Improvements in the Useful Arts*. Providence, 1829.

American Society of Mechanical Engineers. *Transactions*. 1880–. New York.

Barnett, George E. *Chapters on Machinery and Labor*. Cambridge: Harvard University Press, 1926.

Bernal, J. D. *Science and Industry in the Nineteenth Century*. London: Routledge and Kegan Paul, 1953.

Bishop, J. Leander. *History of American Manufactures from 1608 to 1860*. 3d ed. revised. 2 vols. Philadelphia: Edward Young and Co., 1868.

Blake, William P. *History of the Town of Hamden, Connecticut*. New Haven: Price, Lee and Co., 1888.

Brozen, Yale. "Invention, Innovation, and Imitation," *American Economic Review*, XLI (May 1951), 239–257.

——. *Some Economic Aspects of Technological Change*. Chicago: University of Chicago Press, 1945.

227

Burn, D. L. "The Genesis of American Engineering Competition, 1850–1870," *Economic History*, II (Jan. 1931), 292–311.

Byrn, Edward W. *Progress of Invention in the Nineteenth Century.* New York: Munn and Co., 1900.

Chapman, Sydney J. *Work and Wages: Part I, Foreign Competition.* London: Longmans, Green and Co., 1904.

Clark, Victor S. *History of Manufactures in the United States.* 3 vols. Washington: Carnegie Institution, 1929.

Cole, Arthur H. "An Approach to the Study of Entrepreneurship: A Tribute to Edwin F. Gay," *Journal of Economic History*, VI, *The Tasks of Economic History* (1946), 1–15.

——. "A New Set of Stages," *Explorations in Entrepreneurial History*, VIII (Dec. 1955), 99–107.

Coxe, Tench. "Digest of Manufactures," *American State Papers: Finance*, II, 666–812. (Based on returns for the census of 1810.) Washington, 1832.

Depew, Chauncey M., ed. *One Hundred Years of American Commerce.* 2 vols. New York: D. O. Haynes and Co., 1895.

Dickinson, H. W. *A Short History of the Steam Engine.* New York: Macmillan, 1939.

Domar, Evsey D., and Richard A. Musgrave. "Proportional Income Taxation and Risk-Taking," *Quarterly Journal of Economics*, LVIII (May 1944), 388–422.

Fleming, Marcus. "External Economies and the Doctrine of Balanced Growth," *Economic Journal*, LXV (June 1955), 241–256.

Francis, James B. *Lowell Hydraulic Experiments.* Boston, 1955.

Frankel, Marvin. "Obsolescence and Technological Change in a Maturing Economy," *American Economic Review*, XLV (June 1955), 296–319.

Franklin Institute. *Journal.* Monthly, 1826–. Philadelphia.

Gallatin, Albert. "Manufactures," Report of the Secretary of the Treasury, April 17, 1810, *American State Papers: Finance*, II, 925–939.

Georgescu-Roegen, Nicholas. "Choice, Expectations, and Measurability," *Quarterly Journal of Economics*, LXVIII (Nov. 1954), 503–534.

Gilfillan, S. C. *The Sociology of Invention.* Chicago: Follett Publishing Co., 1935.

Glover, John G., and William Bouck Cornell, eds. *The Development of American Industries.* New York: Prentice-Hall, 1932.

Goodrich, Carter. "The Revulsion against Internal Improvements," *Journal of Economic History,* X (Nov. 1950), 145–169.

Great Britain, House of Commons. *New York Industrial Exhibition: Special Reports of Mr. George Wallis and Mr. Joseph Whitworth.* (Parliamentary Papers, vol. XXXVI, 1854.) London, 1854.

——. *Report of the Committee on the Machinery of the United States.* (Parliamentary Papers. vol. L, 1854–1855.) London, 1855.

Hamilton, Alexander. *Industrial and Commercial Correspondence.* Arthur H. Cole, ed. Chicago: A. W. Shaw, 1928.

——. "Report on the Subject of Manufactures," Dec. 5, 1791, *American State Papers: Finance,* I, 123–145.

Hamilton, Walton. *Patents and Free Enterprise.* (U.S. Temporary National Economic Committee, Monograph 31.) Washington, 1941.

Hardy, Charles O. *Readings in Risk and Risk-Bearing.* Chicago: University of Chicago Press. 1924.

——. *Risk and Risk-Bearing.* Chicago: University of Chicago Press, 1923.

Hart, A. G. *Anticipations, Uncertainty, and Dynamic Planning.* Chicago: University of Chicago Press, 1940.

Hart, Amos Winfield. *Digest of Decisions of Law and Practice in the Patent Office and the United States and State Courts in Patents, Trademarks, Copyrights, and Labels, 1886–1898.* Chicago: Callaghan and Co., 1898.

Hill, Forest G. "The Role of the Army Engineers in the Planning and Encouragement of Internal Improvements." Unpublished doctoral dissertation, Columbia University, 1950.

Howe, Henry. *Memoirs of the Most Eminent American Mechanics.* New York: Harper and Brothers, 1858.

Iles, George. *Leading American Inventors.* New York: Henry Holt and Co., 1912.

Jefferson, Thomas. *The Writings of Thomas Jefferson.* Andrew A. Lipscomb and Albert Ellery Bergh, eds., 20 vols. Washington: Jefferson Memorial Association, 1903.

Jerome, Harry. *Mechanization in Industry.* New York: National Bureau of Economic Research, 1934.

Jewkes, John, David Sawers, and Richard Stillerman. *The Sources of Invention.* London: Macmillan and Co., 1958.

Kaempffert, Waldemar, ed. *A Popular History of American Invention.* 2 vols. New York: Charles Scribner's Sons, 1924.

Keirstead, Burton. *An Essay in the Theory of Profits and Income Distribution.* Oxford: Basil Blackwell, 1953.

Knight, Frank. *Risk, Uncertainty, and Profit.* Boston and New York: Houghton Mifflin Co., 1921.

Larson, Henrietta M. *Guide to Business History: Materials for the Study of American Business History and Suggestions for Their Use.* Cambridge: Harvard University Press, 1950.

McLane, Louis. *Report of the Secretary of the Treasury, 1832: Documents Relative to the Manufactures in the United States* (House Executive Documents, 22d Congress, First Session, no. 308.) Two vols. Washington, 1833.

Maclaurin, W. Rupert. "The Sequence from Invention to Innovation and Its Relation to Economic Growth," *Quarterly Journal of Economics,* LXVII (Feb. 1953), 97–111.

Oliver, John W. *History of American Technology.* New York: Ronald Press Co., 1956.

Rae, John B. "The Engineer as Businessman in American Industry: A Preliminary Analysis," *Explorations in Entrepreneurial History,* VII (Dec. 1954), 94–104.

——. "The Engineer-Entrepreneur in the American Automobile Industry," *Explorations in Entrepreneurial History,* VIII (Oct. 1955), 1–11.

Redlich, Fritz. "The Business Leader as a 'Daimonic' Figure," *American Journal of Economics and Sociology,* XII (Jan., April, 1953), 163–178, 289–299.

——. *History of American Business Leaders.* 2 vols. Ann Arbor, Mich.: Edwards Brothers, 1940. Vol. I.

——. "Innovation in Business: A Systematic Presentation," *Amer-*

ican Journal of Economics and Sociology, X (April 1951), 285–291.

Reports of the United States Commissioners to the Paris Exposition, 1867. Washington: Government Printing Office, 1870.

Rostow, W. W. "The Interrelation of Theory and Economic History," *Journal of Economic History,* XVII, *The Tasks of Economic History* (1957), 509–523.

Sawyer, John E. "Entrepreneurship in Periods of Rapid Growth: The United States in the 19th Century," *Entrepreneurship and Economic Growth.* Papers presented at a conference sponsored jointly by the Committee on Economic Growth of the Social Science Research Council and the Harvard University Research Center in Entrepreneurial History, Cambridge, Mass., Nov. 12 and 13, 1954.

——. "The Social Basis of the American System of Manufacturing," *Journal of Economic History,* XIV, *The Tasks of Economic History* (1954), 361–379.

Schmookler, Jacob. "The Changing Efficiency of the American Economy, 1869–1938" *Review of Economics and Statistics,* XXXIV (Aug. 1952), 214–231.

——. "The Level of Inventive Activity," *Review of Economics and Statistics,* XXXVI (May 1954), 183–190.

Schumpeter, Joseph A. *Business Cycles.* New York and London: McGraw-Hill, 1939.

——. *Capitalism, Socialism, and Democracy.* 2d ed. New York: Harper and Brothers, 1947.

——. "The Creative Response in Economic History," *Journal of Economic History,* VII (Nov. 1947), 149–159.

——. "Economic Theory and Entrepreneurial History," in *Change and the Entrepreneur.* R. Richard Wohl, ed. Cambridge: Harvard University Press, 1949.

——. *The Theory of Economic Development.* R. Opie, trans. Cambridge: Harvard University Press, 1934.

Scientific American. Weekly, 1845–. New York.

Scitovsky, Tibor. "Two Concepts of External Economies," *Journal of Political Economy,* LXII (April 1954), 143–151, LXIII (Oct. 1955), 450–451.

Shackle, G. L. S. *Expectations in Economics*. Cambridge: Cambridge University Press, 1952.

——. "A Non-additive Measure of Uncertainty," *Review of Economic Studies*, XVII (1949–1950), 70–74.

——. "Professor Keirstead's Theory of Profit," *Economic Journal*, LXIV (March 1954), 116–123.

——. *Uncertainty in Economics*. Cambridge: Cambridge University Press, 1955.

Shlakman, Vera. *Economic History of a Factory Town: A Study of Chicopee, Massachusetts*. (Smith College Studies in History, vol. XX, nos. 1–4, Oct. 1934–July 1935.)

Shubik, Martin. "Information, Risk, Ignorance, and Indeterminancy," *Quarterly Journal of Economics*, LXVIII (Nov. 1954), 629–640.

Tariff Acts Passed by the Congress of the United States from 1789 to 1909. Washington: Government Printing Office, 1909.

U.S. Bureau of the Census. *Census of Manufactures, 1905*. Washington, 1907.

U.S. Census Office. *Tenth Census* (1880): *Manufactures*. Washington, 1883.

——. *Twelfth Census* (1900): *Manufactures*. Washington, 1902.

Usher, Abbot Payson. *A History of Mechanical Inventions*. Rev. ed. Cambridge: Harvard University Press, 1954.

——. "Technical Change and Capital Formation," in *Capital Formation and Economic Growth*. (A Conference of the Universities—National Bureau Committee for Economic Research.) Princeton: Princeton University Press, 1955. Pp. 523–550.

Vaughan, Floyd L. *Economics of Our Patent System*. New York: Macmillan, 1925.

Veblen, Thorstein. *Absentee Ownership and Business Enterprise in Recent Times: The Case of America*. New York: B. W. Huebsch, 1923.

——. *The Place of Science in Modern Civilization and Other Essays*. New York: B. W. Huebsch, 1919.

——. *The Theory of Business Enterprise*. New York: Charles Scribner's Sons, 1904.

——. "Why Is Economics Not an Evolutionary Science?" *Quarterly Journal of Economics*, XII (July 1898), 373–397.

Wohl, R. Richard, ed. *Change and the Entrepreneur*. Cambridge: Harvard University Press, 1949.

Iron and Steel

American Institute of Mining Engineers. *Transactions*. 1871–. New York.

American Iron and Steel Association. *Bulletin of the American Iron and Steel Association*. Weekly, 1866–. Philadelphia.

Bridge, James Howard. *The Inside History of the Carnegie Steel Company*. New York: Aldine Book Co., 1903.

Carnegie, Andrew. *Autobiography of Andrew Carnegie*. Posthumously arranged for publication by John C. Van Dyke. Boston: Houghton Mifflin Co., 1920.

——. The Papers of Andrew Carnegie. Manuscript Division, Library of Congress, Washington, D.C.

Durfee, William F. "The First Bessemer Steel Works in the United States," *Bulletin of the American Iron and Steel Association*, XVIII (Nov. 12, 1884), 291.

Evans, Henry Oliver. *Iron Pioneer: Henry W. Oliver, 1840–1904*. New York: E. P. Dutton, 1942.

Fackenthal, B. F. "John Fritz, the Ironmaster," *Pennsylvania German Society*, XXXIV (Oct. 1923), 95–112.

Firmstone, William. "Sketch of Early Anthracite Furnaces," *Transactions of the American Institute of Mining Engineers*, III (1874–1875), 152–156.

French, Benjamin Franklin. *History of the Rise and Progress of the Iron Trade of the United States from 1621 to 1857*. New York: Wiley and Halsted, 1858.

Fritz, John. *The Autobiography of John Fritz*. New York: John Wiley and Sons, 1912.

Goodale, Stephen L. *Chronology of Iron and Steel*. 2d ed. Cleveland: Penton Publishing Co., 1931.

Harvey, George. *Henry Clay Frick, the Man*. New York: Charles Scribner's Sons, 1928.

Hendrick, Burton J. *The Life of Andrew Carnegie.* Garden City, N.Y.: Doubleday, Doran and Co., 1932.

Holley, A. L. "The Inadequate Union of Engineering Science and Art," *Transactions of the American Institute of Mining Engineers,* IV (Feb. 1876), 191–207.

——. "Some Pressing Needs of Our Iron and Steel Manufacturers," *Transactions of the American Institute of Mining Engineers,* IV (Oct. 1875), 77–99.

Hunt, Robert W. "History of the Bessemer Manufacture in America," *Transactions of the American Institute of Mining Engineers,* V (June 1876), 201–207.

Hunter, Louis G. "Influence of the Market upon Technique in the Iron Industry in Western Pennsylvania Up to 1860," *Journal of Economic and Business History,* I (Feb. 1929), 241–281.

Inland Steel Company. *Fifty Years of Inland Steel, 1893–1943.* Chicago: Inland Steel Co., 1943.

Iron Age. Weekly, 1859–. New York: Iron Age Publishing Co.

King, Willis L. "Recollections and Conclusions from a Long Business Life," *Western Pennsylvania Historical Magazine,* XXII (Dec. 1940), 223–242.

Korn, Bernhard. "E. B. Ward." Unpublished doctoral dissertation, Marquette University, 1942.

Morrell, Ben. *"J. & L.": The Growth of an American Business.* New York: Newcomen Society, 1953.

Nalle, Richard T. *Midvale—and Its Pioneers.* New York: Newcomen Society, 1948.

Nevins, Allan. *Abram S. Hewitt, with Some Account of Peter Cooper.* New York: Harper and Brothers, 1935.

The Otis Steel Company—Pioneer, Cleveland, Ohio. Cambridge, Mass.: privately printed, 1929.

Pearse, J. B. *A Concise History of the Iron Manufacture of the American Colonies Up to the Revolution and of Pennsylvania Up to the Present Time.* Philadelphia: Allen, Lane, and Scott, 1876.

Proudfit, Margaret Burden. *Henry Burden: His Life.* Troy, N.Y.: Pafraets Press, 1904.

Raymond, R. W. "Alexander Lyman Holley," *Transactions of the American Society of Mechanical Engineers*, IV (1883), 64.

Redlich, Fritz. *History of American Business Leaders*. 2 vols. Ann Arbor, Mich.: Edwards Brothers, 1940. Vol. I.

Reese, Jacob. "The Basic Steel Process and Its Possibilities in the United States," *Bulletin of the American Iron and Steel Asoscia-tion*, XXIII (July 3, 1889), 177.

Steel. Weekly, 1867–. Cleveland.

Swank, James M. *Cambria County Pioneers*. Philadelphia: Allen, Lane, and Scott, 1910.

——. *History of the Manufacture of Iron in All Ages and Particularly in the United States from Colonial Times to 1891*. Philadelphia: American Iron and Steel Association, 1892.

Thurston, George H. *Pittsburgh's Progress, Industries, and Resources*. Pittsburgh: A. A. Anderson, 1886.

U.S. Bureau of the Census. *Census of Manufactures, 1905*. Washington, 1907. Bull. 78.

Weeks, J. D. "Biographical Notice of William Powell Shinn," *Transactions of the American Institute of Mining Engineers*, XXI (1892), 394–400.

White, Charles M. *Blast Furnace Blowing Engines, Past Present— and Future*. New York: Newcomen Society, 1947.

White, Josiah. *Josiah White's History, Given by Himself*. Philadelphia: Lehigh Coal and Navigation Co., 1904.

Textiles

Appleton, Nathan. *Introduction of the Power Loom and Origin of Lowell*. Lowell: B. H. Penhallow, 1858.

Bagnall, William R. *The Textile Industries of the United States*. Cambridge: Riverside Press, 1893.

Batchelder, Samuel. *Introduction and Early Progress of the Cotton Manufacture in the United States*. Boston: Little, Brown and Co., 1863.

Chase, William H. *Five Generations of Loom Builders*. Hopedale, Mass.: Draper Corporation, 1950.

Cole, Arthur H. *The American Wool Manufacture*. 2 vols. Cambridge: Harvard University Press, 1926.

Copeland, Melvin Thomas. *The Cotton Manufacturing Industry of the United States.* Cambridge: Harvard University Press, 1912.

Crompton, George. *The Crompton Loom.* Worcester: privately printed, 1949.

Day, Clive. "The Early Development of the American Cotton Manufacture," *Quarterly Journal of Economics,* XXXIX (May 1925), 450–468.

Draper, George Otis. *Labor-saving Looms.* 3d ed. Hopedale, Mass.: Draper Company, 1907.

Draper, William F. *Recollections of a Varied Career.* Boston: Little, Brown and Co., 1908.

Equipment and Labour Utilization in the Cotton Industry. Manchester: Cotton Board Labour Department, 1947.

Gibb, George Sweet. *The Saco-Lowell Shops: Textile Machinery Building in New England, 1813–1949.* Cambridge: Harvard University Press, 1950.

Gibson, Roland. *Cotton Textile Wages in the United States and Great Britain: A Comparison of Trends, 1860–1945.* New York: King's Crown Press, 1948.

Hayes, John L. *American Textile Machinery.* Cambridge: Cambridge University Press, 1879.

Lincoln, Jonathan Thayer. "Beginnings of the Machine Age in New England: Document Relating to the Introduction of the Power Loom," *Bulletin of the Business Historical Society,* VII (Oct. 1933), 6–13.

——. "The Cotton Textile Machine Industry—American Loom Builders," *Harvard Business Review,* XII (Oct. 1933), 94–105.

——. "Material for a History of American Textile Machinery: The Kilburn-Lincoln Papers," *Journal of Economic and Business History,* IV (Feb. 1932), 259–280.

Montgomery, James. *A Practical Detail of the Cotton Manufacture of the United States.* Glasgow: John Niven, Jr., 1840.

——. *The Theory and Practice of Cotton Spinning.* Glasgow: John Niven, Jr., 1833.

National Association of Cotton Manufacturers. *Transactions.* 1906–. Boston.

Navin, Thomas R., Jr. "Innovation and Management Policies, The

Textile Machinery Industry: Influence of the Market on Management," *Bulletin of the Business Historical Society,* XXIV (March 1950), 15–30.

——. "The Wellman-Woodman Patent Controversy in the Cotton Textile Machinery Industry," *Bulletin of the Business Historical Society,* XXI (Nov. 1947), 144–152.

——. *The Whitin Machine Works since 1831: A Textile Machinery Company in an Industrial Village.* Cambridge: Harvard University Press, 1950.

New England Cotton Manufacturers, Association of. *Proceedings.* 1866–1905. Boston.

Orth, F. "Der Werdegang wichtiger Erfindungen auf dem Gebiete der Spinnerei und Weberei," *Beiträge zur Geschichte der Technik und Industrie,* XII (1922), 61–108, XVII (1927), 89–105.

Rockey, Howard. "From Plantation to Loom," in *A Popular History of American Invention.* Waldemar Kaempffert, ed. 2 vols. New York: Charles Scribner's Sons, 124.

Taft, Royal C. *Some Notes upon the Introduction of the Woolen Manufacture into the United States.* Providence: Sidney S. Rider, 1882.

Textile World Record. Monthly, 1903–1915. New York. Absorbed *Textile Manufacturers' Review and Industrial Record,* 1868–1896, and *Textile Record of America,* 1880–1903.

U.S. Bureau of the Census. *Census of Manufactures, 1905.* Washington, 1907. Bull. 74.

Ware, Caroline F. *The Early New England Cotton Manufacture: A Study in Industrial Beginnings.* Cambridge: Riverside Press, 1931.

Webber, Samuel. "Reminiscences of Early Machine Practices," *Transactions of the American Society of Mechanical Engineers,* XVI (1896), 742–761.

White, George S. *Memoir of Samuel Slater: The Father of American Manufactures.* 2d ed. Philadelphia, 1836.

Machine Tools

Accuracy for Seventy Years—Pratt and Whitney. Hartford: Pratt and Whitney Co., 1930.

American Machinist. Weekly, 1877–. New York.

Benét, Stephen V., ed. *A Collection of Annual Reports and Other Important Papers Relating to the Ordnance Department, Taken from the Records of the Office of the Chief of Ordnance, from Public Documents, and from Other Sources.* Washington: Government Printing Office, 1878.

Bond, Russel A. "Automatic Machine Tools," in *A Popular History of American Invention.* Waldemar Kaempffert, ed. 2 vols. New York: Charles Scribner's Sons, 1924.

Brearly, Harry C. *Time Telling through the Ages.* New York: Doubleday, Page and Co., 1919.

Buxbaum, Bertold. "Der amerikanische Werkzeugmaschinen- und Werkzeugbau im 18. und 19. Jahrhundert," *Beiträge zur Geschichte der Technik und Industrie,* X (1920), 121–155.

——. "Der englische Werkzeugmaschinen- und Werkzeugbau im 18. und 19. Jahrhundert," *Beiträge zur Geschichte der Technik und Industrie,* XI (1921), 117–143.

Chapin, Frederic H. *National Acme: An Informal History.* New York: Newcomen Society, 1949.

Copley, Frank Barkley. *Frederick W. Taylor, Father of Scientific Management.* 2 vols. New York: Harper and Brothers, 1923.

Deyrup, Felicia J. *Arms Makers of the Connecticut Valley.* (Smith College Studies in History, vol. XXXIII.) Northampton, Mass., 1948.

Durfee, William F. "The History and Modern Development of the Art of Interchangeable Construction in Mechanism," *Transactions of the American Society of Mechanical Engineers,* XXII (1893), 1225–1257.

Engineering. Weekly, 1866–. London.

Fitch, Charles H. "Report on the Manufactures of Interchangeable Mechanism," in U.S. Census Office, *Tenth Census: Manufactures,* vol. II. Washington, 1883.

Fourscore Years of Bevel Gearing: The Story of the Gleason Works. Rochester, N.Y.: Gleason Works, 1945.

Herkimer County Historical Society. *The Story of the Typewriter.* Herkimer, N.Y., 1923.

Hubbard, Guy. "The Development of Machine Tools in New England," series of articles in *American Machinist*, LIX–LXI (July 5, 1923–Sept. 18, 1924).

——. "100 Years of Progress in the Development of American Metalworking Equipment," *Automotive Industries*, CXIII (Sept. 1, 1955), 84–87, 281, 298, 300, 315–317.

Jerome, Chauncey. *History of the Clock Business for the Past Sixty Years and a Life of Chauncey Jerome Written by Himself*. New Haven: F. C. Dayton, 1860.

Lathrop, William G. *The Brass Industry in the United States*. Rev. ed. Mount Carmel, Conn.: William G. Lathrop, 1926.

Mirsky, Jeanette, and Allan Nevins. *The World of Eli Whitney*. New York: Macmillan, 1952.

Moore, Charles W. *Timing a Century: History of the Waltham Watch Company*. Cambridge: Harvard University Press, 1945.

New Haven Colony Historical Society Papers. 1865–. New Haven. Vol. V (1894).

North, S. N. D., and R. H. North. *Simeon North, First Official Pistol Maker of the United States*. Concord, N.H.: Frumford Press, 1913.

Olmsted, Denison. *Memoir of Eli Whitney, Esq*. New Haven: Durrie and Peck, 1846.

Roe, Joseph Wickham. *English and American Tool Builders*. New Haven: Yale University Press, 1916.

——. *James Hartness*. New York: American Society of Mechanical Engineers, 1937.

——. "Machine Tools in America," *Journal of the Franklin Institute*, CCXXV (May 1938), 499–511.

Sellers, William. "Machinery Manufacturing Interests," in *One Hundred Years of American Commerce*. Chauncey Depew, ed. 2 vols. New York: D. O. Haynes and Co., 1895. Vol. II, pp. 346–352.

Taylor, Frederick W. *On the Art of Cutting Metals*. New York: American Society of Mechanical Engineers, 1907.

Tymeson, Mildred McClary. *The Norton Story*. Worcester: Norton Co., 1953.

U.S. Bureau of the Census. *Census of Manufactures, 1905*. Washington, 1907. Bull. 67.

Electric Power

Adams, Edward Dean. *Niagara Power: History of the Niagara Falls Power Company, 1886–1918.* 2 vols. Niagara Falls, N.Y.: Niagara Falls Power Co., 1927.

Broderick, John T. *Forty Years with General Electric.* Albany, N.Y.: Fort Orange Press, 1929.

Carr, Charles C. *Alcoa, An American Enterprise.* New York: Rinehart and Co., 1952.

Chesney, C. C., and Scott, C. F. "Early History of the A. C. System in America," *Electrical Engineering,* LV (March 1936), 228–235.

A Chronological History of Electrical Development. New York: National Electrical Manufacturers Association, 1946.

Compton, K. T. "Elihu Thomson: 1853–1934," *Biographical Memoirs.* Washington: National Academy of Sciences, XXI (1941), 143.

Dyer, F. L., Martin, T. G. and Meadowcroft, W. H. *Edison: His Life and Inventions.* 2 vols. New York: Harper and Brothers, 1929.

Electrical World. Weekly, 1883–. New York.

——. Editorial Staff. *The Electric Power Industry, Past, Present, and Future.* New York: McGraw-Hill, 1949.

Greene, S. D. "Distribution of the Electrical Energy from Niagara Falls," *Cassier's Magazine,* VIII (July 1895), 333–362.

Hammond, John W. *Men and Volts: The Story of General Electric.* New York: J. B. Lippincott, 1941.

Jackson, D. C. "Frank Julian Sprague, 1857–1934," *Scientific Monthly,* LVII (Nov. 1943), 431.

Jehl, Francis. *Menlo Park Reminiscences.* 3 vols. Dearborn, Mich.: Edison Institute, 1937, 1938, and 1941.

Jones, Payson. *A Power History of the Consolidated Edison System, 1878–1900.* New York: Consolidated Edison Co. of New York, 1940.

Lamme, Benjamin Garver. *Benjamin Garver Lamme, Electrical Engineer: An Autobiography.* New York: G. P. Putnam's Sons, 1926.

——. "The Story of the Induction Motor," *Journal of the American Institute of Electrical Engineers,* XL (March 1921), 203.

——. "The Technical Story of the Frequencies," *Transactions of the American Institute of Electrical Engineers*, XXXVII (1918), 65–89.

Leup, Francis E. *George Westinghouse: His Life and Achievements.* Boston: Little, Brown and Co., 1918.

Lincoln, P. M. "Some Reminiscences of Niagara," *Journal of the American Institute of Electrical Engineers*, LIII (May 1934), 720.

MacLaren, Malcolm. *The Rise of the Electrical Industry during the Nineteenth Century.* Princeton: Princeton University Press, 1943.

Martin, Thomas Commerford. "The Electric Industry in America in 1887," *Electrical World*, IX (Jan. 29, 1887), 50.

——. *Forty Years of Edison Service.* New York: New York Edison Co., 1922.

O'Neill, J. J. *Prodigal Genius: The Life of Nikola Tesla.* New York: Ives Washburn, 1944.

Parsons, R. H. *The Early Days of the Power Station Industry.* Cambridge: Cambridge University Press, 1940.

Passer, Harold C. *The Electrical Manufacturers, 1875–1900.* Cambridge: Harvard University Press, 1953.

Prout, Henry G. *A Life of George Westinghouse.* New York: Charles Scribner's Sons, 1922.

Rickey, James W. "Hydro Power for the Production of Aluminum," *Transactions of the Electrochemical Society*, vol. LXX (1936).

Sprague, Frank Julian. "Digging in the Mines of the Motors," *Journal of the American Institute of Electrical Engineers*, LIII (May 1934), 695–706.

Sprague, Harriet. *Frank J. Sprague and the Edison Myth.* New York: William Frederick Press, 1947.

Stanley, William. "Alternating Current Development in America," *Journal of the Franklin Institute*, CLXXIII (June 1912), 561–580.

Thompson, R. L. *Wiring a Continent: The History of the Telegraph Industry in the United States, 1832–1866.* Princeton: Princeton University Press, 1947.

Thomson, Elihu. "The Pioneer Investigations on Dynamo Machines Fifty Years Ago," *Journal of the Franklin Institute*, vol. CCVI (July 1928).

Thomson, Elihu. "Some High·Lights of Electrical History," *Journal of the American Institute of Electrical Engineers,* LIII (May 1934), 758.

U.S. Bureau of the Census. *Census of Manufactures, 1905.* Washington, 1907. Bull. 73.

Woodbury, David O. *Beloved Scientist: Elihu Thomson.* New York: McGraw-Hill, 1944.

———. *A Measure for Greatness: A Short Biography of Edward Weston.* New York: McGraw-Hill, 1949.

Index